The Cruise of the German Raider Atlantis

THE CRUISE OF THE
GERMAN RAIDER ATLANTIS

Joseph P. Slavick

NAVAL INSTITUTE PRESS
ANNAPOLIS, MARYLAND

Naval Institute Press
291 Wood Road
Annapolis, MD 21402

© 2003 by Joseph P. Slavick
All rights reserved. No part of this book may be reproduced or utilized in any form or by any means, electronic or mechanical, including photocopying and recording, or by any information storage and retrieval system, without permission in writing from the publisher.

Library of Congress Cataloging-in-Publication Data
Slavick, Joseph P., 1964–
  The cruise of the German raider Atlantis / Joseph P. Slavick.
    p. cm.
  Includes bibliographical references and index.
  ISBN 1-55750-537-3 (alk. paper)
    1. Atlantis (Commerce raider). 2. World War, 1939–1945—Naval operations, German. 3. Rogge, Bernard, 1899–1982. 4. Germany. Kriegsmarine—Officers—Biography. 5. Admirals—Germany—Biography. I. Title.
  D772.A73 S53 2003
  940.54'5943—dc21
                                                               2002009787

Printed in the United States of America on acid-free paper ⊚
10 09 08 07 06 05 04 03   9 8 7 6 5 4 3 2
First printing

To the men of *Atlantis*

Nur Nicht Weich Werden

CONTENTS

	Foreword	ix
	Acknowledgments	xiii
1	Bernhard Rogge	1
2	A Sheep Becomes a Wolf	13
3	*Atlantis* Goes into Action	36
4	The Secret Gets Out	54
5	Captured Sisters	77
6	Hell Ship *Durmitor*	98
7	A Nearly Fatal Landfall	117
8	A German Battleship and an International Incident	142
9	The Noose Tightens	159
10	Pacific Waters	174
11	*Atlantis* Is Lost	190
12	Sunk and Rescued—Twice	200
13	Back to Germany	218
14	After *Atlantis*	225
	Notes	231
	Bibliography	247
	Index	255

FOREWORD

I am privileged to write the first few words that a reader may see before embarking on a fascinating voyage with the officers and crew of *Atlantis*. The author, Capt. Joseph Slavick, has put together a modern study of the operations of a German warship that left port in 1940 and was sunk in 1941 after 622 days at sea, and at war. *Atlantis* left Germany and never found another port.

During that war cruise *Atlantis* traveled more than 100,000 miles, far more than even Jules Verne's fictional *Nautilus*. *Atlantis* picked its way through the snow, fog, and ice of the Denmark Straits until it had eluded the British blockade, and then hunted merchant ships in the Atlantic, Pacific, and Indian Oceans. *Atlantis* sowed mines off South Africa and sank or captured twenty-two enemy merchant ships, eluding British patrols all the while. The tankers *Atlantis* captured formed the basis of a raider and submarine resupply network on the opposite side of the world from Germany. The ship and its crew endured both the stifling heat of the equatorial doldrums and the freezing temperatures near the polar extremes of the earth, and found relative safety from the British by braving weather and seas where no pursuer would follow and no trap would be set.

Atlantis's 622 days at sea were spent in oceans dominated by British warships hunting for a raider and among merchant ships ready to sound the alarm if they were at all suspicious of a stranger. The true story of *Atlantis* compares favorably with the best fictional stories of adventure at sea. The German ship's only protection was its utterly common and harmless appearance, which was changed by adopting one camouflage scheme after another.

Succinctly stated, *Atlantis*'s mission was to sink enough ships to draw search patrols to its area of operations, and then to move on to another area where it could operate free of interference, changing its disguise whenever descriptions of its appearance began to circulate. The longer *Atlantis* was at sea, the more costly the raider's existence to the enemy.

The unique record of *Atlantis* can be attributed to its commander, Kapitän-zur-See Bernhard Rogge. His experience as a naval officer began in World War I. He served in the Kaiser's navy, the navy of the German republic following the monarchy, the Kriegsmarine, and the Bundesmarine of the former West Germany. Rogge's star remained in the ascendant throughout his life. Luck does not explain his survival. Only character, intelligence, and initiative can carry a man successfully through the events that Rogge experienced. More important, he succeeded in saving other lives as well—at both ends of the cannon.

The story of *Atlantis* is one of those rare historical phenomena that endear themselves to historians and adventure readers alike. It is timeless because it is a tribute to the endurance, humanity, and initiative of humankind. The sense of duty and loyalty demonstrated by the crew, their rescue of defeated enemies at risk to themselves, and their capacity to endure life on a ship less than five hundred feet long for twenty-two months demonstrates Rogge's uncanny skill at handpicking his crew. They were separated from their families, wives, and children during a terrible war with only sporadic news of home, yet they never lost sight of their goal. Just as the appeal of the story of *Atlantis* transcends time, it also extends to both sides of the war and goes a long way toward dispelling the hateful propaganda that was spread by all of the warring nations.

To attempt an examination of World War II by examining events on the national level rather than the actions of individuals is to cause the real lessons to become lost or confused. The historian who thinks only in terms of nations will learn nothing about the forces that cause individuals to act.

Captain Slavick masterfully tells the story of *Atlantis*. He studied what books could be found—some quite rare—and then went beyond those sources and pored over a microfilm copy of the ship's log. He also located and consulted British Intelligence reports. To expand the scope of his story Captain Slavick studied the other German commerce raiders, in sufficient depth even to explore a sunken wreck.

For the nagging questions that research could not answer, Captain Slavick consulted surviving crewmen, a group who cared little for personal recognition and wanted only to help tell the story. The survivors freely shared their insights, recollections, photographs, and friendship over the years.

Military leadership is a topic that has no limits, for no two leaders boast identical characteristics. In the case of Rogge, however, Captain Slavick's story offers insight into how a commander managed to keep his men focused on their mission for 622 days at sea in wartime. Each man, regardless of his position aboard the ship, properly considered his job indispensable and performed it dutifully throughout the cruise.

Merchant sailors who spent time as prisoners on *Atlantis* formed friendships with the crew. After the war, former captors and prisoners called on each other. The German officers and crew of the *Hilfskreuzer* continued to meet as the family of *Atlantis,* and to remember their ship and its commander, who died in 1982.

Bryan H. Burg

ACKNOWLEDGMENTS

Because this project began from personal interest and slowly grew into a manuscript over the course of nine years, the list of those to whom I am indebted is quite lengthy. I gratefully express my appreciation to those who assisted me and offer sincere apologies to those I may have omitted.

First, I must thank my mother. Without her love and support I would have not learned the life lessons of perseverance, drive, and determination. These lessons have carried me not only through the process of writing this book, but through life as well.

Great thanks to the crewmen of *Atlantis* who assisted me with information, corrections, guidance, photographic support, and encouragement: Hans Bartholomay, Heinrich Fleischner, Rudolf de Graaf, Heinrich Keller, Gerhard Kühl, Johann Meyer, Eberhard Reiners, Emil Weber, and Martin Zscheile. Each man's assistance was invaluable. The fine details and personal insights they shared make the finished work more alive, complete, and accurate.

Graham McBride of the Maritime Museum of the Atlantic unselfishly spent hours of his personal time compiling data on Allied merchant ships for me. His significant contribution early in the research provided a solid foundation from which the research grew.

Adm. Attilio Duilio Ranieri, a retired Italian naval officer and submariner, shared his personal knowledge of Italian submarine operations in the Atlantic and the boats operating from Betasom. His son, Lt. Giampiero Ranieri, an officer currently serving in the Italian submarine force, provided historical details, archival materials, and much-needed translations.

I owe a special debt of gratitude to Col. Robert F. Simmons, my friend and mentor. His ideas and input regarding the strategic implications of the ship's activities helped round out the book.

Others who assisted with information, research assistance, photographic support, critical review, or encouragement include Lt. Col. (Ret.) John R.

Angolia, USA; Keith Birtwhistle, England; Horst Bredow, Germany; Claudio Cappello-Mambelli, Italy; Harry Cooper, USA; Don Frailey, USA; Gudmundur Helgason, Iceland; William Huber, USA; Jürgen Oesten, Germany; Michael Stephan, Germany; and Gordon Williamson, England. The professional and friendly reference staffs of the following institutions unfailingly answered all of my requests and almost always offered additional guidance and help: Australian War Memorial, Canberra; Bibliothek für Zeitgeschichte, Stuttgart, Germany; Bundesarchiv Militärarchiv, Freiburg, Germany; Deutsches Schiffahrtsmuseum, Bremerhaven, Germany; Deutscher Marinebund e.V., Laboe, Germany; Her Majesty's Coastguard Museum, Bridlington, England; Imperial War Museum, London; Library of Congress, Washington, D.C.; Marine-Offizier-Vereinigung, Bonn, Germany; Marineschule-Mürwik, Flensburg, Germany; Maritime Museum of the Atlantic, Halifax, Nova Scotia; National Maritime Museum, London; National Museum of American History, Smithsonian Institution, Washington, D.C.; Naval Historical Center, Washington, D.C.; South African Maritime Museum, Cape Town; U-Boot Archiv, Cuxhaven-Altenbruch, Germany; U.S. National Archives, Washington, D.C.; U.S. Naval Academy Library, Annapolis, Maryland; U.S. Naval Institute, Annapolis, Maryland; Volksbund Deutsche Kriegsgräberfürsorge, Berlin; and Yale University Library, New Haven, Connecticut.

A few sentences of text cannot explain how important the assistance, generosity, and friendship of Bryan H. Burg, Esquire, have been to the completion of this book. During the long process of research and writing Bryan graciously shared intelligence reports, unpublished reference materials, research guidance, out-of-print books, photographs, and, most important, his friendship. He carefully proofed the entire manuscript and made significant and valuable suggestions on content, clarity, and style. Bryan's contributions and expertise on the subject matter made him the ideal person to write the book's foreword. I was quite pleased when he obliged and agreed.

I cannot adequately convey my appreciation to my wife, Karen. The process has been just as long for her as it has been for me. She quietly accepted my absences on research trips, endured many hours in libraries, tolerated late-night phone calls and even later nights of writing, all with patience, grace, a smiling face, and an understanding that, although unspoken, drove me to finish the book. Without her faithful support, this book never would have gone to press.

Finally, to my children: Meghan, Spencer, and Kaitlin, who missed out on hours of playtime with Dad. I now can finally answer your question: "Yes! I finished my book!"

The Cruise of the German Raider Atlantis

Bernhard Rogge

As the 1930s drew to a close, most European nations were still hoping to avert another war, but they were preparing for the worst. International tensions rose daily as definitive alliances began to form and Europe began to polarize. Germany's actions continued to be unpredictable, but England's promised response to any aggression or act of war was quite evident to the world. England's strategy, unchanged for two hundred years, called for confining conflict to the European continent and defending the British Isles with the Royal Navy. This had not changed since 1765, when Sir William Blackstone wrote: "The Royal Navy of England hath ever been its greatest defense and ornament; it is its ancient and natural strength—the floating bulwark of our island."[1]

What had changed, however, was the level of complexity in the implementation of this plan. England's empire had grown. Instead of simply controlling the coastal waters around Great Britain, the Royal Navy was assigned a much more difficult task. Protecting England in the modern era required not only controlling the North Sea and the Atlantic Ocean, but also containing the unknown and unchallenged power of Italy's Regia Marina within the Mediterranean Sea and defending the ships and ports along the detour route around the Mediterranean—the eleven-thousand-mile route around the Cape of Good Hope.

These modern adaptations were clearly apparent to those interested in such matters. German naval planners of the Seekriegsleitung (SKL), who worked under the direction of the Oberkommando der Kriegsmarine (OKM; the Naval High Command and General Staff), could not miss the buildup of Freetown, Cape Town, Durban, Mombassa, and other port towns along the African coasts as these facilities expanded to support warships and handle the increased mercantile traffic. SKL planners also realized that the most powerful portions of the British fleet would remain centered in the main areas of the European conflict. To ensure the safety of their homeland the British would provide the maximum protection for the North Sea and North Atlantic Ocean. This strategy would leave the far-flung supply lines and the hundreds of individual merchant ships plying them relatively unprotected and vulnerable. With this in mind, the SKL decided to revisit a successful tactic from the First World War: the use of auxiliary commerce raider ships. These armed converted merchant ships would attack the relatively unprotected flow of raw materials, food supplies, and munitions, causing fear among the merchant sailors and embarrassing England in the eyes of the world.

Just before the actual outbreak of the war, the Oberkommando der Kriegsmarine ordered the SKL to assign German officers and crews to all existing and planned Kriegsmarine warships, including the covert commerce raiders. Tall, soft-spoken Fregattenkapitän Bernhard Rogge was one of the select few chosen to command one of these secret ships.

The future captain of one of the world's most successful warships began life on 4 November 1899, in Schleswig-Holstein. The son of a working professional, Rogge attended *Gymnasium*—the equivalent of a college preparatory high school with a curriculum that concentrated on mathematics, the sciences, and Latin—in a small northern village near the border of Denmark. Rogge's grandfather, also named Bernhard Rogge, was a Lutheran scholar who served as the cleric in the court of Kaiser Wilhelm II and wrote many books about the Lutheran Reformation, German history, and the family of the Kaiser. Grandfather Rogge was an influential man in Germany, and he had a strong influence on the future naval officer as well. The deeply rooted moral standards and unflinching sense of duty he learned from his namesake would serve the younger Bernhard Rogge well.

Growing up in a coastal town with a great tradition of seafaring, Rogge heard many exciting and alluring tales of the seas. As he entered his teenage years, a yearning for the sailor's life of adventure and exotic locations began to overwhelm him. At the age of sixteen, Bernhard Rogge answered Germany's call to duty and submitted his application as a wartime volunteer for a career as a sea officer in the Imperial German Navy. A few years earlier, he could not have aspired to such a career. Only men of the Prussian aristocracy and noble bloodlines were allowed to become officers in the German military services. Kaiser Wilhelm II had abandoned that policy, however, and opened the commissioned ranks to loyal and cultured German young men regardless of their family's social standing. The Kaiser's decree allowed Rogge, the son of a professional, to apply for officer's training.

Rogge was accepted into the program and ordered to report for duty at the Marineschule in Mürwik. He entered military service as a sea officer candidate on 1 July 1915, and, after four days of initial inprocessing, began his military training.

The first phase of the new cadets' training consisted of a month's tutoring in infantry tactics, physical conditioning, and military customs and courtesies. At the end of their infantry training, the cadets who had been selected for advancement embarked on actual warships for short on-the-job training stints. Sea Officer Candidate Rogge was one of those chosen to continue. He began months of cycling between duty on operational warships and attending classes at the Marineschule in Mürwik. Rogge's first training assignment came on 8 August 1915, when the still-green recruit boarded a cadet training ship, the old battle cruiser SMS *Freya*, for his initial practical training session.[2]

The cadets changed vessels often and were rotated through the ships' various stations and divisions while at sea. During these alternating postings the cadets were actually assigned to the ships as crew members, remaining on board through all of the vessel's assignments and actions. When the first sea rotation period ended, the cadets returned to the school for one day to pick up their new posting orders. Cadet Rogge received another posting to a sea cadet training ship.

On 24 October 1915, the young cadet boarded Blohm and Voss's majestic 22,979-ton battle cruiser SMS *Moltke*.[3] The young officer candidate's work on *Moltke* included learning some of the more undesirable aspects of naval service. He stoked and tended engines, scrubbed decks, mended cloth, and heaved lines more often than he accompanied officers at their duty stations, yet he was gaining practical experience in the operation of German naval vessels. On 19 April 1916, Rogge was promoted to Fähnrich-zur-See (i.e., cadet or midshipman, a rank usually attained after completing more than one year of initial training). While serving on *Moltke* Rogge experienced a naval battle firsthand when the ship took part in the major naval engagement at Jutland.

After nearly ten months aboard *Moltke* Rogge was reassigned to a warship in fleet service. On 29 August 1916, he boarded the three-year-old SMS *Stralsund*, a twenty-five-knot, 4,557-ton light cruiser from the Magdeburg class, for a short cruise.[4] After a short stint at sea, Rogge was transferred from *Stralsund*. He left the ship on 4 October 1916, and boarded the 4,390-ton light cruiser SMS *Pillau* the next day for more training and practical experience.[5]

For the next twenty-seven months Rogge alternated between serving in combat actions aboard *Pillau* and completing classroom sessions back at the Mürwik Marineschule. During one of *Pillau*'s engagements with the enemy, Fähnrich-zur-See Rogge distinguished himself and earned the Iron Cross, First Class. It was presented to him by his commanding officer on 21 November 1917.

During the training rotations the Fähnrichs remained assigned to their current ship while they made return trips to Mürwik for academic classroom sessions. The classroom instruction became increasingly more difficult, and the instructors began exposing the cadets to the responsibilities of officership. The academic pressure was intense. Initially, the cadets learned the principles of maneuvering, gunnery, navigation, supply, and torpedo warfare. The cadets were expected to absorb a great deal of information in a short time and immediately be able to recite and elaborate on the subject matter. The instructors expelled cadets who could not maintain the pace of the academics or the physical training. Rogge excelled and secured a place in the class.

When the instructors decided the cadets had mastered the book knowledge of the subject matter, they began training them in realistic drills and field practice. During this phase of the training the instructors evaluated the cadets' ability to put their knowledge to practical application. As the cadets advanced, the school's officers showed them how to conduct and lead such exercises. Each student was given opportunities to lead other cadets during the drills and maneuvers. All the while, the officer-hopefuls were being critiqued and graded, and if successful, identified for future responsibilities.

At the end of the training sessions, the remaining cadets were approved for commissioning. On 13 December 1917 (later backdated by the naval personnel staff to 10 January), Bernhard Rogge was commissioned a Leutnant-zur-See (equivalent to ensign or second lieutenant) in the Imperial German Navy.

Leutnant Rogge completed a short naval mine warfare course in Cuxhaven before reporting back to *Pillau* as a full-fledged member of the ship's company. The commission came without fanfare because there was little opportunity for fame or glory near the end of the First World War. The entire German fleet had been rendered all but useless, bottled up in port by the superior power of the Royal Navy. To add to the degradation, the German navy's last planned assault was thwarted from within by mutinous crewmen no longer willing to risk their lives in combat. Most sailors had become apathetic and demoralized. As the war drew to a close, Leutnant Rogge felt similar despair and dejection, but he never lost sight of what he had been trained to be—a sea officer. The collapse of military discipline during the war's final months, although disappointing, provided Rogge with valuable lessons that would serve him well later in his naval career. By the time World War I paused for the Armistice on 11 November 1918, Rogge had earned his commission, served on an active warship, participated in combat operations in both the Baltic and North Seas, and earned the Iron Cross, Second Class, and the Iron Cross, First Class, for his conduct under fire.

On 28 November 1918, Wilhelm II agreed to the near abolition of German military power imposed by the Allied powers. The Kaiser decreed that all German military personnel were released from their oath of allegiance and were free to return home.[6] This shattering announcement compelled Rogge to begin considering life as a civilian merchant sailor.

The Armistice expired on 12 June 1919, and Germany was forced to decide whether to accept the terms of the Treaty of Versailles or immediately resume hostilities. When the Kaiser ordered the German delegation to sign the treaty, the officers and crews of the remaining ships of the Imperial Navy carried out one last great act to redeem their historical legacy. In the largest mass scuttling in history, the sixty-six ships interned at Scapa Flow defiantly went down together rather than surrender to the Royal Navy. The commander of the interned German naval force, Adm. Ludwig von Reuter, later explained that the fleet "was sunk undefeated in the harbor of Scapa Flow in a grave of its own choosing."[7]

The German fleet's defiant act overshadowed the navy's other failures and the recent mutinous conduct of its sailors: "At last," notes historian Charles S. Thomas, "the sailors had shown that they were prepared to obey orders again. At last the honor of the navy had been restored. Indeed, with a little imagination, the 'deed at Scapa Flow' could be used to gloss over the Imperial navy's failures in the First World War altogether."[8] The scuttling enraged the British and gave them reason to hold the German crewmen until January 1920, but it could not sustain the morale of the German navy's beaten sailors.

Admiral Trotha tried to keep the navy alive under the constraints of the treaty. He handpicked each of the token fifteen hundred naval officers Germany was allowed to retain. Rogge was selected to remain as an active naval officer, as were other notables such as Günther Lütjens, Karl Dönitz, Rolf Carls, Otto Ciliax, and Erich Raeder.

Despite being one of the few selected to remain, Leutnant-zur-See Rogge tendered his resignation on 13 November 1919, and secured employment on a cargo ship. Less than one year later the expanding Reichsmarine, without mentioning his resignation, asked Rogge to return to active duty, and Rogge accepted. He returned to active status on 20 September 1920, as the aide-de-camp and company officer for the 4th Coastal Defense Garrison near the outskirts of Bremerhaven in the small town of Lehe.

Promotions followed quickly. On 14 May 1921, Rogge was advanced to Oberleutnant-zur-See. As a special thanks for returning to the service, the naval staff decided to backdate Rogge's promotion date to 10 January 1921 (and later backdated it again to 1 January 1921). Rogge remained at the coastal defense garrison in Lehe until 1 April, when he moved to the coastal defense office in Cuxhaven.

Following his coastal defense assignments, Rogge returned to Mürwik on 1 October 1922, to attend torpedo operations school. On completion of the course there, Rogge reported for initial training to the 4th Flotilla, 2d E-boat Flotilla, on 1 January 1923.

During training he stood out as an extremely motivated and capable officer. Based on his performance, the flotilla commander assigned Oberleutnant Rogge as a Wachoffizier (a watch officer or duty officer) on the small torpedo boat *T 153*. On 25 August 1923, the navy elevated Rogge's responsibility level again by assigning him as the watch officer on the 2,706-ton light cruiser *Arcona*.[9] This assignment lasted barely three months before Rogge was once again singled out for advancement.

On 1 December 1923, Rogge was transferred to the 2,659-ton Gazelle-class cruiser *Amazone* to continue his training in handling ships and commanding sailors.[10] During his nearly three years on that ship, Rogge served in various capacities and completed a fifteen-day Norwegian cruise and a thirty-five-day Spanish and Atlantic islands cruise. It was aboard *Amazone* that Rogge began to truly understand the intricacies of making a warship at sea run smoothly.

Just a couple of months short of his three-year anniversary aboard the cruiser, Rogge received orders to proceed to another shore assignment. Oberleutnant Rogge reported to Wilhelmshaven to begin his duties as the adjutant for the marine commander of Wilhelmshaven and the North Sea Station on 27 September 1926. He remained at this post until shortly after his promotion to Kapitänleutnant on 1 January 1928.

His next assignment, as the sailing officer on the sailing yacht *Asta*, forever established Rogge's love for wind-powered ships. Although he served on the yacht for only five months, from 1 May to 2 September 1928, Rogge found both delight and satisfaction in sailing; moreover, his superiors noted his exceptional skill at handling a sailing vessel. His mastery of the wind-driven vessel may seem anachronistic, but it would serve to advance his career.

In the spring of 1928, Rogge moved to the 13,191-ton battleship *Schleswig-Holstein* for a short period, again serving as a watch officer and deck officer.[11] Before long, however, the naval personnel staff took advantage of Rogge's sailing skills and moved him to the 373-ton cadet training sailing ship *Niobe*, a converted old Danish freighter. During his tenure there he served as the sailing officer, artillery training officer, and watch officer.[12] Rogge was delighted with the two-year assignment. He enjoyed the elegance and majesty of the sails and got great satisfaction from mentoring the young cadets and introducing them to the art of seamanship under sail.

Continuing in cadet training, Kapitänleutnant Rogge next reported for duty aboard the new light cruiser *Emden* on 10 October 1930.[13] The 6,065-ton ship's complement under the command of Fregattenkapitän Witthoeft-Emden consisted of nineteen officers, three hundred crewmen, and 162 sea cadets. As the ship's training officer, Rogge was responsible for ensuring that the cadets were taught properly and became proficient in all of their required skills. *Emden*'s principal function was to take the cadets on world cruises, exposing them to life at sea and showing the German flag in foreign ports.

During Rogge's tenure the warship made an extended training cruise. *Emden* departed Wilhelmshaven on 1 December 1930, and sailed to thirty-five ports of call in sixteen countries. The ship made stops in the Canaries, Spain, Greece, Egypt, Japan, China, Guam, Borneo, and ports on the South African and West African coasts before returning to Wilhelmshaven more than a year later on 8 December 1931.

Just weeks after completing the training cruise, Kapitänleutnant Rogge received another shore assignment. He moved to the naval staff to work as an inspector and examiner in the training and education branch. He remained at this post until shortly after his promotion to Korvettenkapitän on 1 October 1934.

His subsequent assignment sent him back to teaching cadets at sea. Rogge became the executive officer—the second in command—of the 6,750-ton light cruiser *Karlsruhe* on 20 August 1935.[14] Rogge sailed with *Karlsruhe* on a thirty-two-thousand-mile training cruise in October 1935. The cruiser departed the snowed-over northern port of Bremen, crossed the Atlantic, made an extended call at the hot, tropical, and indiscreet port of Rio de Janeiro, and then returned to Germany.

Karlsruhe's return to Germany completed Rogge's obligatory tour as an executive officer. The personnel staff then selected him for what he considered one of the navy's best assignments: the command of a navy sail training ship. On 10 December 1936, Korvettenkapitän Rogge became captain of *Gorch Fock,* a fully rigged bark named for a martyred poet-sailor who went down with his ship during the Battle of Jutland.[15] The assignment pleased Commander Rogge very much because it combined three things he considered highly desirable: command of a ship, cadet training, and the majesty of a large sailing ship.

Gorch Fock was only a year out of Blohm and Voss's Hamburg shipyard when Rogge took command. The boat was built with safety in mind, designed for the rigors and unexpected stresses of having inexperienced cadets as the crew. With a displacement of only 1,392 tons and a mainmast rising 98 feet above the wooden and steel decks, the 243-foot-long *Gorch Fock* had better sea-keeping qualities than most large cargo ships. Sharing with the cadets the power, beauty, and intensity of wind harnessed in twenty-three sails totaling 18,400 square feet of canvas gave Rogge a great sense of pride and satisfaction. Nor could the cadets hide their awe, respect, and admiration for the regal ship.

Rogge was promoted to Fregattenkapitän on 1 November 1937, and shortly thereafter received orders to report to Hamburg to conduct tests and evaluations on Germany's newest sail training ship. *Albert Leo Schlageter* was larger than *Gorch Fock* in almost every respect.[16] Its mast was 50 feet taller, it weighed about 300 tons more, and it could bridle nearly 1,000 more square feet of sailcloth. Rogge was very excited at the prospect of testing Blohm and Voss's newest sailing ship, but he did not leave his first command without regret.

Any sadness Rogge may have felt at leaving *Gorch Fock* quickly faded when, on 12 February 1938, eleven days after boarding the pristine white *Albert Leo Schlageter*, the naval staff notified him that he had been selected to command the new ship! Rogge could not have been happier. He had been chosen to captain the flagship of Germany's training vessels. Rogge took to his new command and duties with enthusiasm. He planned several years' worth of local training cruises and extended worldwide cruises. In the end, however, world events and the loss of his wife would intervene to change Rogge's plans just over one year after he took command of *Albert Leo Schlageter*.

Fregattenkapitän Rogge was enjoying the beginning of a Baltic cruise with a crew of petty officer candidates when he received a solemn order from Naval High Command on 25 August 1939, instructing him to return to Kiel immediately because "enemy" submarines were operating in his area. Rogge would have preferred to stay at sea, but his unarmed training vessel was defenseless. Commander Rogge placed his men on high alert and instructed his navigation officer crew to turn the square-rigger toward home.

Earlier, in late July, just prior to setting sail on his Baltic trip, Rogge had checked with the naval personnel office for information regarding his future postings. Because world tensions were increasing with each passing day, Rogge wanted some idea of his next assignment in case hostilities should erupt. To his delight Rogge learned that if the navy received orders to transform from peacetime to wartime operations, he was slated to command a warship! The clerk pulled Rogge's card and held it out for him to read:

"Rogge, Bernhard, Commander. War Appointment: SHK II, in command."[17] That terse line meant that if war came, Rogge would command a Schwerer Hilfskreuzer II, a heavy, armed merchant cruiser—in other words, a merchant raider, a high-seas pirate!

Rogge readily accepted this assignment. Although a commerce raider was not as glamorous as a battleship, it offered the challenge of true command. Like the famous raider captains of World War I, Rogge would be solely accountable for his ship's successes and failures. His operational latitude would stem from communications security concerns, which allowed raiders to operate almost completely independent of the stifling control of the SKL. Unlike many of his contemporaries, then, Rogge knew his wartime assignment in advance and was completely satisfied. His skill as a seaman, a naval officer, and a leader of men would certainly be tested.

Albert Leo Schlageter was still sailing toward Kiel on 1 September 1939, when Rogge learned via the ship's radio that German troops had invaded Poland in response to hostile gunfire. War had come. As they neared port, Rogge prepared to leave behind his beloved sailing ship.

Two days later, Great Britain declared war on Germany and World War II officially began. The following day, the SKL ordered Rogge's future command, the 7,862-ton Deutsche Dampfschiffahrts-Gesellschaft Hansa-line freighter *Goldenfels*, to report to the Weser shipyard in Bremen.

After *Albert Leo Schlageter* arrived in Kiel on 6 September, Rogge released his men to their mobilization stations and immediately made his way to the naval headquarters building. The local naval headquarters staff provided Commander Rogge with a full briefing concerning the arrangements made for his warship. The operations officers assured Rogge that his ship, codenamed *Ship-16*, was posted at Bremen, that the conversion from freighter to warship had begun, and that a pool of potential crewmen awaited his approval. Although he was impressed by the seemingly flawless efficiency of the naval staff, Rogge doubted that all of these things had actually been accomplished during the confusion of the first days of the war. Fregattenkapitän Rogge decided to follow up on the naval staff's information and personally check on the status of his new ship.

When Rogge phoned the Bremen port authorities, identified himself, and explained his reason for calling, he was flatly informed that no ship of the sort he described was waiting for him anywhere in Bremen. The call worried Rogge and confirmed his suspicions regarding the SKL's efficiency and actual knowledge of events occurring outside its own office buildings. He decided that his only option was to go to Bremen and find the ship for himself. As soon as he was assured that his crewmen had secured *Albert Leo Schlageter* and stood down, Rogge was on a train bound for Bremen.

Commander Rogge looked nothing like a career officer of the German navy as he stepped off the train at the central station. He wore a plain, dark civilian suit and a heavy wide-collared overcoat and dark brown derby hat. He had opted to remove his uniform to prevent spies from acquiring any information that could endanger his command. Rogge checked into the Hotel Columbus directly across the square from the main train station, just as any merchant captain in the area would have done, then walked toward the ship works lining the Weser River.

At the river, he trudged along the piers and docks looking for his ship. It was a lengthy task; Bremen was filled to capacity with German merchant ships stranded in port by the British blockade. When he finally found *Goldenfels* docked at the Deschimäg Werke shipyard, he was not surprised to see that no conversion work was being carried out on the ship, which sat seemingly lifeless. Contrary to the SKL's briefing, *Goldenfels* was nowhere near a dry dock or refit facility.

Despite his disappointment, Rogge liked what he saw. The ship was a simple, single-stacked freighter. It looked like any one of a hundred other merchant vessels that crossed the oceans each day—truly the perfect disguise for a warship in hiding. Even better, his ship came from the Hansa line, which had an excellent reputation dating back to 1881 for putting modern and efficient ships to sea.[18]

Rogge found the port authorities, presented his Kriegsmarine paperwork, and officially took control of *Goldenfels*. Before long he had made arrangements for a tug and a harbor pilot to move the ship to a nearby naval yard. Rogge felt more secure with his ship at a military dock, where the conversion could be made free from prying eyes and loose gossip.

Once satisfied with the new berth for his ship, Rogge reported to naval headquarters in Bremen to receive his operational orders, crew list, and any other information that might be available for him. When he arrived at the headquarters building Rogge discovered that the bustling administrative office had a processing area for the region's mobilized crewmen operating right out in the open. Rogge approached and noted the orderly rows of tables bearing cards with names and crew listings. Each table was labeled with the name of a ship. When Rogge found his ship's table, he was appalled to see the card lettered in heavy black letters: Schwerer Hilfskreuzer II. Rogge was about to oversee a highly secret transformation, and the administrative office was openly announcing that his ship was a high-seas raider!

The astonished Commander Rogge quickly ensured that the staff changed the tags to a more suitable reference—his ship's simple naval designation: *Ship-16*. Rogge also asked the naval office to assign a barracks for the men who had already reported for duty. Rogge wanted to give his crew a place to congregate and limit their milling about the town. When they had all assembled at the barracks, Rogge surveyed his crewmen and they examined their new captain. Years later, Oberleutnant Johann-Heinrich Fehler, the man destined to be the raider's demolition officer, recalled his first look at his new commander: "A man in a bowler and a civilian suit and overcoat; a tall, broad-shouldered fellow with keen hard eyes of the professional officer tempered by the good-humored lines round the firm, decisive jaw . . . such was my initial impression of the captain of Ship Sixteen. Which was immensely reassuring."[19]

When he had completed the billeting arrangements for his crew, Rogge returned to his hotel with a few of his officers and began to conceptualize and draft plans for the construction and transformation of the ship. Rogge also wrote down some ideas about crew selection. As he began to contemplate all of the requirements, tasks, and particulars that lay ahead of him, he was almost overwhelmed by the magnitude of the job. Yet, he had a keen sense of purpose as well, and a well-defined goal to achieve. Rogge was about to embark on one of the most epic and fascinating naval adventures in the history of the world's modern navies. He would set a new standard for endurance, seamanship, and leadership.

2

A Sheep Becomes a Wolf

BERNHARD ROGGE RECOGNIZED that a good crew was vital to the success of his mission. Service on an auxiliary cruiser demanded a special type of crewman. Rogge was very selective as he tried to ensure that all of the men he chose had certain intangible traits on which he and the officers could build during the cruise. He later explained what he was looking for: "It is the moral qualities of the crew, their ability to withstand strain and overcome difficulties as long as possible. The limits of what is possible in this sphere [life on an auxiliary cruiser] coincide with the limits of human endurance, of the extent to which men are able to bear up under physical hardships and emotional stress."[1]

The captain also realized that he needed a mix of officers and crewmen with training that covered every area of naval expertise. These men must be willing to face and overcome the expected strain and difficulty of raider warfare. They would traverse enemy-filled waters far from home for extended periods. They would have to endure the cold of Antarctica and the Arctic and swelter in equatorial heat; live within the confines of a small, cramped, stuffy ship; tolerate long periods of sheer boredom and then instantly plunge into a heated battle. They had to be ready to carry out their superior officers' commands without hesitation or complaint, regardless of their personal feelings or commitments. Finding the right men for the ship was certainly no small task.

The navy personnel office allocated slots for twenty officers on *Ship-16* and automatically assigned a man to fill each one. Bernhard Rogge did not immediately accept each man. He was extremely careful to ensure that each officer was suited both personally and professionally for the unique duty. The personnel staff's selections that he deemed unacceptable were firmly refused; Rogge accepted only those officers who met his standards.

Rogge had no complaints about Kapitänleutnant Erich Kühn's selection as the ship's executive officer. Kühn came from the regular navy and was very experienced. Rogge had known him since 1936, when Kühn was a warrant officer. The captain was impressed not only with Kühn's professional abilities, but also with his strong character and firm leadership style. Rogge unquestionably approved Kapitänleutnant Kühn's appointment.

Captain Rogge also readily accepted the appointment of Oberleutnant Lorenz Kasch, another experienced career naval officer, as the gunnery officer. Rogge likewise confirmed the selections of Oberleutnant Adolf Wenzel as the radio officer and the spirited Leutnant Johann-Heinrich Fehler as the demolition officer. Although these men lacked experience, Rogge okayed them based on his observations of their demeanor and officership. Other officers hoping to serve aboard Rogge's auxiliary cruiser were not as fortunate. The captain politely but emphatically informed several men that they did not have the qualities or abilities for which he was searching.

Rogge not only turned down selections made by the personnel office—he went one step further and had the effrontery to request other officers specifically by name! He even asked the navy to have some men already assigned to other warships transferred to his new command—men who possessed specific abilities or skills that he considered essential to the operation of his ship. Rogge had personal knowledge of each man's abilities and qualifications, having previously served with each, and he would not accept "no" as an answer.

He fought his case, argued, and called in many favors and markers to secure the men he wanted. Fortunately, Fregattenkapitän Rogge was on good terms with Fregattenkapitän Winther, the officer in charge of the officer assignments branch at Wilhelmshaven. Rogge persisted, and with Winther's help the men he wanted reported for duty one by one: Leutnant-zur-See Dr. Ulrich Mohr came as the ship's adjutant, Korvettenkapitän Fritz Lorenzen as the administrative officer, and Dr. Wolfgang Collmann as the weather officer. Mohr was especially pleased to be selected because his family and Rogge's family were friends.

Most of the ship's other officers came from the civilian merchant fleet. The navigation officer, Kapitänleutnant Paul Kamenz, was an experienced merchant captain and a welcome addition to the crew. The other newly commissioned naval officers were all civilian merchant seaman who held either a master pilot's certificate or first mate's certificate. These men would pilot valuable captured ships back to German-controlled waters or act as division chiefs within their areas of specialization. The navy commissioned these men at the temporary reserve rank of Leutnant-zur-See. The new naval officers added a breadth of experience and proven seamanship abilities to the crew. Two medical doctors—Dr. Georg Reil and Dr. Hans-Bernhard Sprung—were assigned to the ship to ensure high-quality medical care for the crew and any prisoners they might take. The ship's strong officer corps gave Rogge a solid foundation on which to build his crew.

Once Rogge was satisfied with his ship's officers, he moved to the task of selecting the enlisted crew members. The captain wanted men with even temperaments and quiet confidence. He needed true sailors and soldiers. Adventurers, Nazi party functionaries, and the apathetic were undesirable.[2] Rogge searched for men who had learned careers or trades and had shown direction and focus. To ensure that his requirements were met, Rogge started the selection process with a review of each of the assigned men's naval personnel records, followed by a personal, one-on-one interview. The interview was generally very short, consisting of only three or four questions. Based on the results of the meeting and the man's records and general military bearing, Rogge made a final decision. Funkgefreiter Johann Meyer recalled the selection process: "One day in October 1939 he came to us in Bremerhaven and had a small talk with each man. If after that he said, 'O.K., thank you,' you belong to the crew. If he said, 'Thank you, go out to the left side,' you were not his man."[3]

Rogge rejected 104 of the initial 214 prospective crewmen sent by the SKL, complaining about the quality of the candidates that were offered to him. Rogge sensed that the navy was trying to unload undesirable or inferior sailors on what it considered a lower-priority assignment. The new raider was not a battleship, after all. Rogge repeatedly made it clear that he would not crew his ship with any sailor not meeting his standards. He stood his ground and firmly requested new lots of candidates each time he exhausted the previous roster.

To top it all off, Rogge then followed his successful officer-acquisition technique and requested certain enlisted men by name. One of these specially requested men was Stabsobermechaniker Willi Lender, a big Viking of a man who had served under Rogge on both *Karlsruhe* and *Gorch Fock*. Lender's exceptional mechanical abilities would be of incalculable value during the long and unpredictable cruise that lay ahead, and Rogge demanded that he be assigned to *Ship-16*.

Rejecting officers and crewmen and then demanding specific replacements by name was not the normal outfitting procedure for a ship in the German Kriegsmarine, and complaints echoed up the chain of command. Rogge held steadfast to his requests. The Naval High Command, recognizing that Rogge was not outfitting a normal ship, finally relented and approved the transfers of all the crewmen Rogge requested. The SKL supported Rogge's outrageous demands because the admirals knew from their own World War I experiences that Great Britain's economic links to North America and its other trade routes were its lifeblood. England was dependent on the sea lanes for its survival. Rogge's auxiliary cruiser could help pinch off the flow of goods, and the quality of its efforts would depend on the quality of its crew.

As crew selection slowly progressed, Rogge secretly shifted his ship to the AG Weser Deutsche Schiff und Maschinenbau shipyard, where the conversion from merchant ship to commerce raider began. The shipwrights had no idea how to convert the ship; no plans or blueprints existed. How was a merchant freighter to be made into an effective weapons platform while still maintaining the outward appearance of a cargo ship? The job was immense and seemingly impossible.

When the workmen looked to Rogge for guidance and instruction, Rogge looked to the raiders of the previous war. He had lengthy conversations with Fregattenkapitän Karl August Nerger, the skipper of the highly successful World War I raider SMS *Wolf*. Nerger had been through the entire process years earlier when he converted the single-screw Hansa-line steamer *Wachtfels* to the merchant raider *Wolf*. Nerger offered valuable insight on the conversion along with battle-proven wisdom about raider operations.

Rogge also had frequent meetings with the captains of other planned World War II raiders and the naval staff in Berlin. At each meeting Rogge learned more about the requirements for his ship and the art of camouflage, deception, attack, and survival. After each gathering Captain Rogge would return, confer with his officers, and work out the plans for each successive portion of the ship's conversion. Rogge and the crew would then explain or show the Weser workmen precisely what was required.

At the completion of each step, the cycle repeated itself. Nothing was left to chance. As a problem was identified, the Weser engineers and Rogge and his officers had to develop an answer. Their solutions and decisions were put to paper and became the blueprints for the workers to follow. Countless hours passed as the officers worked out solutions in briefing rooms, at dockside, and over bottles of beer and schnapps. Rogge knew that even problems that seemed insignificant in port could become overwhelming obstacles under the pressures of a long cruise, so he tried to consider all potential trouble areas.

Even the concept of raider operations created problems. The fact that the ship was supposed to operate on its own for extended periods required it to be entirely self-sufficient. The fuel capacity of the old *Goldenfels* had to be more than doubled to hold the three thousand tons that *Ship-16* required. The water capacity needed to be tripled to twelve hundred tons. Guns had to be installed, and in such a way that they would be hidden yet could be quickly employed in battle.

An aircraft hangar, prisoners' quarters, crew quarters, a nine-hundred-book library,[4] mess halls, recreation rooms, ammunition magazines and hoists, and four hundred tons of provision stores had to be worked, cut, welded, and riveted into the ship's interior. And every detail, from the type of wallpaper in the seamen's quarters to the location of the guns and ranging equipment, required careful consideration and lengthy discussion. Rogge tried to take into account how every aspect of the crew's life would affect his mission. He later explained his rationale:

> The official German Navy Record of 1914–1918 already contains the passage: "Service conditions on an auxiliary cruiser must be judged in a completely different light from those on a regular warship.... [T]he many days a raider operates without achieving any visible success, the long period it remains at sea and the monotony of life on board are aspects which must be given careful attention."[5]

Fregattenkapitän Rogge took the old lessons to heart and attempted to outfit his ship accordingly. Day after day, the workmen cut, hammered, welded, and pounded. Slowly, the new ship began to take shape.

On 1 November 1939, the German Naval High Command promoted Fregattenkapitän Rogge to the four-stripe rank of Kapitän-zur-See, or full captain. Although Rogge detailed some officers to monitor the progress of the conversion, the new captain continued personally to oversee all the minute details.

While some officers concerned themselves with converting the freighter to a warship, others struggled to meet the equipment requirements. Leutnant Mohr was faced with the monumental task of equipping the ship through normal naval channels. Mohr's job required him to plan for each contingency and need, and then to work all of the materials, tools, and equipment into the ship's storage spaces. Leutnant Fehler recalled an incident that describes Mohr's task perfectly:

> I found Mohr working in his cabin. One hand was pressed to his brow, the other, holding a pen, was describing extraordinary maneuvers over a much scribbled-upon note pad. His usual urbanity had deserted him. He was mumbling to himself.
>
> "Going mad?" I asked. "Or are you composing music?"
>
> He looked at me with a savage despair. "Neither. I'm trying to work out just how much toilet paper this blasted company will need. And the space it will occupy—making due allowance for its daily diminishment."
>
> I tip-toed out.[6]

Equipping the ship with basic necessities proved to be a daunting and challenging task. In one glaring example of bureaucratic efficiency, Mohr telephoned headquarters, then Wilhelmshaven, then Berlin, and finally spoke to the admiral commanding the naval dockyards in an attempt to secure four simple flare pistols for his ship. The answer was the same each time. The supply depot firmly refused to give *Ship-16* the requested equipment because there was no need for a naval depot ship to have even a single flare pistol, let alone four. Finally, frustrated and at his wit's end, Mohr elevated the problem to Captain Rogge. Rogge sent a special dispatch directly to Grand Admiral Raeder explaining the problem. The flare pistols arrived a day after the admiral received the report.

Meanwhile, Kapitänleutnant Kühn was using his twenty-five years of naval service experience to procure needed materials for the ship. Kühn was "finding" the items he needed on nightly raids around the piers, docks, and naval storage yards. It is doubtful that he generated as much paperwork as Mohr, but he was just as effective. Through both Mohr's and Kühn's efforts, the necessary equipment items and supplies arrived daily and began to fill the ship's interior. Every bit of available space served a specific purpose. Every nook, cranny, and corner stored spare parts, paint, lumber, supplies, machinery, water, and even live pigs!

By the first week of December, crew selection was nearly complete and the conversion had progressed to the point that the last items, the guns, were ready to go aboard the ship. The ship's main guns came from the dilapidated old German battleship *Schlesien*.[7] When Adjutant Mohr attempted to procure modern guns and ranging equipment to replace the forty-year-old guns and antiquated range finders allocated to *Ship-16*, the Admiralty refused his request, flatly stating that the ship would likely be sunk before it ever had the opportunity to use them. This lack of confidence in his new ship angered Mohr. He told Rogge of the callous comment and suggested that a protest was in order. Rogge simply dismissed the comment and ordered the old guns mounted.

The gun placement, the last task in the conversion effort, proved far easier than the shipwrights had anticipated. Surprisingly, the ship already had existing reinforced sections for gun mounts built in at strategic locations. The German government, with remarkable forethought, had secretly subsidized Hansa's construction of the ship in 1937 under the provision that specifically strengthened areas be built into the ship. Once the guns were in place, the conversion was completed by the addition of concealing doors that opened upward.

The German Admiralty commissioned its newest warship on 19 December 1939, fourteen weeks after *Goldenfels* pulled into Bremen as a merchant freighter. The ship's official military name was *Ship-16*, but Rogge told his crew that he was giving the ship an unofficial name: *Atlantis*. He explained that the fabled city of Atlantis had been one of the great mysteries of the seas throughout history. Rogge hoped the ship *Atlantis* would become a mystery of the seas for the duration of the war.

Crewed by 347 men, *Atlantis* measured 488 feet in length and 61 feet in width, and drew 31 feet of water. The two huge MAN diesel engines coupled to a single shaft could drive the ship at seventeen and a half knots at flank speed. The hidden armaments consisted of six SK L/45 150-mm cannons, one 75-mm bow gun, two twin-mounted 37-mm guns, and four single-mounted 20-mm antiaircraft guns. In addition, *Atlantis* carried four single 533-mm torpedo tubes and two Heinkel seaplanes, and had room for ninety-two naval mines. The 150-mm guns were installed so a four-gun broadside could be brought to bear on the enemy. Although short in gun range, *Atlantis* was well equipped for a close-in fight.

The new warship sat in Bremen as Rogge allowed his crew to settle in and become accustomed to life aboard the ship. The men learned to navigate the many passageways and decks to find their quarters, the mess rooms, their battle stations, and the other necessary areas of the ship. Once the crew had become comfortable with *Atlantis,* Rogge initiated battle drills.

For two days the captain sharpened the crew's reflexes and instincts through a nearly endless string of drills and simulations. Captain Rogge carefully balanced the training regimen with personal attention to each man's individual concerns, realizing that each man's personality would affect his actions during the course of an extended cruise. He later explained his leadership technique as follows:

> The problem therefore was—especially on an auxiliary cruiser whose foremost task was to remain at sea as long as possible—to find the key to the personality of every individual aboard. . . . Superiors had to gain the confidence of their subordinates. To this end, the officers and petty officers on board had to become acquainted with every man as soon as possible. Greeting a person without addressing him by name is impersonal. An ordinance expressly forbade adding a name to the Hitler salute. So for this reason alone, if for no other, we had no use for the Hitler salute. We formed a community based on the motto which I learned in peacetime from the captain of a training cruiser: "You cannot be everyone's friend, but you can be a good comrade to all."[8]

Rogge also began teaching the men the art of deception and camouflage. Additionally, he held meetings with the entire crew to impress on them his strong desire to maintain proper discipline and order as they conducted their raiding. The ship would comply strictly with international law in its tactics. Rogge explained that the use of false flags and disguises to deceive the enemy was a permissible ruse as long as the warship hoisted its true colors before firing.[9] Captain Rogge made it clear to all that he would settle for nothing less than honorable conduct toward the enemy. He instructed the crew to comply with all established rules and conventions concerning contact with the enemy during battle and the handling of prisoners afterward. Any man who violated the rules would be punished. The captain reiterated that the goal of *Atlantis* was to conduct high-seas raiding actions in support of the German war effort while keeping loss of life to an absolute minimum and remaining within the constraints of international law.

As the initial preparations were ending, the shore-based administrative office suggested that Rogge take along a supply of Iron Crosses to issue during the cruise. Captain Rogge politely refused and replied that he would rather put the ship to sea first and present Iron Crosses at the end of the cruise, if they were earned.

On 21 December 1939, the Admiralty ordered Rogge's warship moved from the Weser yard in Bremen to the naval yard in Kiel, a more secure location, where the crew could begin final preparations for the cruise. It was dark before *Atlantis* cast off, cleared its berth, and began to sail down the Weser. The ship was steadily picking up speed when a noticeable stagger reverberated throughout the interior. Within seconds the ship came to a full stop. The newly commissioned warship had started its glorious career by sailing outside the deep navigation channel and plowing firmly into the thick mud of the river bottom.

Captain Rogge was not at the helm at the time; an experienced river pilot was in command. Nonetheless, the incident was highly embarrassing for Rogge as the ship's captain. The other officers feared that news of the grounding might reach the Admiralty or the Führer. The result could be the appointment of another commander. There was certainly a precedent for that. When the World War I raider *Wolf* ran aground in the Elbe as it sailed out on its maiden cruise, the captain was relieved of his post and Fregattenkapitän Nerger was appointed as commanding officer in his place.

Although Rogge ordered the engines run in full reverse and tried everything else he could think of, *Atlantis* remained solidly stuck. The crew understood as well as the officers that their captain could be replaced for the incident. They had grown loyal to Rogge and feared that any possible replacement would lack his command abilities and even temperament. The officers asked Rogge to wait for the next high tide before calling for assistance. The incoming tide might raise the ship just enough to pull it free from the mud. Rogge agreed, and the ship's company anxiously awaited the rising tide. To everyone's relief, the incoming water slowly lifted the ship and finally released it a full six hours later.

Once free, the ship sailed down the Weser into the open waters around Cuxhaven, up the Elbe, and finally north up the Kiel Canal. All the while, the crew continued their silent prayers that their captain would not be replaced as a result of the grounding incident. The ship pulled into its assigned position without any further misfortune on mid-morning of 23 December 1939. Rogge ordered Kühn to set the ship's disguise to appear as a naval support ship.

As December passed into January, one of the worst winters in recent history put an icy grip on all of northern Europe. The approaches and waterways to and around the North Sea froze solid. *Atlantis* sat docked in Kiel disguised as a naval auxiliary ship. The dark gray paint and large deck-mounted searchlights, guns both fore and aft, and two funnels created a very credible disguise. Rogge noted that it was nearly impossible to distinguish the fabricated guns and funnel from real ones. The crew openly wore their Kriegsmarine uniforms as they went about the mundane tasks sailors the world over perform when their ships are in port. Clearing the docked ship of snow and ice and keeping the machinery operational became a priority for the crew. All the while, Captain Rogge intensified the frequency and duration of the practice drills.

Even though it flew the German battle ensign, the ship's true identity remained hidden. When in town, the crew tolerated heckling and teasing from shore-based naval personnel and crewmen from ships of the line who had no idea of the "depot" ship's real purpose. Rogge did his best to praise his men and bolster their spirits throughout the month. He told them that their duty was extremely important and they must endure the ribbing because secrecy was their strongest ally. Nevertheless, Rogge worried that one of the men might lose control and announce the ship's true identity. Each day in port added to the risk.

As January drew to a close, the ship began to receive its final supply requisitions. The officers were beginning to see conditioned responses and instant reactions during the ever-increasing number of drills. They were pleased to see the men building skills that would serve them well in battle.

On 31 January, the crew stood proudly on their spotless ship as Grand Adm. Erich Raeder, Naval Supreme Commander in Chief, boarded the ship for an inspection. The admiral, wrapped in his long greatcoat, quickly toured the ship, inspecting both personnel and equipment. The inspection pleased him. It also pleased the officers, as the admiral did not mention the grounding incident that had occurred a month earlier. His silence on the subject finally put to rest the crew's fears of losing their captain.

The day following the inspection, the practice drills resumed. Throughout February the crew perfected the art of changing their ship's exterior appearance. Under the cover of darkness the crew practiced the various deception techniques, always returning *Atlantis* to its depot ship disguise by daybreak.

Atlantis had a variety of disguises from which to choose. The men could alter the ship's silhouette using wood framing, canvas sheeting, and paint. The masts and king posts moved up and down. Other masts could be erected in various positions about the deck. The funnel could be lengthened or shortened; if needed, a false one complete with smoke could be added. Fake ventilators could be set up and the real ones moved or removed. The exposed deck guns wore the disguise of cargo or deckhouses. Erecting dummy guns allowed the ship to pass as a minesweeper or an armed merchant ship. The ship also had one novel attribute that Mohr thought was truly impressive: *Atlantis* possessed two sets of navigation lights, of opposite colors, mounted side by side. With the flip of a switch, the opposite set of lights illuminated, making it appear that the ship was sailing in one direction when in fact it was sailing in the other! *Atlantis* also carried paints of all types and shades and flags of many nations, which all combined to offer a wide repertoire of possible guises. Each facade had to be good enough to prevent detection even at close range, yet not hinder the guns from springing instantly into action.

The first week in March saw *Ship-16* top off the fuel stores and secretly begin to take on ammunition and naval mines. Munitions and magnetic mines were loaded only in small parcels and always at night. Rogge broke up the shipments to ensure that no one would wonder why a naval auxiliary ship was taking on so much ammunition. Yet, despite all of Captain Rogge's efforts, security began to slip. Rumors about a merchant raider began to drift around the piers. Rogge became doubly concerned about security. His crew had been sitting in port for too long; it was time to put to sea.

Finally, the captain was recalled to Berlin for his final briefing and last-minute updates. Rogge's orders were no surprise to him. In concept, they were the same as those of any other merchant raider in the history of naval warfare. His mission was to disrupt the enemy's transport, trade, and shipping operations, keeping the British Admiralty constantly on guard and off balance. *Atlantis* was to appear unexpectedly, pounce on the enemy, and quickly melt back into the vast expanses of the sea. The SKL expected Rogge's actions to force the British to employ escorted convoys where it was undesirable for them to do so. The High Command also wanted *Atlantis* to compel the enemy to waste capital ships in remote areas searching for a ghost warship. *Atlantis* was to avoid enemy warships, convoys, and passenger ships, which were often too fast, too heavily armed, or too well escorted for a raider to approach or outfight. Rogge acknowledged his orders, received final good luck wishes from Berlin, and boarded a train bound for Kiel.

On the captain's return, the crew anxiously waited for word of the date when they would set sail. Rogge piqued their curiosity by hinting that their departure was close at hand, but he would tell them no more. Two days later, on 12 March 1940, Rogge broke the tension. He called the crew together and notified the men that they would sail the following day, then ordered First Officer Kühn to prepare the ship for sea. A cry of horror and disbelief rose from the crew. March 13! Surely *Atlantis* was not going to sail on the thirteenth of the month—unlucky 13! What was the Admiralty thinking?

Rogge laughingly announced that he had predicted the crew's reaction and obtained permission to sail at 11:55 P.M. on 12 March instead. Apprehension and excitement raced through the crew as they realized that their long-awaited voyage would begin in only a few hours.

Just before midnight on Tuesday, 12 March 1940, *Atlantis* pulled clear of a German port for the last time. There was no dockside crowd, no band, none of the jubilant fanfare that normally accompanied a German warship leaving port. *Atlantis* just slowly pulled away from the berth and faded from view, following the old battleship *Hessen* into the night.[10] The thirty-seven-year-old battlewagon's armor plates were now good only for breaking ice. Following *Atlantis* were two other raiders: *Ship-36—Orion* and *Ship-21—Widder*, both disguised as minesweepers. The convoy of secret warships followed *Hessen* through the ice-choked Kiel Canal to the North Sea.

Rogge left one trusted chief petty officer behind at Kiel. The petty officer's job was to report to the naval support office and collect the mail addressed for the naval depot ship called *Ship-16*. Each day the man picked up the mailbags and transported them to a secret storeroom, where he stacked them to remain hidden and unread. This was a harsh security procedure in terms of the crew's morale, but having mail pile up in the naval support office would adversely affect the ship's operational security. The support personnel would have tried to locate the ship to attempt delivery of the mail. This in turn would provide British intelligence agents with a wealth of information. Rogge chose to store the mail, a much easier and more secure solution than allowing its delivery.

The ships crept along the German coastline to a position just off the Jade Inlet. Rogge and the other captains wanted to complete some routine gunnery practice and exercises as soon as possible; the practice drills for the main guns, antiaircraft defenses, and the range-finding equipment were of primary concern. Unfortunately, circumstances dictated otherwise. When the ships arrived at the designated training location, there were no targets for them. The tugs assigned to tow the targets had been dispatched to help locate survivors from a U-boat recently sunk in action. The bitter cold and continuous buildup of ice made the operation of the guns all but impossible in any case.

Rogge decided to run the gun routines regardless of the weather. He worked the crew and the ship intensely for the next two days. Each day he tested a different gun crew for proper timing and ranging while he maneuvered the ship in hard turns at various speeds. The big exercise was planned for dusk on the last day in the practice area. At the appointed time, First Officer Kühn once again called the gun crews to their posts for the last firing exercise. The plan called for the employment of all the ship's guns in a grand finale.

On Rogge's order, Gunnery Officer Kasch signaled for the firing to begin. Almost instantly, the main guns belched black smoke and boomed, lighting up the sky with brilliant orange-red plumes as they sent their 100-pound shells screaming out to sea. With each volley, the recoil from the big guns produced a pronounced shudder that resonated throughout the ship. The rest of the ship's armament joined in. The 20-mm antiaircraft batteries shot rapid-fire volley after volley, creating bright red arcs all around the ship. The 75-mm bow gun crew busied themselves putting shots across imaginary bows. Machine-gun positions opened up and joined the fanciful battle while other crewmen launched illumination flares high into the sky.

Shortly after the firing began, a radioman, Funkmaat Heinrich Wesemann, notified the bridge that German naval coastal stations were reporting a heavy naval engagement taking place within German coastal waters. To the amusement of the crew, one alarmed station even reported that the British navy was attacking in force!

Having completed the gun trials and successfully stirred up the coastal defenses around Wilhelmshaven, *Atlantis* slowly crept toward the Süderpiep, a small inlet north of the Elbe. The crew silently wondered if they would return to port or attempt to break through the British blockade. On 19 March, Rogge gathered his men and announced that they would not be returning to Kiel. Morale skyrocketed as the men realized they were about to sail against the enemy blockade.

The British blockade circled the North Sea and its approaches within a very tight ring of three overlapping defenses. A breakthrough required first passing the Gap, a giant minefield that extended from the Frisian Islands up to and along the Norwegian coast. The British had sown a very dense and complicated screen of mines all along the edges and approaches to the North Sea. The minefields gave English warships a significant tactical advantage over any adversary who tried to operate in the North Sea area.

The next obstacle was a long, narrow stretch of water running between the Shetland Islands and Norway called the Neck. The Neck allowed no escape for a ship caught there. Once inside the area, a ship that was spotted or pursued had nowhere to go. The narrow stretch of water funneled vessels into an easily monitored and controlled traffic channel. The British patrolled the Neck with warships, picket boats, and reconnaissance aircraft. If the enemy approached *Atlantis* there, Rogge would have no option but to unmask his guns and attempt to fight his way out to open water.

The third and last major barrier was the heavily patrolled and dangerous waters of the Denmark Strait, known for their unpredictable ice floes. Floating ice and near-zero visibility were constant threats in this region. To add an additional concern, British cruisers had begun to run war patrols through the strait.

The blockade was considerably more difficult to breach now than it had been during the First World War. The British had less area to cover because of the extensive minefields. Technological improvements in reconnaissance gear and ranging equipment allowed them to monitor the reduced surface area more closely. All of these factors increased the probability that the British would discover most passing ships. To succeed, Rogge needed foul weather, stormy seas, and limited visibility to mesh with his skill, luck, and cunning. Even if all of these factors came together favorably during the breakout attempt, *Atlantis* still had only a slight chance of making the open ocean.

On 23 March, *Atlantis*, outfitted as an innocent depot ship, slowly moved into Süderpiep Bay unnoticed, anchored, and waited for nightfall. During the cold night the crew swarmed over the ship and changed its facade. A gray, two-funneled, nameless naval auxiliary ship became the single-funneled, 5,749-ton, fourteen-year-old Norwegian freighter *Knute Nelson*. The crew labored all night at the task. They removed false structures, added others, and then repainted the entire ship. The immense task of changing the ship's disguise required all the strength and stamina each man possessed. It was an undertaking that no one aboard looked forward to, yet all performed without complaint when called on to do so.

By morning, the ship displayed an entirely different deck profile. The crew had moved the stacks, masts, poles, and stanchions and put a coat of fresh green paint on the hull and one of bright white on the superstructure, the colors of the Oslo-based Fredolsengaten and Company line. To top off the deceit, the disguised *Atlantis* flew a yellow flag of quarantine warning others to stay away or risk catching some dreaded disease.

Atlantis sat at anchor for seven more days while Rogge waited for the weather to deteriorate. During the wait, British reconnaissance planes occasionally swooped in to inspect the anchored Norwegian freighter. *Atlantis*'s disguise as *Knute Nelson* held up against this scrutiny despite the one occasion when a young crewman darted out on deck in full Kriegsmarine uniform while trying to catch a glimpse of the enemy plane. Apparently the young man went unnoticed, as the plane did not broadcast a report.

Each day of waiting increased the chance of discovery, but the weather was not yet to Rogge's liking. It was 31 March before Kapitän-zur-See Rogge decided to attempt the breakout. The first task was to change the raider's costume again. In the dead of night and under the driving of the taskmaster Kühn, scaffolding was erected around the ship. Men scampered up and down, repainting, rerigging masts, and moving structures here and there.

By morning on the first day of April, *Knute Nelson* had metamorphosed into the high-masted Russian naval auxiliary vessel *Kim*. The Russian navy had recently commandeered the 5,114-ton *Kim* from Moscow's Sovtorgflot line, and the ship's true whereabouts were unknown. This recent change in *Kim*'s status from a civilian merchant vessel to a naval auxiliary gave Rogge the perfect cover. The Russian military was notoriously secretive. It was highly unlikely that the British knew much about the types and locations of Russian ships. Furthermore, some ships simply did not show up in the international registers, and the language barrier presented its own set of problems. The new ship boldly wore hammer and sickle insignias, large red stars, and the only Cyrillic inscription Adjutant Mohr could find to copy: СТЕРЕТАИТЕСЬ ВИНТСВ.

The Russian writing, which warned other ships, "Keep clear of our propellers," was a believable addition to the disguise. Rogge thought the wording a nice touch and applicable enough for those few who could read it. Perhaps the most convincing part of the new camouflage was one of Flying Officer Richard Bulla's HE-114 seaplanes, firmly lashed on hatch number two and realistically painted in a Russian color scheme.

Rogge inspected the new disguise by circling the ship in a small motor launch. He scrutinized *Kim* from all angles, up close and from a distance. Captain Rogge returned to the ship with only one criticism: the Russian flag was flying upside down! A crewman quickly corrected the small but dangerous mistake and completed the disguise.

At mid-morning, *Atlantis* weighed anchor and started moving slowly northward up the coast, filling the airwaves with useless radio chatter, as would any unconcerned merchant vessel pulling away from port. The ship picked up its escort of two E-boats—*Leopard,* under the command of Kapitänleutnant Hans Trummer, and *Wolf,* under Oberleutnant-zur-See S. Broder-Peters—and a submarine, *U-37*.[11] Soon the four ships would enter the first danger area: the Gap.

All available hands maintained a sharp lookout on deck despite the buffeting winds and icy drizzle. Occasionally, a lookout would spot a rusty, slimy, horned menace and *Atlantis* would alter course to turn away from the dangerous sphere. The Luftwaffe provided intermittent air cover as the weather allowed. The small escort group gave the impression that the Germans were giving a Russian ship a proper send-off as it headed for home. Their actual task was to protect *Atlantis* as it made for the narrows between the Shetlands and Norway.

The weather was exactly what Rogge needed for a successful breakout. Visibility varied between zero and one-half mile. The sky was a foggy, featureless expanse of gray. The ships pitched in the fast, heavily rolling waves, which sent powerful flows of icy green water rushing over *Atlantis*'s lookouts. The men battled and cursed the cold and ice; Rogge welcomed it.

By late afternoon the ships were past the most dangerous parts of the minefield and the escorting E-boats had reached their operational range limits. The two nimble boats flashed signals to Rogge and requested permission to end their escort. Rogge had *Atlantis*'s signalman reply with his approval. The two E-boats turned and raced off toward home without a further word or signal, leaving *Atlantis* and *U-37* alone to face whatever might come next.

As day melted into darkness, the calm was broken when a lookout reported ships off the starboard bow. Through his binoculars, Rogge could clearly see three small fishing vessels outlined against the Norwegian coast. He decided to allow the Russian disguise to act as the ship's defense. First Officer Kühn altered course slightly to feign a heading toward Murmansk as they continued to sail on.

Slowly, the vessels passed astern of *Atlantis* and faded from view. Shortly thereafter Funkgefreiter Franz Ott excitedly reported that the fishing boats were broadcasting coded messages in the enemy's five-letter group format —the code used by British Naval Intelligence. Rogge hoped the intelligence boats were reporting a routine departure of a Russian freighter from a German port and not the sailing of a Kriegsmarine warship. Regardless of what the spy ships reported, *Atlantis* and *U-37* pushed on into the night.

As the night advanced, so did a storm front. The waves formed deep troughs with steep sides that engulfed the ships and then crashed down on them with blows so sudden and so sharp that the men could not keep on their feet. Visibility dropped to zero as the tremendous wind swept the heads off the waves and drove them into sheets of stinging, blinding, icy spray. Rogge was pleased; the weather was allowing him to make good his escape without the worry of discovery. The two vessels passed the first danger area and entered the approach to the Neck right on schedule.

Captain Rogge wanted to pass the second danger point by the following morning, but the seas forced both ships to slow their progress. The latest intelligence report for the narrow Neck area warned of three known British cruisers assigned to continually scour the small stretch of sea. Rogge ordered maximum vigilance, which kept a large percentage of the crew out in the brutal weather watching for enemy ships. Very few crewmen would rest or sleep that night. The officers did not leave their posts at all, and the sailors were required to man lookout positions when their other normal duty shifts were complete. It was a drastic measure, but the threat level was very high.

The weather worsened until it reached gale force 10 at midnight. The waves pummeled the ships. Korvettenkapitän Werner Hartmann, the thirty-eight-year-old commander of *U-37*, signaled that his boat could not keep up. The U-boat was iced over and unable to maintain speed or crash dive. Hartmann feared the heavy seas would break up or capsize his boat. Rogge agreed, and via signal lamps the two commanders quickly made arrangements for their ships to part ways and meet again east of the Denmark Strait.

U-37 dropped back while *Atlantis* pushed on, the big ship's plates rattling each time another immense swell crashed down on the deck. Within hours of losing the marginally protective U-boat escort, the lookouts on *Atlantis* spotted two sets of masts clearly silhouetted against the gray dawn sky. Sirens posted belowdecks wailed, calling the men to their action stations. Crewmen frantically scrambled through gangways, up and down ladders, and about the decks to reach their assigned posts.

Captain Rogge could barely see the two vessels across the heavy seas, but he was able to see enough to identify them. One ship ran blacked-out. The other was illuminated with lights, but not just navigation lights—command lights. The two ships were definitely warships! Rogge knew that no German warships were operating in the Neck. The ships on the horizon were unquestionably hostile enemy ships of the line.

Within moments of being sighted by the German lookouts, the two enemy ships turned hard onto an intercept track. Rogge summoned his chief engineer, Oberleutnant Wilhelm Kielhorn, to the bridge. The slightly overweight, round-faced Bavarian officer reported a few minutes later, winded from his race from the stiflingly hot bowels of the ship and nearly overcome by the sudden intense cold. Nevertheless, he stood at rigid attention to receive his orders. The instructions Rogge rapped out were simple. Kielhorn was to nurse every available bit of power out of his diesels, get the ship up to full speed, and keep it there until told to do otherwise. Kielhorn acknowledged his orders, and Rogge slid the engine telegraph to register flank speed.

The chief engineer returned to his post and pulled out all stops. He worked the engines up to full speed and *Atlantis* reached its maximum of seventeen and one-half knots. The vibrations from the huge engines inside combined with the seas battering the hull outside seemed certain to tear the ship apart. Again and again *Atlantis* smashed into wave crests with brutal force and then plummeted into their deep troughs. Loose items flew around the inside of the ship, clanking, banging, and shattering everywhere.

The men fought a losing battle to maintain their positions at their designated stations as the ship drove straight into the gale-force wind. The bruised, cursing gun crews continually burned and chipped away at the ice in an attempt to keep their guns and counterweighted doors operational. The ride was sheer agony for all those aboard. And all the while, the warships continued their merciless pursuit.

The ship was consuming fuel at an alarming rate, but Kielhorn kept the engines at maximum capacity. The engineer knew that he was driving the newly refurbished engines too hard, too hot, and too fast; they might come apart at any moment. The men feared the ship would break up; Leutnant Kielhorn feared the engines would fail; and Rogge feared the enemy warships would close the gap and decide the issue by gunfire. Escape was the only alternative for *Atlantis*. Equipment failure or any other problem that slowed the ship would bring about death or capture.

Finally, in the late afternoon, the pursuing ships slowly began to fade astern. Whether the German ship was too fast, the storm too violent, or the cost of fuel too much for the English ships, *Atlantis* had won the race. A cheer went up from the crew when the lookouts announced that the two masts had slipped below the horizon and faded out of view.

Rogge ordered *Atlantis* slowed as soon as it was safe to do so. He secured his ship from action stations and ordered normal operations resumed. As they had practiced, teams of men hustled around the ship to check for signs of leaking or damage. The crew found no damage to the ship or the engines. In its first test, *Atlantis* had held firm.

Rogge pressed on at the slower pace. He kept the phony Russian ship headed in a direction that continued to imply Murmansk as its destination. Within hours of losing sight of the warships, the lookouts reported yet another vessel in view. Rogge inspected the ship through his long-range binoculars. The two distinctive long masts made identification quite simple. The ship was the 7,003-ton German merchant ship *Taronga*, originally a Wilhelmsen Company freighter that the Germans had seized and pressed into service. *Taronga* turned to give the apparently Russian ship a wide berth and within a short time passed by without incident, acknowledgment, or report to German authorities. Rogge felt secure in the Russian disguise.

Not long after *Taronga* sailed over the horizon, the lookouts reported yet another sighting. A set of two tall mastheads belonging to another warship turned and approached from a course off the normal shipping lanes. Mohr sounded action stations. Rogge decided to allow the Russian disguise to protect *Atlantis* in the event of contact. The crew waited to spring into action as the officers anxiously watched the suspected warship approach at high speed. Suddenly, the unknown ship turned hard and made off with a burst of speed. With the crew breathing a sigh of relief, *Atlantis* once again secured from action stations and continued north as the stormy gray sky began to give way to a dark, blustery night.

The next morning brought an end to the storm. Although the waves were still very high, the pounding brutes of the previous days had eased into long, slow swells. The Russian merchant ship drove steadily northeast, making very good time in the rolling seas, finally alone and sailing hard. As the day ended, the swells stopped and the sea lay virtually flat. *Atlantis* picked up speed as it headed north. Still feigning Murmansk as its destination, the ship crossed the Arctic Circle.

The temperature was almost unbearably cold. To accomplish the necessary deck work, the crew dressed in multiple layers of heavy clothing. The men fought both the subzero temperatures and their bulky clothing to perform routine maintenance and the required functional checks. And all the while, the lookouts manned their posts, bundled against the cold, continually scanning the horizon for any sign of another ship.

In the dead of the night, the lookouts rousted the entire crew to witness the spectacle of the northern lights. The crew threw on their cold-weather clothing and huddled on the deck as they delighted in the immense aerial light show of the aurora borealis. The phantom lights jumped and streaked miles above their heads. The Wagnerian display of beauty and power temporarily broke the tension and the fears of impending battle.

In the early morning hours, *Atlantis* finally approached the point at which it would be impractical to continue in the direction of Murmansk. Kühn ordered the ship turned sharply westward. After the drastic course change, the ship followed the track of the Murmansk-to-Iceland shipping route and steamed away from Murmansk. Any ship that caught sight of *Atlantis* would assume it had sailed from Murmansk and was heading toward Iceland. This was Rogge's ploy. He masked his true destination, the area just off Jan Mayen Island, perfectly.

Jan Mayen was where Rogge expected to rendezvous with *U-37*. At midday the lookouts reported the island off the raider's starboard side. *Atlantis* tracked the precise course plotted by Kapitänleutnant Kamenz on his maps. Considering the extreme weather and the chasing warships, the pinpoint arrival confirmed the balding navigation officer's abilities, experience, and skill.

Almost immediately after sighting the island, the lookouts identified the unmistakable profile of a surfaced submarine cruising slowly and floating high in the water. A submarine resting on the surface of a smooth sea creates a dangerous silhouette. In a strict military sense it was a tactical blunder, but Korvettenkapitän Hartmann did not expect any enemy ships in those waters and he wanted *Atlantis* to find him as quickly as possible. He took a risk, but a well-calculated one.

Atlantis drew up near the submarine and the two ships sat close together for the next several hours while the two captains met to discuss their plan of action for crossing the third danger area. As the commanders conferred, the crews heaved long, flexible fuel lines between *Atlantis* and *U-37*, and twenty-five tons of fuel were passed to the U-boat. Rogge and Hartmann had two options available to them. The two ships could go north of Iceland into the Denmark Strait. There they would encounter rough seas, dangerous floating ice, and very low visibility. The advantage afforded by this route was a very low probability of contact with an enemy warship. The other route, south of Iceland into the North Atlantic, offered smoother seas, no ice pack, and increased visibility, but it also meant crossing a sea dotted with British mines and swarming with enemy cruisers. The two commanders reviewed the weather forecasts and the updated enemy strength reports to weigh the odds of successfully piercing the final barrier. After much deliberation and discussion, Rogge made the decision: they would transit the treacherous Denmark Strait.

When the crews completed the refueling operation, *Atlantis* and *U-37* started north around Iceland. As nightfall approached, the crews spotted the first floating chunks of ice. Once again Rogge ordered maximum vigilance on deck. The ships steamed due south through the heart of the strait. This was by far the coldest weather *Atlantis* had experienced so far. The water temperature was well below freezing at 27 degrees Fahrenheit, and the air temperature was 20 degrees below zero.

The mountainous seas kept pace with the harsh cold; every few seconds they lifted the ships high and then abruptly dropped them into deep troughs. White-capped monsters regularly crashed over *Atlantis*'s bow, coating the decks in thick sheets of ice. The men, working in clothing nearly frozen solid, used axes, picks, and torches to break the ice off the decks, guns, and hatches, only to see them coated again within minutes. The work was dangerous and exhausting, but it was necessary.

U-37 was icing badly too. Even with safety lines, the submarine crew could not clamber out to the submarine's exposed areas to clear away the ice. The U-boat was nearly iced over and incapable of taking any offensive action. A rogue wave could have instantly foundered and sunk the ship.

At 67 degrees, 24 minutes north latitude and 24 degrees west longitude, the submarine signaled that it could go no farther. *U-37* managed to stop and slowly turn around in the dangerous waves. Between the wave crests crashing over the small conning tower, *U-37* flashed the message "Best of luck and a safe return," then sailed off in the opposite direction, bobbing on wave crests and dropping into troughs until it was out of sight.[12]

Atlantis plowed on. The lookouts watched more for icebergs than for enemy warships. The night seemed endless. The cold was nearly unbearable and there was no respite from the punishing ocean. As dawn came, the men were beginning to reach the limits of their endurance when the ocean began to calm considerably and the temperature rose noticeably. Rogge described the change in temperature as being as sudden as stepping out of a cold winter night into a warm room. The calm water and warm air meant *Atlantis* had successfully made it to the waters of the Gulf Stream. Within an hour of crossing into the Gulf Stream, the water temperature had jumped to 42 degrees Fahrenheit and the air temperature was quite bearable.

The third danger area lay behind them, and the raider's secrecy remained intact. *Atlantis* had not been identified by any other ship or attacked by British warships. At around noon, *Atlantis*'s radio operators picked up a message from *U-37* to the naval staff at the German Admiralty. The report notified the Admiralty of *Atlantis*'s status and relieved Rogge of the requirement to break his radio silence and make a report of his own.

Atlantis continued to sail south along the coast of Greenland for the rest of the day and all the following night. At 8:00 A.M. on Saturday, 8 April 1940, Kapitänleutnant Kamenz and Kapitänleutnant Kühn reported to their captain that *Atlantis* was past the southern tip of Greenland and through the blockade. *Atlantis* had reached the open waters of the North Atlantic Ocean.

3

Atlantis Goes into Action

HAVING ATTAINED HIS first objective, the open waters of the North Atlantic, Captain Rogge reviewed his orders. They instructed him to sail south, avoid all contact unless fired on, sow his mines, and then begin raider actions only after he entered his assigned operational area.

The SKL had given *Atlantis* the task of creating a physical barrier to impede Allied shipping around Cape Town. *Atlantis* was to lay ninety-two naval mines in an area just off the South African coast where ships rounding the tip of the African continent were funneled by currents and channels. A minefield at such a shipping bottleneck would tie up British minesweeping forces, create confusion and delay for the enemy, and potentially scatter ships—making them easy prey for a commerce raider. Captain Rogge intended to do just what his orders specified. He was in complete agreement with the tactical elements of the plan, and he certainly wanted to empty the mine stowage bays of their volatile cargo before embarking on any other operations.

The raider cruised steadily southward toward its destination, Cape Agulhas, on one engine at the leisurely pace of ten knots. Each passing hour brought higher temperatures and warmer seas. As the ship moved farther and farther south, the radio room picked up an ever-increasing stream of messages from passing ships of all nationalities. Some of the broadcasts, sent in the clear, gave Rogge important weather data or clues concerning how the British Admiralty directed Allied merchant ships or conducted naval operations. Other transmissions relayed only trivial facts or consisted of banter between ships, which still would be of interest to a disguised raider. The remainder of the broadcasts were in unreadable Allied code groups. These gave Captain Rogge reason for concern because he did not know if they originated from a large enemy capital ship with powerful modern guns or an English tramp freighter sailing for the Royal Navy. Every coded signal had to be treated as a hostile warship threat.

Each time *Atlantis* received another ship's transmission, Rogge would alter course to avoid contact. He also decided to order a slight change in his ship's appearance. Rogge had First Officer Kühn shorten the topmast and remove the conspicuous crow's nest to make the raider appear less like a warship and more like a merchant.

Early on the morning following the completion of these small adjustments *Atlantis* caught sight of a large and brightly lit ship on the far horizon. With the use of their powerful optics, the Germans could clearly make out the other ship's neutrality markings, distinctly illuminated by the ship's own lights. Rogge turned *Atlantis* away, giving the unknown neutral a wide berth. As the two ships drew farther apart, the neutral transmitted a wireless message identifying itself as the Italian vessel *Oceania*, a 19,507-ton liner sailing from Genoa, Italy, to Buenos Aires, Argentina. *Atlantis* did not respond.

As the days passed, the men packed away their heavy cold-weather gear and broke out their light summer uniforms and pith helmets. The tropical sunshine sent spirits soaring. The crew accomplished their daily tasks with newfound vigor and stimulation. Rogge was decidedly gladdened at the SKL's choice of a warm South Atlantic patrol area for his ship instead of an icy North Sea assignment.

The short-lived leisure ended when a radioman reported to the bridge on 17 April and handed his commander a decoded message from the SKL that changed Rogge's plans. The wireless dispatch instructed *Atlantis* to rush to its area of operations and begin raiding as soon as possible. British pressure on German naval forces in the North Sea region was escalating, and the High Command wanted Rogge to draw some of the British attention farther south.

Rogge was clearly displeased with the order. Hastening the pace meant a significant increase in fuel consumption. As the ship's speed increased a few knots, its demand for fuel rose almost exponentially. Resupply at sea was questionable at best, and Rogge knew he could endanger his entire mission by running low on fuel. Beginning attacks before reaching his assigned area of operation was also a bad idea. Early engagements would alert the British to his presence while *Atlantis* was still outside the southern shipping lanes. This would eliminate Rogge's tactical advantages of surprise and shock and negate the strategic benefit of a prowling raider ship in the far-removed South Atlantic. He would be better off blending into the normal shipping lanes rather than appearing as a conspicuous stranger from the open sea.

Captain Rogge also knew that the SKL had dispatched order 1814/16/17 to *Orion*. This order instructed *Ship-36* to simulate a pocket battleship preying on Allied merchant shipping in the North Atlantic. *Orion* alone was fully capable of pulling the British away from the German forces in and around Norway and disrupting Allied operations in the North Sea.

Rogge considered all of the factors involved and decided to follow the order, but with slight modifications according to his judgment and current tactical situation. He was not insubordinate in doing so. During Rogge's final briefing, Grand Adm. Erich Raeder himself had given him this unique flexibility. Captain Rogge resolved to speed up slightly but still to operate on one engine. This action would put *Atlantis* in its operational area sooner, as the SKL wanted, and at the same time continue to save fuel. The captain also advised the helm to discontinue steering away from enemy shipping. If *Atlantis* was presented with an opportunity to attack an enemy ship quickly and silently, it would do so, but it would not yet actively seek targets or hunt down any ship. This plan would suit the SKL's purpose without compromising the secrecy of the ship. Rogge assembled the ship's officers and briefed them on their new orders, then released them to make final inspections and preparations for combat.

The captain took advantage of the continued flat seas and clear skies to pilot a cutter around the ship to inspect its disguise. The paint, applied in subzero temperatures and then immediately subjected to a storm's wicked battering, had flaked off in great patches, leaving the ship looking old and weatherworn. Despite the huge patches of discoloration and missing paint, the ship remained quite convincingly Russian in appearance. While they continued to slowly sail south, the captain put Kühn and his work parties into action repairing the disguise and repainting the few areas badly in need of it.

During the late afternoon of 22 April, the ship crossed the equator. Because *Atlantis* was between Freetown and Bahia in a very narrow portion of the South Atlantic, Rogge decided to delay the traditional "crossing of the line" ceremony until they were farther south and in a more open area of the sea.

Rogge gave his men a few days of relief from the simulations and drills. Some men had small additional duty requirements such as repainting the camouflage or performing the ship's routine maintenance. For the most part, however, the men spent their time playing cards, chatting, or simply relaxing on deck chairs. The humid tropical weather dictated very light clothing —shorts, light shirts, and pith helmets or cloth overseas caps. Some men swam in the deck pool built from planks and sailcloth; others fished for sharks or ambled around the various deck levels.

On Wednesday, 24 April, *Atlantis* passed 8 degrees south latitude and entered the wider part of the South Atlantic, where the seasoned seafarers could finally initiate those crossing the equator for the first time. After much fuss, an old salt dressed as King Triton appeared on deck. To the tempo of heavy drumbeats and cheers, the costumed "King of the Sea" formally called for the start of the initiation rites. As horns sounded, the excited veteran sailors, called shellbacks, found 250 uninitiated pollywogs to induct into the Kingdom of Neptune.

King Triton nodded his head, and a shellback dressed as a mermaid began the proceedings by pounding his trident on deck and reading the instructions to the uninitiated from an almost official-looking scroll. The pollywogs moved on deck and stood in a group. One by one they were thoroughly drenched with sea water. Next they moved to the corridor formed by a double line of veteran sailors wielding paddles and were forced to run the gauntlet. Each man received a playful trouncing from the far-from-serious shellbacks. Following the smacking, the pollywogs were subjected to an extended dunking in a slimy liquid of questionable origin. As the pollywogs moved along the deck they were smeared with a noxious mixture of kitchen scraps and oil, and then finally were coated with a heavy layer of feathers.

When the daylong initiation ceremony began to wind down, Rogge made an announcement that revitalized the day's revelry. The captain gave all but the most necessary crewmen the afternoon off and authorized a ration of beer and cake for the crew. Cheers went up and the crewmen carried on their lively celebration into the evening.

While the merriment continued on deck, Captain Rogge and Leutnant Mohr discussed a new disguise for the ship. They had moved too far south to remain in the Russian costume. A Russian ship in far southern waters would draw suspicion rather than avert it.

During the cruise from Bremen, Mohr had immersed himself in Lloyd's *Register of International Shipping,* familiarizing himself with all of the world's ships that resembled *Atlantis.* The adjutant surveyed thousands of ships and then worked through all of the limiting factors to narrow the field. Initially, he looked for ships that grossed about eight thousand tons, possessed a cruiser's stern, and were built after 1927. He cut the list further by eliminating ships that routinely served in *Atlantis*'s assigned area of operation. It would be dangerous, not to mention embarrassing, to cross paths with the actual ship *Atlantis* was pretending to be. It had happened before. During World War I, a British ship and a German ship, each disguised as the other, actually met in battle. The possibility of meeting one's namesake could not be ignored.[1]

Mohr next eliminated ships with white waterlines because the raider's crew would be unable to paint a convincing white waterline at sea. A poorly painted waterline in a highly visible contrasting color such as white would announce *Atlantis* as a fake from a great distance. Mohr also removed ships that had regular contact with the Royal Navy. The chance was far too great that a sharp-eyed sailor would recognize a small error and use it to expose the raider's cover.

Mohr's final list had twenty-six candidates. Five of these were American-flagged ships, which were excluded because the Germans did not know the American call signs. Of the remaining twenty-one ships, Mohr next eliminated the Greek ships because their paint schemes were far too specific and difficult to replicate. Rogge then eliminated the British, French, Belgian, and Dutch ships on the list because their intelligence networks in port still had a good reading on most ships' locations and ports-of-call dates. That left eight ships of Japanese registry. Although they knew almost nothing about Japanese color schemes, the officers decided to choose one of these ships as the subject of the next disguise. Mohr had the most information about the Kokusai Company's color patterns, so he proposed the *Kasii Maru,* call sign JHOJ, a four-year-old, 8,408-ton passenger freighter, as the ship of choice.

Rogge approved Mohr's selection, and on 27 April 1940, First Officer Kühn set his chief petty officers into motion. Barking orders, yelling, and cursing, the petty officers supervised as their work crews climbed masts carrying saws, moved ventilators, or went over the sides of the ship with their paintbrushes and buckets. Slowly, the gray *Kim* changed shape and color. The hull became black, the masts received a bright yellow coat of paint, and the ventilators were painted red and yellow. The deceit even included the Kokusai trademark, a large white *K* on the sides of the red-and-black smokestack.

All things considered, the crew's first complete conversion on the high seas proved easier than expected. Painting the ship's upper works presented no significant problems; however, refinishing the hull and waterline proved very difficult. The paint used for the ship's earlier masquerade had never really dried. It had turned into thick, gray goo impregnated with salt that prevented new paint from adhering to or covering the hull. This caused a great deal of concern. The hull and waterline were extremely important aspects of the ship's camouflage. Without a convincing paint job there, the rest of the disguise would be worthless and the ship's mission and safety would be compromised.

Kapitänleutnant Kühn and Leutnant Mohr took over the wardroom and sat down to solve the hull and waterline problem. Within a few hours the two men had developed a solution, presented it to Rogge, and received his approval. Kühn stopped *Atlantis* and then pumped fuel from one side of the ship to the other; the ship listed slightly to one side exposing the hull down to the waterline. The men scrambled over the high side of the ship on long ropes and scaffolds, free to scrape off the old sludge, prepare, and then repaint the exposed surfaces on the raised side of the ship. When the paint on the raised side of the ship was dry, the crewmen reversed the process and painted the other side. The system did not work perfectly because the paint never had enough time to completely dry and set, but it worked well enough to create credible and realistic disguises.

Painting the overhanging stern presented another logistical problem. The stern could not be raised out of the water, and waves rolled up over the stern section every few seconds. Kühn solved this dilemma too. He dispatched painters armed with large brushes affixed to wooden poles to cluster under the stern in small dinghies. The men timed the waves, swabbing on paint every few seconds as they rode up and down the twelve-foot swells. Soon after the operation began, several black-and-gray fins appeared and slowly cruised amid the small boats. After that, it became standard policy for the officer of the deck to post an armed crewman on the stern to protect the men in the boats from shark attack.

Despite the difficulties, the men completed most of the alterations during the first day. After Sunday church services on 28 April, Rogge halted the work on the disguise and assembled the crew to explain their orders and mission once again. He reminded the men that their job was to cause disruption, alarm, and despondency within the enemy's merchant fleet. To that end, *Atlantis* would not attack every ship it met; each encounter required evaluation based on the current situation. Rogge explained that he might order the ship to do things that the crew considered questionable, such as leave the shipping lanes or go into hiding. He wanted the men to understand that they were not to second-guess him; their duty was to obey his orders. The captain made it clear that he was open to suggestions and ideas from the crew, but the final decisions concerning command and the conduct of operations were his alone to make. The men acknowledged their understanding, and First Officer Kühn released them to return to their posts.

The following day the crew put the final touches on the new disguise and Captain Rogge again launched a cutter to inspect the ship. Using both his naked eyes and binoculars, Rogge inspected *Atlantis* from close quarters and from a distance. He returned very satisfied. The new disguise was quite credible. The flat plating forward of the bridge boldly displayed large flags bearing the rising sun of the still-neutral Japanese empire, and the crewmen manning the bridge were dressed as Japanese sailors. The final credit for the believable costume rested with Adjutant Mohr and Korvettenkapitän Lorenzen, who had left nothing to chance in their planning of the disguise. They had even assigned the shorter, darker crew members to amble about the decks dressed in kimonos. Pilot Officer Richard Bulla walked on the foredeck pushing a baby carriage. The brightly painted ship with its decks full of passengers looked completely harmless.

On 30 April, *Atlantis* entered the Cape Town–Freetown shipping lane and began hunting. The following day, the radio room received several coded intelligence reports from the German naval staff informing Kriegsmarine forces that the British planned to divert all of their merchant shipping around Africa rather than risking passage through the Mediterranean Sea. Rogge did not believe it was practical or possible for the British to implement such a drastic and logistically burdensome undertaking. He initialed the report and decided not to alter his original plan.

As dawn broke on 2 May, the masthead lookout excitedly reported a column of smoke off the port bow. Kühn sounded the call to action stations. The men dashed to their assigned battle stations with well-disciplined precision. Rogge ordered the ship turned 40 degrees to port. The Japanese costumes appeared and the actors took to the decks. Within minutes *Atlantis* was tracking on an intercept course, every man was at his post, and the ship was deadly silent. Only two people, Rogge and the Japanese-garbed Mohr, were on the bridge, as would be normal for a merchant ship. The gun crews manned their weapons, hidden behind fake cargo and quick-acting doors. Other sailors dressed in Japanese clothing lounged lazily or openly sauntered about on deck, their weapons within easy reach. Belowdecks, damage control teams, engine stokers, ammo bearers, mechanics, and engineers, who could not see events evolve on the surface, all waited silently and anxiously for orders from above. The stage was set for *Atlantis*'s first attack.

Slowly the wispy trail of smoke in the sky gave way to mastheads and then to a funnel. Leutnant Paul Kamenz manned the range finder hidden in a false water tank above the wheelhouse. He routinely broke the silence by calling off the ever-decreasing range of the unidentified ship. The radio room reported a Belgian ship, *Thysville*, transmitting nearby.

Rogge raised his binoculars as the ship's black hull and gray funnel became visible. The ship in his sights was not *Thysville*. The straight stem and cruiser's stern identified it as an Ellerman liner, a passenger vessel. Mohr immediately leafed through the shipping registers to compare Rogge's descriptions with known Ellerman-type passenger liners. Within a few minutes he had a probable identity. Based on Rogge's reports, Mohr reasoned that the two-decked passenger carrier was probably the British ship *City of Exeter*.

At a distance of nine miles, Rogge could make out antiaircraft batteries and an aft-mounted cannon through his binoculars. He also noted the many boats secured in davits along the side rails. Rogge altered course to turn away from the British vessel that was steaming up on his ship from the south. At seven miles, *Atlantis*'s deck crew could see the glint of binoculars reflecting in the sun—the raider was being examined just as thoroughly in return. Rogge lowered his glasses and declared there would be no attack. A sigh of disappointment whispered through the crew. There were probably more than two hundred passengers on the ship, the captain explained. *Atlantis* could not accommodate that many passengers, who would inevitably include women, children, the elderly, the infirm, and those with special needs or diets. Such added burdens could hamper the entire cruise. Realizing that their captain was correct, the crew stopped grumbling as they reluctantly secured from battle stations.

The men on deck watched the liner sail by, expecting a gentlemanly signal flag or ensign dip. Such were the normal courtesies passing ships extended to one another on the high seas. The 9,654-ton *City of Exeter* passed *Atlantis* with no acknowledgment at all. The snubbed Germans decided the haughty English had not offered a courtesy signal because they believed *Atlantis* was a Japanese ship that did not warrant courtesy.

The Germans were wrong. The captain of *City of Exeter* did not extend a courtesy signal because he was very suspicious of the "Japanese" ship. He was so wary, in fact, that he broadcast a report to the British Admiralty as soon as the ship was out of sight giving a full description of the ship and labeling it suspicious. In his book *German Raiders of World War II* August Karl Muggenthaler notes that the liner's report had an almost immediate effect on *Atlantis*'s operations, although the Germans would not learn about the report for another two months.[2]

Atlantis sailed southeasterly along the Freetown–Cape Town route until a little after 2:00 P.M. on the following day. About five hundred miles off Cape Frio, Portuguese West Africa, the coxswain sighted a thin smoke cloud rising from the horizon. Rogge sounded action stations and called for full speed from both engines. Slowly, the faint thread of smoke gave way to crosstrees, and at 2:07 Rogge ordered his ship turned to intercept the target.

The unknown ship appeared as a faint smudge at a range of 17,000 yards. Twenty minutes later, the range was down to 10,400 yards and *Atlantis* had apparently remained unnoticed. The merchant ship, however, was clearly visible. The distinctive aft gun enclosed in a protective tub told Rogge the target was definitely an Allied merchant. The Allied ship held a steady course and speed and did not seem to realize that *Atlantis* had changed course and speed three times in the preceding eleven minutes. The target's course would bring it directly across *Atlantis*'s bow from starboard to port.

Rogge waited.

The English ship had a large red band painted on its funnel and flew no flag. *Atlantis*'s gun crews targeted the radio shack. Should the ship begin transmitting a distress call, the first gun salvos would be aimed to destroy the wireless room and immediately end the dangerous broadcasts.

At five minutes before three, Rogge ordered the disguise dropped. Immediately, a crane became a gun, camouflage and false walls fell, and the large steel doors sprang upward to reveal more guns. The Kriegsmarine battle ensign was unfurled and raised along with signal flags spelling out "Heave to or I will fire" and "Do not use your radio." Total time expended in the transformation from an innocent Japanese freighter to a warship: two seconds.

There was no reaction from the target ship, which continued to sail on.

One minute later, Rogge ordered the 37-mm gun crew to fire a warning shot. Due to the angle on bow, however, the small gun could not traverse toward the target. Rogge then ordered the 75-mm gun fired. The larger gun promptly flashed twice, sending a shudder through *Atlantis* and filling the upper decks with the smells of sulfur and hot metal. Both rounds landed ahead of the target vessel and hurled brilliant white-water geysers high into the air.

The Allied ship continued on its track and responded by raising an answering signal flag meaning "half." Rogge, puzzled by the reply, ordered the starboard 150-mm guns to fire across the merchant's bow. The large guns each thundered once, their shells sending an unmistakable warning to the Allied ship.

The British ship responded with the message "I understand your signal" and then blew off a column of steam to appear as if it intended to stop. At 3:03 P.M., the target momentarily feigned a stop and then took off in a sharp starboard turn at flank speed. Rogge ordered the firing to begin in earnest, and the 150-mm guns fired another salvo of two 100-pound shells.

The first shots hit the stern and exploded with a fury. The shells smashed the deckhouses and mangled the area into an unrecognizable mass of twisted steel and burning debris. The merchant ship's stern immediately began to billow a thick cloud of gray and white smoke. Despite the damage, the British steamship resolutely continued its escape attempt, maintaining its head of steam and continuing the tight turn away from the raider.

Atlantis fired another two-shot salvo. Once more, both shells found their mark, tearing through the vessel's port side directly under the bridge. Within seconds of the horrific impact, *Atlantis*'s crewmen watched as dense black smoke poured from the jagged shell holes and large flames climbed up the side of the ship. Rogge, dreading unnecessary loss of life and destruction, ordered a cease-fire to give the merchant crew ample time to surrender and take to the boats.

At 3:05, a radioman reported that the target ship was broadcasting a radio message in defiance of *Atlantis*'s warning. Hugo Gout, the Allied ship's wireless operator, attempted to broadcast "QQQ, QQQ," followed by the ship's position.[3] Gout was trying to alert the British Admiralty that his ship was under attack by a merchant raider. The radiomen on the German ship immediately began transmitting gibberish in order to block the distress call or confuse any listeners.

Rogge ordered Kasch to resume firing. The main guns fired four more salvos toward the ship. The first three missed due to a malfunctioning electrical converter in the fire-control system. During the shelling, the ship continued to broadcast reports and pleas for help. Gout managed to send eight complete distress messages around the jamming until a lucky shell fragment struck the radio mast.

The fourth salvo struck the target directly amidships, smashing the number five hatch. The high-explosive shells not only destroyed the hatch cover, they also set the ship's cargo on fire. After the last series of hits, the ship's master finally allowed his ship to slow to a stop. The ship's gunner, Cyril Burns, a World War I artilleryman who was more than capable of hitting his ship's attacker, did not get the opportunity to engage the aggressor. Once the burning merchant lost way, the crew hastily took to the lifeboats and began to row away from their burning ship, and away from *Atlantis*, too.

At 3:26 P.M., Adjutant Mohr, Leutnant Fehler, and ten others, all heavily armed and wearing the proper Kriegsmarine uniforms, were lowered in boats by Kapitänleutnant Kühn and a detail of seaman. Within ten minutes Mohr's boarding party was climbing up the sides of the T. J. Harrison Company's 6,199-ton freighter *Scientist*. On deck Mohr met the only two men remaining aboard the ship, Captain Windsor and Chief Officer Watson. The three had a curt but proper question-and-answer period concerning the whereabouts of any secret papers. Windsor indicated that he had followed standard procedure and thrown all important papers and maps overboard. Realizing the men would not provide any useful information, Mohr sent them off to pack their belongings, giving them fifteen minutes to return topside.

The boarding party teams went off to accomplish their specific tasks. The red-haired Fehler went deep into the ship's holds to plant charges. He placed forty-pound packs of explosives at the bulkheads between the engine room and the forward and aft holds. Explosions at these critical areas were intended to break the ship's back and cause it to sink quickly.

Mohr's duty was to canvass the ship and gather anything of intelligence value. The adjutant and his men dodged the smoke and burning debris and made their way to the bridge and officers' berthing area. On his way to the bridge, Mohr encountered a dead British crewman on the deck. The man, his skull shattered, lay crumpled in an expanding pool of blood. Despite having some medical training, Mohr found the sight very disturbing. Several members of Mohr's party were beginning to look ill when he sternly ordered them to stop gawking and return to the duty at hand. The search party collected every scrap of paper they could find, even emptying the wastebaskets, to take back to the raider for examination.

Mohr found searching his first deserted ship an eerie experience. His footsteps echoed against the unnatural quiet of the empty ship. He was glad to hear the occasional sounds of other members of his search team as they inventoried the amount and value of the ship's cargo and probed for provisions and equipment. Mohr filled his collection bags and hurriedly assembled the boarding parties back on deck with the two prisoners.

By the time Mohr had his men and the prisoners together, *Scientist* was burning furiously. The adjutant decided it was time to leave and rushed everyone over the side and back to their small boat. The boarding parties used their motor launch to circle around and collect all of *Scientist*'s drifting lifeboats, taking them under tow before returning to *Atlantis*. Once emptied of survivors, the lifeboats were stripped of all valuable items and provisions and all but one of them were sunk with rifle and machine-gun fire. One lifeboat was brought on board *Atlantis* and stowed for future use.

Rogge, who wanted to sink the smoking, burning ship quickly, watched in disappointment as Fehler's charges went off with nothing more than dull pops from deep inside the ship. Captain Rogge directed the 150-mm guns to begin firing on the drifting hulk. Despite the pounding from several shells, the ship refused to sink. Not wanting to waste any more of his ammunition, and very aware that the immense black tower of smoke could be seen for many miles, Rogge finally ordered Kasch to finish the ship with a torpedo.

The torpedo men launched one of their "eels" almost immediately after receiving the order from Kasch. The deck crew of *Atlantis* and the prisoners stopped what they were doing and watched as the torpedo raced toward *Scientist*, its track and progress clearly marked by a distinct track of white froth. Within minutes the torpedo struck *Scientist* amidships, shaking the ship from stem to stern with an exceptionally powerful explosion. The British freighter immediately began to list slightly and then quickly settled into the water up to the boat deck. After a slight pause, *Scientist* slid below the surface with a loud metallic groan, a few gasps of steam, and some muffled pops; just over four hours had passed from the time *Atlantis* first sighted the ship's smoke cloud.[4]

Atlantis steamed away from the scene of the battle, its first victory won, lookouts once again searching the horizon. The raider cruised on its original southern route at twelve knots, zigzagging occasionally to increase the scope of its search area.

The crew's new duties focused on attending to the seventy-seven prisoners, who were searched and given quarters according to their race, rank, and standing, as was customary even on their own ships. The prisoners consisted of twenty Europeans and fifty-seven Asian "lascars."[5] Each prisoner received an issue of blankets, eating utensils, soap, and shaving items. A roll call and accounting of *Scientist*'s crew revealed that two men had died and one was injured during the attack.

One of the deaths had occurred during the shelling; this was the man Mohr and his boarding party discovered. The other casualty had actually died aboard *Atlantis* from serious stomach wounds despite intensive medical care from the German doctors. The injured man was *Scientist*'s wireless operator, who received ghastly wounds from flying wood splinters when shells struck near his radio shack. Doctors Reil and Sprung successfully treated the wounded radioman as soon as he was brought on board.

The captured seamen were taken to quarters three decks down. Their berthing area was deep within the ship, just abaft the bridge and forward of the engine room. This steel-walled area was accessible only through a single, locked sliding steel door. Ventilation was supplied by means of suction pipes. During action, the suction to these pipes was cut off to free every bit of power to drive the screws. This made the prisoners' quarters quite unbearable at times. In his book *Sea Prison and Shore Hell*, Roy Alexander quotes from prisoner John Creagh's diary to describe the accommodations:

> The room consisted of the 'tween decks for'ard of the engine room bulkhead and running for'ard to No. 2 hold.
> Above us were the crew's mess deck, torpedo room, main deck and boat deck; beneath were workshops, drying rooms and other quarters, of which we knew very little. The washroom and lavatories adjoined the main room. The hatch cover in the room was covered with eight large tables and forms for messing purposes.
> Each ship [i.e., the prisoners from each ship] had its own cutlery, etc. and lockers to contain those things. The remainder of the space was taken up by bunks. These were in three rows of double tiers, both sideways and upwards, and were built from a couple of feet from the hatch coamings outwards to the ship's side. Each man had a straw mattress, pillow, blanket, cloth and covering for the bedding. The bathrooms had wash-basins, a steam jet and a salt water jet supplied. Each man drew about one quart of condensed water per day for washing, but could use as much salt water as he wished.[6]

Once the processing of the prisoners was complete, the questioning began. The prisoners were very cordial and cooperative with their German captors. They related that their ship was traveling from Durban via Freetown to Liverpool carrying 2,500 tons of maize, 1,150 tons of chromium, 2,600 tons of wattle bark, and various other mixed goods. *Scientist* was due eventually to join a convoy at Freetown and would not be overdue at Sierra Leone until 10 May.

Atlantis's officers also learned that the Royal Navy had no inkling that merchant raiders were operating in the area and consequently did not provide protection for merchant ships between Durban and Sierra Leone. The British officer who had been on watch when *Atlantis* approached told Rogge that the appearance of the "Japanese" merchant ship had not aroused his suspicion. Captain Windsor, on the other hand, insisted that he would have instantly recognized the raider *Atlantis* as an impostor at a distance of at least five or six miles. Windsor could not, or would not, give a specific reason to explain how he would have recognized *Atlantis* as a fake, so Rogge simply nodded kindly and dismissed his claim without any further comment or action.

As the questioning continued, Mohr, Kamenz, and the senior wireless operator pored over each book, chart, and sheet of paper recovered from *Scientist*. Captain Windsor had thrown all of the secret papers overboard, but the material that remained supplied *Atlantis* with a wealth of information.

When things had settled down, Rogge mustered the officers to review the lessons learned from their first combat experience. First, they had learned that the British fully intended to use their radios, even if instructed by a raider to do otherwise. This critical fact made Rogge modify the strategy of future attacks. From now on, *Atlantis* would try to overwhelm targets suddenly with surprise. If the target ship broadcast any type of radio message, the first salvos would aim for the radio room. Rogge also learned of the British Admiralty's order to run without lights, even navigation lights, and to maintain strict radio silence at all times unless under attack.

While searching *Scientist* the officers found instructions for the standard British painting and color schemes used in wartime operations. They noted that British ships all wore black or gray hulls and yellow-brown upper works. This information made it possible for *Atlantis* to incorporate British disguises into its list of ships to impersonate.

Fehler had discovered that he would need much more explosive power than he had previously estimated to send a ship to the bottom. Rogge ordered him to increase the explosive charges from forty to two hundred pounds. This was an order that the spirited "Dynamite" Fehler found very easy to obey.

When everyone had had a chance to contribute, Captain Rogge ordered his officers to make sure that all these important lessons and facts were disseminated to the entire crew to help guide future operations.

The novelty of having prisoners on board wore off within a few days, and life aboard the raider returned to routine as the ship continued sailing south toward the tip of Africa. The Asian prisoners made it clear that they were just as willing to work for the Germans as for the British, and *Atlantis*'s crew happily turned over to them such distasteful tasks as scraping paint, mending lines, washing laundry, general cleaning, and cooking. The prisoners were happy to continue earning money, and the crewmen were delighted to be relieved of those burdensome jobs.

The new work arrangements even pleased Rogge. With an Asian cook in the galley, the captain was able to enjoy correctly steamed rice and the Asian dishes he had learned to like during his training cruises in the Orient. The ship's German cooks never had mastered the preparation of such foods.

On reaching the tip of Africa, Captain Rogge sailed *Atlantis* around the southern apex of the continent and then turned northeast into the Indian Ocean. Once *Atlantis* had entered the standard shipping lanes in the Indian Ocean, Rogge turned the ship and sailed back in the opposite direction, giving the appearance of having originated in Ceylon or Australia. It was unlikely that anyone who saw the ship would associate it with any suspicious activity farther north in the Atlantic.

By 5:00 on the evening of Friday, 10 May 1940, *Atlantis* was directly off Cape Agulhas and almost in position to begin the mining operation. Visibility was superb and the sea was exceptionally calm and flat. The men on the bridge could distinguish the Cape Agulhas light at a range of more than thirty miles. At 8:30 P.M. Rogge ordered action stations. The crew took their posts, and the lights in the mine compartment were extinguished. Fifteen minutes later, Leutnant Fehler received permission to open the mine-laying ports on the ship's stern. Moments after opening the ports, Fehler's crew pushed the first of the deadly black spheres into the ocean. The remaining Type-C Electric Mines followed the first one down the launching rail at regularly timed intervals. *Atlantis* maintained a constant fifteen knots while following a preset course from as near as five miles to as far as twenty-six miles offshore. The mines were dropped from the twenty-five-fathom line to the sixty-fathom line. The SKL had designed the neat rows of mines to coincide with the routes of ships going around the point of the continent.

The crew was reminded of their dangerous position every time the Cape Agulhas light flashed over the ship. At one point, crewmen watched a car's headlights follow a meandering coastal road. Rogge silently worried that the weather was perhaps too good. He feared the propeller's phosphorescent green wake in the otherwise dark sea would act as a beacon for watchers at shore stations or on nearby warships. The seeding of the minefield continued without incident. Even though the massive mine ports were only five and a half feet above the water, only one wave washed into the openings. The operation took just over four hours and occurred without an interruption, mishap, or problem. Finally, at 1:17 A.M. on 11 May, the last mine rolled out of the ship and the crew cranked the mine-laying ports closed. Ninety-two magnetic contact mines lay deployed in the pattern dictated by the SKL. The mines would not be missed aboard *Atlantis*.

Kapitän-zur-See Rogge next sailed *Atlantis* at ten knots back toward the Indian Ocean with deception in mind. Rogge correctly reasoned that *Scientist*'s experienced officers could estimate his course and speed even when they were confined belowdecks. He further assumed that the prisoners had almost certainly determined that a mining operation had occurred. Captain Rogge decided to mislead the prisoners and provide them with false information about the mine-laying procedure. By mid-afternoon the following day, Rogge had decided how to effect his deception. His plan called for convincing the imprisoned merchant sailors that a U-boat was involved in the mining operation. Rogge knew he could not keep the prisoners from analyzing where the ship was and what it was doing, but he acted to ensure that their calculations were faulty.

After Sunday services on 12 May, the prisoners were quickly ushered belowdecks and locked down with a well-acted sense of urgency from the Germans. As soon as the prisoners were isolated, *Atlantis*'s engines were run to simulate maneuvering alongside another ship. Rogge then hailed an imaginary submarine commander through a megaphone. The crew banged gangplanks against the ship's side and then paraded noisily around the decks as if other comrades were coming aboard. Soon afterward, the wardroom filled with rowdy laughter, and loud, boisterous singing escaped from the crew's quarters. The singing, floor stomping, and increased activity and noise were all meant to suggest that *Atlantis* was entertaining a U-boat crew. The ruse continued for a few hours, and then the crew repeated the entire banging and maneuvering process to simulate the U-boat's departure. To top off the ploy, Rogge had a life jacket soiled and then stenciled "U-37." He pitched the false advertisement into the sea with the hope that it would wash ashore or be picked up by a British patrol boat.

Mohr confirmed Rogge's suspicions that the British prisoners had detected the mining operation. During his conversations with the British officers, they continually prodded him for information or commented on the mine-laying operation, hoping he would reveal something useful. Captain Windsor firmly declared that he was sure a mining operation had taken place and went on to boast that he had also flawlessly calculated the position of the minefield. Windsor told Mohr he was sure the raider and an accompanying U-boat had conducted a joint mining operation off the southwest coast of South Africa near Durban. Mohr maintained a straight face while repeatedly denying either a meeting with a U-boat or a mine-laying mission. The adjutant played his part to perfection; the more he denied their suppositions, the more convinced the prisoners became that their assumptions were correct.

By turning back and altering course in a manner that *Scientist*'s officers could not detect and then staging a false U-boat meeting, Rogge ensured continued operational security for *Atlantis*. Even if the prisoners later communicated with British intelligence agents, the locations in their reports would be hundreds of miles off and would include a nonexistent U-boat rendezvous.

4

The Secret Gets Out

ATLANTIS SAILED AWAY from the minefield on a heading of 80 degrees—almost due east. Captain Rogge wanted to distance his ship from the area as quickly as possible. He intended to cruise to a remote spot where the crew could perform some needed maintenance, stand down from maximum vigilance, and wait in safety for the mines to begin taking victims and drive other victims his way.

As they sailed away, the radiomen searched the frequencies for reports about the mines. The men picked up a wealth of information in the form of gossip between ships, war reports, and coded messages in the standard British five-letter groups, but they intercepted no references to their hidden surprises along the cape. Nor did Adjutant Mohr, who spent much of his spare time in the radio shack listening to the BBC and American news reports. This practice was normally a crime punishable by death, but Mohr had special permission to listen for intelligence-gathering purposes.

Atlantis's listeners received the first indication of activity in their minefield on 13 May when the keeper of the Cape Agulhas light reported an explosion and disturbances in the water. The following day, the radiomen intercepted another report of an explosion. These reports forced the senior naval officer at Simonstown to take action. Although official confirmation was lacking and he was not convinced that a real threat existed, he issued orders to broadcast mine warnings and alter shipping routes.[1] The raider's radio room picked up the announcement: "Important. To all British and Allied merchant ships. In view of unconfirmed reports of an explosion South of Agulhas all ships are warned to keep well clear of the Agulhas Bank. T.O.O 141013."[2]

The senior naval officer also ordered the director of South African Seaward Defence to dispatch a small flotilla of minesweepers to the area. At 9:15 on the morning of 15 May, the flotilla, consisting of *Africana* (with flotilla commander Lt. Cdr. F. J. Dean aboard), *Natalia, Aristea,* and *Crassula,* arrived and immediately began to search the cape's outer bank.[3] The ships searched fruitlessly all day until 5:15 P.M., when a mine unexpectedly exploded and released a column of spray said to be "higher than the lighthouse."[4] This explosion occurred within six miles of the sweepers. The explosion and the setting sun caused Dean to order the ships to cease operations for the night. The following day the sweepers moved their search to the inner bank and the inshore shipping lanes. At the same time, Radio South Africa announced a general caution to all ships to be especially wary of moored and drifting mines around the cape.

Rogge wondered why the announcement mentioned drifting mines. The mines *Atlantis* had sowed were all moored. Rogge assumed that the British report of drifting mines was incorrect. In fact, the report was correct. After the war, Rogge learned that the mines issued to *Atlantis* had mooring lines designed for use in calm water. Many of the lines broke in the rough waters of the cape, allowing the mines to drift away or self-detonate.

As the minesweepers continued their search on the sixteenth, a mine exploded in *Aristea*'s sweep at 9:15 A.M. At 10:45 *Aristea* cut away another mine, and the crew noted its new condition, indicating very recent enemy activity. At the end of the day, the director of South African Seaward Defence recalled the sweepers to port.

Rogge was completely satisfied; the mines had accomplished their task. They had disrupted the Allied merchant shipping routes and altered traffic flow all around the cape. His satisfaction was short-lived. *Atlantis* soon picked up propaganda transmissions from Berlin exulting in the extensive damage a minefield sowed by a raider ship was doing in the South Atlantic and taunting the British for being unable to capture a single raider ship operating right under their noses. Rogge was furious. The secrecy of his mission had been cast aside to broadcast propaganda claims and ridicule the British. This announcement would certainly bring unwanted attention and additional danger to his ship.

Berlin's claims were greatly exaggerated. In fact, not one ship was sunk or even damaged by the mines. The search for them did, however, tie up considerable British assets. Merchant shipping was redirected for months and a total of eleven warship and minesweeper groups were dispatched to search the area for mines. Between July 1940 and March 1941, minesweeping flotillas paid additional visits to the Agulhas area. These operations resulted in four additional mines being discovered and destroyed. The British found only eleven mines altogether, despite these large-scale clearing efforts. Three of them exploded on their own, one washed up onshore, and the British swept up seven. The other eighty-one mines probably sank, floated away, or detonated unnoticed.

On 20 May, the British flag officer at Colombo, Ceylon, flashed a message to all British and Allied ships that caused an immediate change in Rogge's plans. The signal warned of a German raider prowling the southern waters disguised as a Japanese merchant vessel.[5] The message also asked for sighting reports and gave sailing instructions and notices of tightened harbor security.

Atlantis's secret was out. The mines at Cape Agulhas combined with *City of Exeter*'s earlier report of a suspicious Japanese ship and Berlin's reckless propaganda left *Atlantis* exposed and in great danger. Rogge immediately ordered a course change to get the ship even farther away from the Australia-to-Durban route. Because the British report specifically mentioned the Japanese disguise, *Atlantis* would also have to take on an entirely new look. Rogge ordered Mohr to search his registry books and provide recommendations.

That evening Mohr reported to Rogge with another list of possible candidates. Rogge considered each and finally picked the one-year-old, 7,906-ton, two-masted Dutch motor ship *Abbekerk* of Vereenigge Nederlandsche Scheep Vaarts My, NV. Rogge based his decision on his knowledge of the Dutch color schemes and the fairly common silhouette of *Abbekerk*. Due to the late hour, Rogge decided to wait until morning to begin the transformation.

Early on 21 May, Captain Rogge assembled the crew and explained the plan for the change of disguise. He then turned over the project to Kühn and the petty officers. Ignoring a squall blowing up from the east, the crew immediately started work on the immense project. Scaffolding went up and men swarmed over the ship. A deckhouse rose on the stern. The bright colors were exchanged for browns and olive drab. The large white *K* on the funnel was replaced with an orange band and a black boot. On the morning of the twenty-second, the Dutch-flagged *Abbekerk* sailed away from the site where the Japanese-flagged *Kasii Maru* had previously been.

Rogge moved *Atlantis* to the Australia–Mauritius route to intercept ships traveling between Australia and South Africa. Flight Officer Bulla took the seaplane up on several occasions and searched large areas of the shipping routes, but each time he returned to report no sightings. The flights were not a complete waste of time. Every flight provided the crane operators and plane handlers with much-needed practice at the difficult task of recovering the seaplane. The complicated recovery process required the observer who accompanied the pilot to climb out of the cockpit and catch the lifting hooks, which the crane operators dangled near him, and attach the cables to three lifting points: two attachments on the engine cowling and one on the top of the windscreen. When the observer had successfully secured the aircraft to the crane, the pilot could shut down the engine and climb out. Both crewmen then rode on the wings as the crane lifted the plane aboard the ship.

On one occasion the crane operators smashed the aircraft into the ship's hull and destroyed the plane's engine. After a spare engine was broken out and mounted, the craft flew again only to have the recovery crew smash the float and cripple the plane once again. With only a limited supply of replacement parts available, Rogge decided to cease routine aircraft reconnaissance and in the future use the seaplane only when it was necessary.

The ensuing days passed uneventfully aboard the ship. The daily war reports were the only source of excitement. The men crowded around the loudspeakers to listen joyously as the announcers reported success after success for the Wehrmacht. The crewmen were excitedly discussing the conquest of the lowlands and Norway when word of the fall of Paris came over the wireless. The report spread throughout the ship by word of mouth before Rogge could make the announcement over the speaker system. When Rogge's announcement did come, the men gave a rousing cheer. France had fallen! Captain Rogge added to the celebration when he authorized a ration of beer for each man and released nonessential men to their quarters.

In the wardroom the officers loudly debated the probable length of the conflict and laid bets on their opinions. Of all those present, only three officers feared a long, protracted war; the others bet on German victory dates between September and December 1940. Rogge did not enter the conversation; he simply predicted that the war would be much longer and more difficult than they expected. Dr. Reil's suggestion that the war might last for years was met with a rush of opposition. Hoots and jeers likewise met Adjutant Mohr's prophecy of American involvement and an end to the war in July 1945. Rogge allowed the men to continue with their discussions, reminded them that the ration of only one bottle was still in effect, and then retired for the evening, leaving the rowdy men on their own. Within a day, the thrill of the fall of Paris had subsided and the men were back to their daily routines.

One evening a few days later, Mohr relaxed in the radio room as he monitored American news broadcasts from San Francisco, nonchalantly taking short notes every so often. Suddenly, the adjutant heard a report that made him sit up and start taking notes in earnest. The broadcaster announced the sinking of the Dutch ship *Abbekerk*![6] That was bad luck indeed. Mohr ripped the paper from the notepad and rushed to the bridge to find Captain Rogge.

Rogge considered his options. He did not want to change the ship's disguise again so soon. The conversion process placed a great strain on the crew. Furthermore, Rogge had only a small list of ships that *Atlantis* could imitate. He did not want to eliminate another possibility so easily. The officers returned to the wardroom to research other possible disguises while Captain Rogge remained on the bridge, deep in thought. It suddenly occurred to him that the Dutch possessed an entire line of Kerk-class merchants. If spotted, he reasoned, his ship would look like one of many others of the same class. By the time another ship was close enough to read the name, *Atlantis* would be well within gun range. Captain Rogge decided to take the risk and continue, leaving the disguise unchanged. In fact, the report was incorrect; it may have been an intelligence ploy. *Abbekerk* was eventually sunk, but not until 1942.

The morning of 10 June brought *Atlantis* out of its dull routine. A lookout spotted mastheads off the starboard beam. The watch officer sounded the siren that called the men to their action stations. The German crew quickly ushered the lascars belowdecks and raced to their posts. Oberleutnant Kasch, at the range finder, set the present range at thirty-two thousand yards. Rogge ordered both diesels to flank speed and put *Atlantis* on a converging course with the target ship. The foretop lookout called out a description: the ship had five pole masts and a funnel set well aft. Mohr immediately began to search his reference books for ships matching that description.

Within thirty minutes the range had closed to sixteen thousand yards. The crew on deck could easily make out the details of the enemy ship and even noted the unmanned cannon mounted aft. At a range of nine thousand yards, Captain Rogge began to turn *Atlantis* in 5-degree increments, hoping to continue reducing the range without raising suspicion or causing alarm on the target ship.

Just as Rogge began to think he had fooled the target ship's master and was going to close the range on the other ship easily, the enemy altered course away and sped up considerably. A race was on! The two ships were on slightly converging courses; *Atlantis* was running at flank speed, seventeen and one-half knots, and the enemy ship was steaming at its top speed, just under seventeen knots. The ships continued at this pace for more than four hours. *Atlantis* made a slight course adjustment every few minutes and continued slowly to close the gap.

At 11:35, the range was down to fifty-four hundred yards when suddenly the target ship turned off slightly and the range began to open up once again. Rogge ordered a quick 15-degree turn to starboard and had the camouflage dropped. The guns sprang from their hiding places, the Kriegsmarine battle ensign was run up the mast, and the signal flags ordering "heave to" were unfurled.

The target ship showed no sign of acknowledgment. Rogge ordered a 25-degree course adjustment to bring a full broadside of the 150-mm guns to bear if needed. The captain then gave Kasch permission to fire at his own discretion. Kasch did not hesitate. The first salvo landed short, between *Atlantis* and the target. The explosions elicited no reaction at all from the enemy. The big guns fired again. The second salvo was long, and columns of white foam erupted in front of the target ship's bow. The target ship could not ignore the unmistakable message of the exploding shells.

The enemy merchant ship cut into a tight turn and began transmitting a distress call. One of *Atlantis*'s radiomen screamed to the bridge, "Ship transmitting! LJUS Norwegian motor ship *Tirranna*, shelled by . . ."[7] *Atlantis*'s other radioman immediately began to beat out a test pattern to jam the merchant ship's broadcasts, sending a full-power repetitive pattern of "VVV TEST VVV TEST VVV" over and over again. Kasch's gunners continued firing. *Tirranna* began to change speed often and zigzagged so successfully that the next five salvos missed. The target ship even returned fire with its small defensive gun in a vain attempt to hit the attacker.

Atlantis fired more than thirty salvos during the three-and-a-half-hour chase, expending more than 150 rounds before finally scoring enough hits to force *Tirranna* to heave to and surrender. The Allied ship quickly lost way and sat on the slowly undulating sea to await its fate. As soon as it had stopped, Kapitänleutnant Kühn, Adjutant Mohr, and the boarding party crossed the small divide of water and boarded the Norwegian merchant ship.

The boarding party was met by *Tirranna*'s captain, Edvard Hauff Gundersen, and his officers. The crew remained on the ship as well because the bursting shells had splintered most of the lifeboats. The boarding party began its search and inspection of the ship. They found the shattered decks covered with blood. The shelling had killed five men and wounded many others.[8] Most of the casualties occurred when a shell landed among a group of engine stokers just as they were coming up on deck. On learning of the many wounded men on *Tirranna*, Rogge dispatched Kapitänleutnant Kamenz and another detail to lend assistance and speed the evacuation of the injured.

Tirranna, a two-year-old, 7,230-ton fast merchant ship, had departed Melbourne, Australia, on 30 May for Mombasa under British Admiralty orders. The ship sustained six hits from the 150-mm guns. Despite the damaged deckhouses and upper works, the machinery, compass, radios, and engines remained sound. The ship also carried a valuable cargo: three thousand tons of wheat, twenty-seven thousand sacks of flour, six thousand bales of wool, fifty-five hundred cases of beer, 178 army trucks, and mail, tobacco, and other canteen items for Australian troops in Palestine.

Captain Gundersen accompanied Mohr and answered all of his questions as the adjutant probed around the ship, then asked one of his own. Why had the Germans attacked a Norwegian ship? Hostilities between Germany and Norway had already ended. Mohr merely pointed out that *Tirranna* was carrying contraband and provided no further explanation.

On board *Atlantis,* Captain Gundersen and his first officer were taken to Captain Rogge. The two Norwegians were noticeably relieved when Captain Rogge assured them that they would not be harmed and even offered his sympathy for the five crewmen killed in the shelling. He wanted only to question them about the attack. The two explained that they thought they were racing a Dutch ship of the Kerk class for some friendly sport. Not once did they suspect that the ship behind them was anything more than a Dutchman looking for a race. If that was true, Rogge said, why had they not stopped and surrendered when ordered to do so?

Gundersen replied that they saw nothing but *Atlantis*'s outline silhouetted against the sun. The signal flags were unreadable. *Tirranna*'s first mate asked Rogge how he had come to capture *Abbekerk*. The astonished Rogge then realized that the two Norwegians still did not know that they were on board a German ship! If anyone should have been able to see through the raider's costume, it was these men. The old *Goldenfels* and *Tirranna* had berthed next to each other less than a year before in Bombay. The crews of the two ships even competed in a soccer match, yet they still had not recognized *Atlantis* as a German ship. Captain Rogge was very pleased that his disguise had worked so well.

Rogge was also pleased with his booty. *Tirranna* was a fast, German-built ship fitted with an echo sounder and carrying a very valuable cargo. The ship and its contents could make important contributions to the German war effort, and Rogge decided to keep it as a prize ship. He wanted to dispatch *Tirranna* immediately to German-controlled waters, but the ship did not have enough fuel on board to complete the trip. Rogge opted instead to send the Norwegian ship to a position somewhere in the south, hoping to capture a tanker that could provide fuel for both *Atlantis* and its new prize.

During the course of the night, crew members pumped one hundred tons of *Tirranna*'s fuel to *Atlantis* while boats shuttled peaches, marmalade, soap, beer, hams, cheeses, and reams of intelligence papers, sailing regulations, and British policies back to the raider.

Rogge selected Leutnant Waldmann, a civilian merchant captain, to command *Atlantis*'s first prize and allotted a prize crew of twenty-seven:

twelve armed Germans, seven Norwegians, and eight lascars. He summoned Waldmann to his cabin and gave him very precise instructions. Waldmann was ordered to sail *Tirranna* to latitude 31 degrees, 10 minutes south and longitude 68 degrees, 30 minutes east and wait for the arrival of either further guidance or 1 August. If *Tirranna* was sighted at any time prior to the first, Waldmann was to sail to a secondary position. If *Tirranna* did not receive further instructions by 1 August, Waldmann must then sail to another specified location and wait for orders or 31 August. If Waldmann had no orders by the last day of August, Rogge told him to sail *Tirranna* to the closest port sympathetic to the German war effort.

In the event *Tirranna* was stopped by an Allied warship, Waldmann was to report that he was lost, his ship having been attacked, damaged, and chased off course by a German raider. If the ship was boarded, Waldmann and the men were to take to the boats and scuttle the ship immediately. The captain asked Waldmann to repeat his orders and then dismissed him to begin preparations for departure.

Early the next morning the two ships sailed off in different directions, leaving behind only a small patch of oil and some floating boxes. *Tirranna* sailed south; *Atlantis* steamed north toward the shipping lanes once again. Kamenz planned the speed and course to plant *Atlantis* on the traffic routes at the break of dawn. Once on the lanes, Rogge steamed in loose zigzags in an easterly direction. He planned to hunt these waters only until *Tirranna*'s disappearance became known. Rogge knew the loss of a seventeen-knot ship would be a matter of great concern for the British and would draw powerful, fast patrols his way. The captain had no intention of being in the area when the warships arrived.

On the afternoon of 13 June, Rogge mustered the entire crew and administered a good dressing-down. The captain reminded the men that their conduct was to be above reproach at all times. He had personally witnessed things that distressed him during *Tirranna*'s capture. He had seen men belittling and laughing at their prisoners. A prisoner was no longer a combatant, the captain explained. Each man taken captive aboard *Atlantis* was to be treated with respect and dignity.

Rogge went on to say that he had watched men take personal items and souvenirs from *Tirranna* in full view of the Norwegian crew. The captain defined what constituted legitimate spoils of war and what constituted pure theft. He understood and approved of the men taking mementos, but only under legal and approved situations. To counter wanton looting, he issued an order establishing a new procedure for taking souvenirs. No man was to remove any item from a captured enemy ship without the approval of an officer. On gaining an officer's approval, the crewman who took the booty must then issue a receipt written against Captain Rogge. There would be no exceptions. The men acknowledged the new order and Rogge dismissed them back to their posts.

Atlantis continued to sail in the direction from which *Tirranna* had come. Acting on information gleaned from *Tirranna*'s papers, Rogge decided to repaint his ship to better resemble a ship sailing under British orders. He wanted the raider to look like an Allied merchant ship to the maximum extent possible. *Tirranna* had provided a perfect example of a ship painted in accordance with Allied instructions. Work on the disguise refinements began on 14 June.

The men painted *Atlantis* an overall darker color and then painted large Norwegian flags on the forward plates. The flags then received a rough painting over that left them still visible while giving the appearance that the crew had attempted to paint them out. Even the upper works and masts received a darker coat of paint; the only exception was the uppermost topmasts. Rogge had noted how clearly *Tirranna*'s dark topmasts stood out against the light tropical sky. For the added bit of stealth, he decided to leave that portion of *Atlantis* lightly colored.

The log entry for 16 June was the same as the ones for many previous days: "Nothing sighted." Rogge changed course for the intersection of the Australia–Aden and Sunda Strait–Durban routes. Two days later, the crew completed repainting the raider. With the new colors, *Atlantis* loosely attempted to masquerade as the Norwegian Wilhelmsen line's four year-old, 7,229-ton motor ship *Tarifa*. Now the only thing lacking was an opportunity to test the new disguise.

As the daily war updates continued to flow in, the crew heard story after story about their army counterparts in Europe, who seemed unstoppable.

The radio reported victory after victory, conquest after conquest. The men aboard *Atlantis* were impatient for a fight, eager to share in the glory before the war was over.

Rogge called a conference with Korvettenkapitän Lorenzen, Kapitänleutnant Kamenz, Leutnant-zur-See Mohr, and Oberleutnant-zur-See Kielhorn to determine the ship's situation with regard to fuel and provisions. This information was crucial, for Rogge did not know when his ship's next resupply would occur, who would conduct it, or what *Atlantis* would receive. The officers worked through the supply and manifest lists and then applied mathematical formulas to their figures. They determined that water, fuel oil, flour, butter, and sugar were the limiting factors. Rogge's next step was to order the men to draw up a conservation plan and subsistence charts outlining consumption rates and remaining stores. Within days the crew was operating under a strict fuel and ration conservation plan. It was not very noticeable, but the plan did cut into the rations a bit and allowed for few lavish meals.

Monotony prevailed as *Atlantis*'s crew followed their daily routines. The painting, washing, scraping, repairing, and day-in and day-out details began to wear down the crew. Rogge later wrote: "During this period of fruitless search, I was reminded of how Admiral Jellicoe had written that 'Victory depends less upon the stimulant of success than upon the patient performance of one's duty by day and night and in all weathers.'"[9] The crew was struggling to maintain their motivation and dedication.

On 19 June, Radio Australia announced the sinking of the thirteen-thousand-ton liner *Niagara* off Auckland. Rogge knew that *Ship-36*, the raider *Orion*, operating off the Australian coast under Kapitän-zur-See Weyher, had to be responsible. By making its presence known, *Orion* would divert attention away from *Atlantis*'s operating area. Rogge was decidedly gladdened by the appearance of another auxiliary cruiser at the fringe of his operational area.

The days continued to pass, each the same as the one before it. Rogge often ordered the engines shut down to conserve fuel, letting the ship drift silently in the calm, flat currents of the Indian Ocean. The ship's log remained blank except for the daily noontime entry: "Nothing sighted." The period of inactivity was overwhelmingly boring for the men. The damp heat—unrelenting, oppressive, and inescapable—was nearly unbearable. The sun beat down on the ship, heating the metalwork and the decking to temperatures that burned uncovered hands and went right through the navy-issue canvas tropical shoes. The heat belowdecks routinely topped 140 degrees Fahrenheit; the engine room was hotter still. Another raider captain later described the torment: "That heat! Nothing but sun, sweat, weariness, limpness, and the sickening never-ending ship's routine. Only a little comfort was to be found in the sea water showers."[10]

The radio room was the only source of novelty. News of the war came from radio stations in Berlin, San Francisco, Sydney, and Cairo. The radio was often a source of intelligence information too. On one occasion, a clear-text message broadcast from a British station to a Dutch ship gave instructions on how to safely set course through the Sunda Strait, information Rogge noted for future operations. Beginning on 25 June, *Atlantis* began to pick up shore stations from Hong Kong to Mombasa calling the now overdue *Tirranna*.

Hoping to break the unrelenting boredom and find a tanker, Rogge turned his ship onto the Sunda Strait–Mauritius route and sailed toward the Cocos Islands on 2 July; still no luck. On the tenth, when *Atlantis* was within six hundred miles of the large British naval base at Colombo, Ceylon, Rogge ordered the ship brought about, planning to retrace his path and inspect the area once again.

The raider was halfway between Ceylon and Sumatra when, at 6:43 on the morning of 11 July, the month of waiting ended. An ecstatic lookout reported smoke rising from the horizon! Rogge could clearly see the huge, dark cloud. He assumed it had to be coming from a convoy but decided to take the risk and approach anyway. He cleared the ship for action and ordered the engines stopped. Once the engines' vibrations had ceased, Rogge lifted his glasses and strained to see through the morning haze. He saw only one thin pair of masts climbing up over the curve of the horizon. The source of the smoke was a single ship. The attack was on!

Rogge ordered full speed ahead, and the engines immediately came back to life. *Atlantis* started slowly to get under way and then quickly began picking up speed. As the ship accelerated, Rogge began to make small, unobtrusive course changes. Each time he ordered a correction, the range decreased between the two ships. Soon the target was plainly visible. At seventy-five hundred yards, the vessel, a merchant ship, steamed across *Atlantis*'s bow. The target ship had one funnel, a dark hull, and dirty brown upper works. It bore no nationality markings, but the aft gun platform left no mistake as to its identity. It was a British ship. Leutnant Mund, the ex–first officer of *Goldenfels,* commented to Rogge that the British ship in his sights was almost certainly German-built and probably once belonged to the Hansa line. Captain Rogge acknowledged Mund's observation but offered no opinion on its accuracy.

The target ship did not make any effort to steer away and allowed *Atlantis* to close to three thousand yards. Just as Rogge was about to give the command to raise the gun flaps, hoist the battle ensign, and begin the attack, the radio officer advised him that it was near the time when all shore stations tuned to the six-hundred-meter radio band. The time was an internationally recognized period when normal radio traffic ceased to allow all shore stations, regardless of nationality or allegiance, to listen for SOS calls. Rogge decided to wait until the time had passed. When the radio traffic started again, Rogge ordered the disguises lifted. History repeated itself at 7:45 A.M. as the flaps came up and the German battle ensign and the signal flags ordering the target to heave to unfurled in the breeze. Twenty-five years earlier, the World War I raider *Emden* had hunted British ships in the very same waters.

The 75-mm gun snapped out four quick warning shots ahead of the target. Rogge had abandoned using the small, ineffective 37-mm signal gun for the warning shots. When the shells began striking the water, the radioman reported that the ship was broadcasting. "QQQ . . . Shelled by ra—— . . ." The British ship was able to send only that small portion of its message before the 150-mm gun crew silenced it with a direct hit to the radio room. *Atlantis* began to jam the airwaves with test patterns and corrupt Japanese call signs in an attempt to mask the partial message sent by the British merchant ship.

At least one ship heard the abrupt transmission despite all the efforts to cover it. The American ship *Eastern Guide* picked up the distress call and asked, "Shelled by whom?" *Atlantis*'s radio operators immediately responded, "I have nothing for you!" *Eastern Guide,* in close proximity judging by the strength of the signal, then broadcast a message asking *Atlantis* to cease its transmissions and repeated, "Shelled by whom?" A shore-based British station broke in and signaled *Eastern Guide* to stop transmitting and remain quiet.[11] With that, the American ship ceased its efforts to intervene and the British ship's plea went unanswered and unheeded.

The British vessel lost way and the crew promptly began to abandon ship and take to the boats. Mohr and the boarding party launched their cutters.[12] The Allied press had managed to convince nearly all Allied merchant sailors that the Germans were hell-bent on murdering and plundering. Most of the Englishmen decided to risk drifting in the lifeboats rather than wait around for the Germans to murder them. Mohr dispatched some of his boarding party's boats to round up the fleeing crewmen while his boat continued on to inspect the latest prize.

Once on board, Mohr rushed to the captain's quarters to find the skipper with his back to the door. Mohr pulled his military-issue pistol and in very fine English informed Capt. Armstrong White that he was a prisoner of war, then took the English ship's master out on deck for questioning. Captain White informed Mohr that he had been asleep when the attack took place. As soon as the shelling stopped, he had rushed out on deck and tried to stop the men from fleeing. For that reason, he had not had enough time to destroy all of his secret papers. Mohr sent men to locate the official documents and transfer them to *Atlantis* for examination.

The English ship was the 7,506-ton *City of Bagdad*, an Ellerman liner. Mund had been right, however; the ship's former name was *Geierfels*. Britain received the ship at the end of the First World War as a war reparation under the Treaty of Versailles. The ship had left England bound for Penang, Malaysia, carrying 9,324 tons of steel, tubing, chemicals, engine parts, and a small assortment of other goods.

The boarding party reported that the twenty-one-year-old ship was in a sorry state. The machinery showed neglect, wear, and age. Mohr had a signalman flash the information to Rogge, who quickly decided that this was no prize.

Leutnant Mohr sent the *City of Bagdad*'s remaining crew to collect their belongings and began making arrangements to ferry them over to *Atlantis*. Just after noon, the eighty-one new prisoners—twenty-one Europeans and sixty lascars—were aboard *Atlantis*. Only two men had been wounded during the attack; a boatswain lost a foot and the wireless operator sustained superficial cuts to his arms. Then the German raiders picked the English ship clean; fresh water, potatoes, rice, and other food stores were ferried back to *Atlantis*. It was part of the raider strategy. By provisioning from his captives, Rogge could sustain his ship without having to rely on a dangerous rendezvous with a German supply ship.

Later, Rogge and Mohr stood on the bridge of *Atlantis* and watched the demolition party's launch pull away from *City of Bagdad*. Rogge scanned the men in the motor launch through binoculars and mentioned to Mohr that he did not see Fehler in the departing motorboat. The dull rumblings of the demolition explosives pulled their attention back to *City of Bagdad*. The ship quickly began to settle at the stern and list badly. The funnel was still smoking as if the ship was under steam when the bow rose high out of the water. At that point, Rogge noted a lone figure on the sinking ship. The man scrambled over the railing and jumped into a waiting motor launch just as the ship began its descent into the depths. Rogge instantly recognized the figure as his demolitions expert, the red-haired Oberleutnant Johann-Heinrich Fehler.

Soon after returning to *Atlantis*, Oberleutnant Fehler found himself standing at attention in the captain's quarters explaining his actions to Rogge. Fehler told his commander that he had been embarrassed by his failure to sink *Scientist* and did not want to repeat that situation. He had decided to stay with *City of Bagdad* as the demolition charges went off to get a better feel for what happened on board a sinking ship. The scuttling events had unfolded so rapidly that Fehler was forced to jump for his life, cutting his arm in the process.

The problem was that Fehler had used 260 pounds of explosive to sink *City of Bagdad*—60 pounds more than Rogge had ordered him to use, and in fact nearly 100 pounds too much. The resulting explosion caused massive structural damage deep within the ship, which crumbled and began to go under much faster than Fehler had anticipated. Rogge reprimanded Fehler for his daredevil antics and told him never to take such a risk again, then dismissed him to see to his injury.

Atlantis steamed off to the south at high speed. After the crew completed prisoner processing and other tasks, Rogge called a meeting of all his officers. He first commended Oberleutnant Wenzel for reminding him about the period of international radio silence, then began a discussion about the lessons learned from the most recent combat experience, requesting after-action reports from all sections.

The discussion led to some minor modifications to the standard attack procedures. The officers decided to give up using the 75-mm gun for the warning shots. Rogge told Kasch to use two shots from the 150-mm main guns in future engagements. Employing the larger guns would make a stronger statement and would give the gun crews an earlier opportunity to zero in the range. Rogge also gave orders for the boarding parties to immediately carry all dead enemy crewmen belowdecks on stopped ships as a measure of respect. Rogge felt that allowing the boarding parties to walk around and over the dead did not provide the proper level of reverence.

Mohr reported that the secret papers of *City of Baghdad* contained a copy of a report from *City of Exeter* on its 2 May sighting of *Atlantis* that described the German raider in every detail! The release even contained photographs of the Hansa liner *Freienfels*, a ship closely resembling *Atlantis*. Rogge was astonished to learn that the master of *City of Exeter* had not been fooled by *Atlantis*'s Japanese disguise. His failure to offer a courtesy salute had not been snobbery after all.

This new and shocking information led Rogge to decide to alter the profile of the ship. The captain told Kühn to add another gallows mast both fore and aft. Kühn immediately put crews into motion to add the extra masts and make the modifications. The work crews built the phony masts out of empty barrels and other spare parts. When complete, the new masts realistically changed the ship's profile enough to satisfy Rogge.

Once he and his officers had reviewed *Atlantis*'s conduct during the recent capture, Rogge summoned Captain White to his cabin. The master of *City of Bagdad* confirmed that he had seen the report and had also heard rumors about a raider while still in the port city of Lourenço. White explained that he had ignored the report as too old and had discounted the other information as pure gossip. The captured captain chattered on, unknowingly disclosing important information that convinced Rogge that the British did not have a clear idea of any raider's position or area of operation, or even how many actually existed.

Based on the sketchiness of the British information about *Atlantis* and the ship's recently changed profile, Rogge decided there was no need to continue running to the south. He turned *Atlantis* westward and began hunting once again. Two days later, at 9:43 A.M. on Saturday, 13 July 1940, the forward and mainmast lookouts sang out in unison: "Smoke clouds in sight!"

Rogge sounded action stations and scanned the port side. Through his binoculars, he was able to discern a thin thread of smoke against the otherwise misty gray horizon. The unknown ship was abaft and to port of *Atlantis*. Rogge ordered a 20-degree turn to starboard and then slowed *Atlantis* from nine to seven knots. This maneuver forced the other ship to turn so that it would pass astern of *Atlantis* in accordance with the established international rules of movement at sea.

A radioman reported to Rogge that loud tuning noises were coming from the other ship's radio, an indication that it might be preparing to transmit a radio message. Rogge immediately instructed Kasch not to fire any warning shots and to target the radio shack on the first salvo, then put his ship into a slow, nearly unnoticeable turn that quickly began to reduce the range. When the range came under fifty-four hundred yards, Captain Rogge ordered the disguise dropped.

At 10:09, twenty-six minutes after first sighting the unknown ship, *Atlantis*'s flaps and war flag sprang up and the 150-mm main guns began firing. Salvos one, two, three, and four missed their mark! Kasch frantically led his gun crews through calculations and firing adjustments that brought salvos five and six to bear on the target ship. Rogge could plainly see the impacting shells. One entered the ship just above the waterline, another landed just below the bridge, and a third crashed down on the deck, piercing a steam pipe and boiler. The unknown ship began to burn at once and hoisted a flag for "I am stopping." It appeared as though there would be no resistance.

Rogge was delighted that the surprise attack had worked so well, even if the gunnery was somewhat ragged. There were no radio transmissions, and the ship's surrender was achieved quickly and safely. *Atlantis* secured gun flaps and slowly steamed up to the stopped vessel. All was quiet as Captain Rogge stood on the bridge and watched the stopped passenger freighter's crew and passengers take to the lifeboats and row away.

Through his binoculars, Rogge could plainly see that the passengers included women and children. He decided to put a prize crew on this ship and relieve *Atlantis* of the burden of more than two hundred additional prisoners. Rogge could read the ship's name without his binoculars: *Kemmendine*.

Suddenly, *Kemmendine*'s deck puffed a small cloud of smoke, and a report from its 75-mm gun carried to *Atlantis*. A shell screamed passed Rogge on the bridge and crashed into the water next to *Atlantis*. Rogge was furious at the deception. He instantly put *Atlantis* into evasive action, called for full speed, and ordered his guns into action again. *Kemmendine*'s stern was pelted with a withering fire until the officers on deck convinced Rogge that the attack might have been an accident or the work of a lone gunner disobeying orders. By that time, however, fires raged aboard *Kemmendine* and immense arms of white, black, and gray smoke billowed off the port side and stretched skyward.

After the raider's guns halted their fire again, the boarding party made its way to the fiery ship. The second round of shelling had changed *Kemmendine* from a prize ship to a total loss. The boarding party found the ship badly shot up and burning furiously. They could not get belowdecks to plant the demolition charges and had to beat a very hasty retreat to ensure their own survival. The doomed ship sat dead in the water, continuously spewing mile-high plumes of thick smoke that might be acting as a beacon directing enemy warships directly back to *Atlantis*.

Rogge decided that torpedoes would be the best solution because they would quickly sink the ship and put an end to the dangerous smoke clouds. Kamenz maneuvered *Atlantis* to give Kasch's torpedo men an easy shot. Within a few moments two torpedoes were streaking toward the enemy ship. The first torpedo struck high amidships, just at the waterline. The explosion was thunderous, shaking those on *Atlantis*'s decks and sending a shock wave through the water, yet the ship held steady and showed no sign of sinking. The second torpedo hit was submerged and caused a much less impressive explosive display than the first, but it was far more damaging. It struck well below the waterline just aft of amidships. Although the only visible result was a small fountain of dirty water along the side of *Kemmendine*, the explosion caused significant structural damage. Under the stress of the heaving waves and the blasts of the two torpedoes, *Kemmendine* released a great cloud of steam, smoke, and flying debris, then, with an ear-splitting calamity of collapsing decks and failing beams, broke into two ragged halves. The sinking halves formed an immense V as *Kemmendine*'s separate bow and stern groaned loudly and rose up on end before sliding beneath the waves.

Miraculously, no one was injured in the attack, but most of *Kemmendine*'s survivors were still floating in lifeboats as their ship disappeared below the surface. The heavy seas made the job of transferring the prisoners from the boats to *Atlantis* both difficult and dangerous. The men were able to time the swells and jump to the boarding ropes hanging over the raider's side. The women and children presented a problem because they could not jump from the lifeboats or climb up the sides of the ship, especially in the heavily rolling seas. The German crew solved the problem by rigging a hoist system using large coal buckets and the davits to lift the women and children aboard. After several hours of lowering and raising the dirty buckets, the entire complement of crew and passengers from *Kemmendine* was safely aboard *Atlantis*.

When Rogge met *Kemmendine*'s master, R. B. Reid, to conduct an accounting of the passengers and crew, he learned that the sixteen-year-old, 7,769-ton vessel had belonged to the British India-Burma line. Its only cargo was a small amount of beer and whisky. *Kemmendine* was sailing from Glasgow to Rangoon via Gibraltar and Cape Town with 147 souls on board: a crew of twenty-six officers and eighty-six lascars, and thirty-five passengers —five women and two children among them. The passengers were either well-connected aristocrats, family members of British officers from Gibraltar, or wealthy Indian merchants. Rogge saw to it that the prisoners were given separate quarters and assigned Commander Reil to care for and supervise the women and children.

As soon as the crew had moved the prisoners to their quarters, Rogge set out to ascertain why *Kemmendine* had fired on *Atlantis* a full nine minutes after surrendering. Captain Rogge assembled a board of inquiry to determine if court-martial proceedings were in order against the British ship's gunner. The board was composed of Captain Rogge, Kapitänleutnant Kamenz, Leutnant-zur-See Mohr, and Capt. R. B. Reid and his first mate. Capt. Armstrong White of *City of Bagdad* served as the witness.

During the course of the proceedings, the officers determined that the gunner had no way of knowing that *Kemmendine* had surrendered. The scream of a ruptured steam pipe drowned out all communication to the stern. The gunner was not a merchant sailor or mariner. He was a window washer from London who ran up to the gun and pulled the lanyard without orders. The board attributed the incident solely to the confusion of battle. Captain Reid signed a document confirming that *Kemmendine*'s gunfire after surrender was unintentional and that the conduct of Rogge and his crew had at all times been honorable and in accordance with the established rules of naval warfare. Captain White concurred and signed as a witness to the board of inquiry's findings. Rogge filed the documents, made an extensive log entry surrounding the facts, and put the matter to rest.

That evening Rogge once again mustered the entire crew. He thanked them for their dedication and announced that the Naval High Command had allotted thirty Iron Cross, Second Class, authorizations to the ship. The standard German naval practice was to award decoration authorizations to the ship but to leave the individual selections to the captain's discretion. Rogge explained that he would not choose thirty men above the other crewmen. In his view, every crew member on the ship had earned the award, and Rogge did not want to arouse ill feelings or start a competition by issuing individual awards while at sea. The decorations would be awarded at the end of the cruise. Three months earlier, of course, when the ship was fitting out in port, Rogge had turned down the SKL's offer to take a supply of Iron Crosses on board. He had none to present even if he had wanted to do so. The crew's morale rose noticeably after Rogge's announcement.

Later that evening Rogge mentally reviewed the performance of his men and decided that Leutnant Adolf Wenzel and Funkmaat Heinrich Wesemann each deserved one of the Iron Crosses. The two men had taken information from the captured British codebooks and compared them with coded British messages. Wesemann, using his three years of experience in a military decoding unit, worked carefully with Wenzel to slowly piece together the British merchant code. The two men cracked nearly 50 percent of the British code, giving Rogge the significant tactical advantage of being able to read a good portion of the British message traffic.

The following morning *Atlantis* received an order from the SKL to transmit an immediate cruise and action update to Berlin. This was the second such order Rogge had received; the first had arrived five weeks earlier on 8 June. Rogge had ignored the order, fearing that use of the radio transmitter would allow Allied radio detection gear to triangulate a position fix on his ship. The German naval staff was aware of Rogge's reluctance to transmit messages. Up to this point the SKL had not required Rogge to transmit because it could easily track *Atlantis*'s progress using information gleaned from reports about the minefield, dispatches, signals from the British Admiralty, and open-band calls to missing merchant ships. The German staff had a good idea of what was happening and why Rogge was silent, but the SKL's strict bookkeeping and accounting regulations required an official report.

Captain Rogge relented and dispatched a report to Berlin on 14 July, and then a duplicate one on the sixteenth. Those messages were his first transmissions to Berlin in three and one-half months. The short messages gave his position as 6 degrees south latitude and 77 degrees east longitude, and told the SKL that he had provisions for eighty-five more days and had sunk thirty thousand tons of enemy shipping to date. The British navy did pick up the coded transmission and attempt to locate the sender. However, the fix they worked up had no longitudinal point and was 3 degrees off on the latitude, making the threat to *Atlantis* minimal.

From 14 July to 22 July, *Atlantis* lazily zigzagged south of the Chagos Archipelago on the Mauritius–Sabang route, steaming at thirteen knots at night and slowing to nine knots during daylight hours. The gathering point for crew and prisoners during these days was around the forward dummy hatch, which the crew had turned into a play area for the children. They lined the hatch with a tarp, filled it with sand from the ballast area of the ship, and put chairs and chaise lounges around the edges. Each day the children would run to the sandbox to play with toys carved from wood scraps or with *Atlantis*'s mascot, Rogge's dog, a Scottish terrier named Ferry. The mothers would follow their children and sit in the tropical sun as they supervised their young ones. The German crewmen gathered around to talk with the women or, more often, to watch the children play. The officers took pains to ensure propriety, yet the children would frequently follow the men around the ship or ride piggyback as crewmen carried out their duties.

On the twenty-third, *Atlantis* turned back to cruise up along the Australia–South Africa shipping lane and into the general area where Rogge had ordered *Tirranna* to wait for a rendezvous. Rogge was relieved when a lookout spotted the prize ship at 7:22 on the morning of 29 July. He was eager to get *Tirranna* seaworthy and transfer *Atlantis*'s prisoners to the prize ship. As soon as *Atlantis* came to a stop near *Tirranna*, Kühn got the work under way. Within a short time both ships were covered in scaffolding and rigging as men sanded, hammered, and riveted. Motor launches and cutters moved continually shuttling supplies and people between the two ships.

Leutnant Kielhorn was responsible for the work on both ships' machinery. He dispatched a crew of ratings over to *Tirranna* to ensure that the engines were mechanically sound and personally supervised the first major overhaul on *Atlantis*'s huge MAN diesels himself. His machinist's mates and mechanics disassembled, cleaned, and rebuilt the diesels piece by piece, beginning with the starboard one.

First Officer Kühn, who was accountable for the structural repairs on the ships, literally converted both ships into floating construction sites. He earned the nickname "Captain Bligh" for the manner in which he relentlessly drove the men under the hot tropical sun.

Kamenz transferred 420 tons of precious fuel to *Tirranna*, topping off the fuel stores at 650 tons. With that much fuel, the prize could easily reach the German-held ports in the Bay of Biscay. Rogge did not want to part with so much fuel, but neither did he want to keep more than 330 prisoners confined on his ship. They consumed a large amount of his food stores each day and added additional safety concerns to his raiding. Rogge felt it better to part with the fuel and allow *Tirranna* to take over the prisoners.

The boats and launches slowly transferred the prisoners. The women and children went over first, then the Indian passengers, and finally most of the British and Norwegian crewmen. The work on the two ships and the prisoner transfers progressed well until the fifth day, when Mohr made a disturbing discovery on board *Tirranna*. The prize crew had ransacked the mail room. The men, led by a chief petty officer, had rifled through the packages and done a considerable amount of looting. When Leutnant Mund, the prize captain, learned of the incident, he had ordered the men to clean up the mess and return everything except for three pairs of socks, two shirts, and a pullover each. Mohr and Mund searched the prize crew's lockers and found that eleven men had disobeyed orders by retaining extra items. Rogge was disappointed by the men's conduct. He held himself and his men to a high standard, and he expected them to live up to that standard at all times. He issued an order of reprimand against the eleven men involved.

This incident was immediately followed by the theft of Capt. Armstrong

White's personal binoculars from the secure storage area aboard *Atlantis*. Captain White politely explained to Rogge that he had a great sentimental attachment to the binoculars and would like to have them returned to the storage area. Captain Rogge published a general request to the crew appealing to their sense of honor. If the person possessing the binoculars came forward and returned them, Rogge promised that the matter would end with no questions asked or other actions taken.

The response to Rogge's request was a posted note saying the binoculars had been thrown overboard. Leutnant Mohr investigated and narrowed the possible suspects down to five. Mohr then conducted handwriting samples and identified a close match. Under the increasing pressure, the suspect confessed when questioned. Rogge preferred court-martial proceedings against the confessed thief despite Captain White's plea for leniency. The court-martial board, consisting of Leutnant Mohr, Pilot Officer Bulla, and a boatswain, judged a severe punishment against the rating: two years' imprisonment, a dishonorable discharge, repayment of losses to Captain White, and removal from *Atlantis* on the next available transport. Rogge personally felt that the punishment was overly harsh, yet he also knew it was entirely necessary. His mission relied on the strength and integrity of the crew, and he could not allow discipline to slip.

Captain Rogge called the crew together and reaffirmed his intention to take strict action against any man who looted for the sake of personal gain. The captain explained again that souvenir collecting must be done under the supervision of an officer, who would see that the items were distributed in a fair and equal manner. The allocation policy ensured that the engine gangs and other crewmen working belowdecks would have the same mementos of the cruise as their counterparts working on the boarding parties.

Once the matter of discipline was put to rest, attention quickly turned back to the work on *Tirranna* and *Atlantis*. Both ships, freshly painted and nearly overhauled, sat on calm seas under the morning sun of 2 August. The decks buzzed with activity as men swarmed over the ships to complete the refurbishment. Suddenly, a lookout on *Tirranna* blew the ship's warning siren, and all heads turned to see mastheads approaching at high speed from the misty haze of a rain cloud less than four hundred yards away!

5

Captured Sisters

Atlantis's crew leaped into action as the alarm bells sounded. The men dropped their tools, brushes, and buckets and rushed to their posts. The unknown ship drove steadily toward *Atlantis* and *Tirranna* under a full head of steam. Kielhorn cranked up the one assembled diesel engine and got *Atlantis* under way, leaving a good portion of the crew still on board *Tirranna* or in motor launches and cutters in between the two ships. *Tirranna* started its engines and got under way to follow *Atlantis*. The crewmen caught in small boats between the ships as they were shuttling supplies and equipment back and forth turned and motored determinedly after the larger ships.

Rogge warily noted that the approaching ship had a manned gun pointing in the direction of *Atlantis*. The captain turned to order Kasch to open fire and realized that his gunnery officer was still aboard *Tirranna*. Rogge ordered the petty officer who replaced Kasch to open fire. The first salvo missed the target by four hundred yards. In the clearest possible terms, Rogge expressed his demand for accuracy to the petty officer commanding the gun crews. The gunners' second near misses straddled the target with white columns of foaming white water. After more encouragement from Captain Rogge, the third and fourth salvos found their mark. The shells struck the target and exploded in great red-orange flashes. The target ship's gunners deserted their gun, and Rogge immediately ordered his men to cease firing.

Atlantis steamed directly toward the enemy vessel just as it ran for the cover of a thick, low-hanging squall. Rogge drove *Atlantis* into the rainstorm directly after the fleeing ship but could not locate it for ten very tense minutes. As the patch of rain moved across the ocean and away from the vessels, visibility improved and exposed the mysterious ship, which lay hove to just ahead of *Atlantis*. Rogge had his gunners train their cannons on the vessel as he cautiously brought *Atlantis* alongside and stopped.

The captain ordered boarding parties over to the obviously Allied merchant ship, but one of Kühn's petty officers informed him that the boarding teams had no boats in which to make the crossing. All three of the big ships lay stopped while they waited for the motor launches and cutters to catch up. Once the small boats arrived, the boarding parties formed up and went over to the still unknown ship.

The captain of the newly captured ship was brought back to meet with Rogge. Capt. Mathias Foyn, the ship's master, readily gave Rogge the details of his ship. *Talleyrand* was a thirteen-year-old, German-built, 6,732-ton Wilhelmsen liner, a typical Norwegian-flagged freighter with a cargo of wool, wheat, steel, and teak from Fremantle en route to Cape Town and the United Kingdom.

The Norwegian captain explained that his second officer had spotted the familiar silhouette of *Tirranna* stopped next to another ship. The officer noted the boats shuttling between the two freighters and assumed that one was experiencing engine trouble and the other had stopped to assist. *Talleyrand*'s second officer decided to close in and offer assistance to his sister ship. Rogge listened in disbelief as he heard what the fortunes of war had brought to him. He had successfully captured *Tirranna*, and now its nearly identical sister ship, *Talleyrand*, had dropped right into his lap!

The thirty-five men and one woman of *Talleyrand* were brought on board *Atlantis*, reuniting friends and family who had not seen each other for quite some time. Between the two Norwegian crews there were old friends, acquaintances, and even family members, including a pair of brothers. Finn Bjørneby, third officer of *Talleyrand*, greeted his younger brother Svenn, third officer of *Tirranna*, on the deck of *Atlantis*. It was a happy occasion for all, despite their current surroundings and status. A German warship was certainly a strange place for a Norwegian family reunion!

Rogge wanted to keep *Talleyrand* as a prize, but the ship carried only enough fuel to take it to the next port of call. Rogge would have to fill *Talleyrand*'s fuel tanks from *Atlantis*'s supply if it were to travel to a worthwhile destination. As he could not afford to spare any more fuel, he decided to sink the captured ship instead. By 10:00 A.M. a German boarding party was stripping *Talleyrand* of its remaining fuel and food stores while the Norwegian crewmen collected their belongings to take over to *Tirranna*.

Pilot Officer Bulla saw an opportunity to test his plane and went to Rogge with a request. Bulla thought he could heavily damage or even sink a ship with his aircraft and asked Rogge to allow him to test his theory. Captain Rogge agreed and dispatched the delighted Bulla to ready his aircraft for flight. While the boats were busy emptying *Talleyrand* of food, water, and fuel, Bulla's airmen broke out and reassembled the floatplane.

By early afternoon, the German crewmen had completed the transfer of *Talleyrand*'s 420 tons of fuel and returned to *Atlantis* with the last load of supplies. Not long afterward Bulla lifted his Heinkel-114 seaplane off the surface of the water and circled overhead, testing and adjusting the compass. The pilot and his observer, Stabsfeldwebel Georg Borchert, found that the magnets had been disrupted by their long-term storage in the ship's metal-walled hanger. Bulla compensated for the magnetic errors, recorded the ship's coordinates and drift, and noted the time.

Once satisfied that he could successfully navigate back to the ship, Bulla piloted the craft high and away from *Atlantis*, looking for ships beyond the range of *Atlantis*'s visibility limits. After checking a large arc around *Atlantis* and seeing nothing but open ocean, Bulla and Borchert returned to *Atlantis*'s location and swooped the HE-114 downward at the deserted *Talleyrand*.

Bulla's first attacks were low glides over the masts and posts. The seaplane trailed a grappling hook intended to tear out the ship's radio aerials. Bulla streaked over the empty ship in several passes, trying to determine the optimum altitude and speed needed to hook the aerials, but was unable to snag them. Next he flew the plane off into the distance and got into position to conduct an attack. The aircraft returned at high speed, circled the three ships several times gaining altitude, and then broke into a bombing run against *Talleyrand*.

Atlantis's deck rails were crowded as both captors and captives vied for the best positions to watch the action. The spectators let out a communal groan of disappointment when the bombs landed wide of their mark and splashed harmlessly into the sea. Bulla put his machine into several tight turns and circled back for some very successful strafing runs over *Talleyrand*'s bridge and radio room. Using the plane's 7.92-mm MG-17 machine guns, Bulla and his observer caused significant damage to the deckhouses, upper works, and funnel. His attack completed, Bulla climbed upward and flew away to conduct another over-the-horizon search. At the same time Rogge ordered Fehler over to *Talleyrand* to sink it via more conventional means.

Fehler's first scuttling charge went off at 5:46. A second large explosion immediately followed the first, and then a series of smaller blasts erupted from deep within the engine room. *Talleyrand* visibly shuddered and then started to sink by the stern until the deckhouses were awash with waves. The stricken ship puffed several small clouds of dark gray smoke, then rolled over on its starboard side as it continued to sink slowly beneath the surface.[1]

Rogge turned next to completing the refit work and preparing Leutnant Waldmann to sail the prize ship *Tirranna* to German-held waters. He detached Leutnant Mund, the highly experienced ex–first mate of *Goldenfels*, to assist Waldmann on the voyage. Rogge instructed the two officers to stay away from other ships and outlined a course that would steer *Tirranna* mostly clear of German U-boat and British submarine patrol areas, past Cape Finisterre, and finally to their destination port: either Saint-Nazaire or Lorient. Rogge instructed the officers when to sail at high speed, when to slow, when to zigzag, how he wanted the prisoners maintained, and even how to process *Atlantis*'s outgoing mail on reaching port. The two men assured their captain that they were indeed prepared to complete the cruise to German-controlled waters.

When the workmen completed *Tirranna*'s refit on 4 August, Rogge instructed Waldmann to prepare to sail at midnight. At five minutes past midnight on the fifth, *Tirranna* sounded its siren signifying the start of the cruise. *Atlantis* responded with its own siren as a farewell wishing fair winds and calm seas. The prize ship carried off most of *Atlantis*'s prisoners: all of the women and children, the men over age fifty, most of the Indian merchants, a fifteen-year-old sea cadet, the crews of both *Talleyrand* and *Tirranna*, as well as a prize crew of eighteen armed German guards. The crews and prisoners lined the rails of both ships waving and singing as if they were friendly passenger ships parting company and not a warship sending off captives to an unknown future.

Atlantis remained stopped on the water while its repairs and refurbishment continued. Kühn's work crews had very nearly completed the maintenance, repair, and repainting of the ship's structure. Belowdecks, Kielhorn's mechanics had already completely stripped, cleaned, lubricated, and reassembled the starboard engine, and began working on the port-side engine. The mechanics found that the engines really needed the overhaul despite the relatively short time since *Atlantis* had left port. The pistons were burnt and fouled, the gaskets leaked, and carbon filled all the open spaces. After viewing this, Kielhorn established a regular reconditioning schedule to ensure that the engines were kept at their peak condition.

Atlantis was strangely quiet without all of the prisoners, especially without the children running around the decks or playing loudly in the kindergarten's sandbox. The only prisoners remaining on board were just under a hundred British officers and seaman and sixty-two Asian stokers.

On the morning of 8 August, *Atlantis* received a wireless transmission from the German naval staff confirming the receipt of Rogge's signal of three weeks earlier. The message had arrived through very roundabout means: it was forwarded by the surface raider *Pinguin* and then relayed to a shore station by U-boat *UA*. *Atlantis* could receive Berlin's powerful transmissions, but the ship's two 125-watt shortwave radios and 200-watt low-frequency radio lacked the power to transmit directly back to Germany.

At about noon the same day, Oberleutnant Wenzel picked up a message sent in the clear from Mauritius instructing all Allied ships hearing a distress call or wireless jamming to report their own location and the bearing toward the source of the distress call. The message explained that the Allied naval powers believed it better to receive reports of hundreds of contacts, even if most were mistakes or bogus, than to allow one legitimate SOS to go unheeded.

Rogge deduced several facts from this message. First, it convinced him the British were now aware that one or more raiders were operating in the Indian Ocean. Second, it indicated that the British forces detached to secure the region were not of sufficient strength or numbers to mount continuous patrols to search out the raiders. The warships had to respond from wherever they were posted along the coast only after a sighting or other pertinent information was received from an Allied ship. This meant the British strategy against the raiders was one of response and reaction rather than active searching.

Rogge eagerly accepted the challenge of the new British countermeasure. In fact, the strategy could actually help *Atlantis* to locate Allied merchant ships. The raider had two radio rooms. *Atlantis* could transmit a false SOS and then have the second wireless station attempt to jam the first's transmission. All Allied ships in the vicinity would respond with their present position and bearing relative to *Atlantis*. Rogge could then follow a bearing back to an Allied ship's location if it seemed to be a choice, solitary target. Better yet, the British plan provided Rogge with the security of knowing that the responding British cruisers would be too far away to catch *Atlantis* when it struck.

On 11 August, *Atlantis* set out for the sea lanes again. The newly refurbished engines pushed the ship smoothly through the water; when they were brought up to flank speed, the vibrations were noticeably less severe. Rogge used his fresh engines to set out on the path taken by *Tirranna*, east toward the shipping lanes of Colombo, Singapore, and the Sunda Strait.

For two weeks the lookouts watched the horizon but saw nothing to report. The men began to grow weary of the boredom and monotony. They picked up many signals from other ships, but the reports were always distant and weak. The days dragged on, one into the next, until 2:45 A.M. on 24 August. *Atlantis* was about two hundred miles north of Rodriguez Island when a lookout on the starboard wing sighted the smudge of a ship breaking the horizon. The watch officer sounded action stations and turned the raider to begin closing on the ship. Within a few moments of hearing the alert siren, Mohr appeared on the bridge, followed quickly by Captain Rogge.

Rogge moved *Atlantis* to a course abaft of the unknown ship and increased speed to fourteen knots to slowly close the distance between them. On the bridge, the petty officers strained through the patches of thin mist to identify the new target. One man exclaimed that it was an aircraft carrier. A second claimed it was another German raider ship. Another countered that it was undoubtedly a destroyer. The old chief petty officer put down his binoculars and told his captain that he was sure the ship was a British merchant vessel.

As *Atlantis* closed the distance, Rogge confirmed the chief's identification. The ship was a merchant ship, but it was sailing very erratically, changing speed from nine knots to five knots to one knot and then going back to nine knots—very suspicious behavior. The odd speed changes made Rogge think the ship might be a British Q-ship: a heavily armed disguised man-of-war. Q-ships cruised the oceans posing as crippled or aged merchant ships, hoping to lure German U-boats or surface raiders into close range and then spring a devastating attack on them. The suspicious vessel stopped, drifted for a short while, and then started off again under power. Rogge was now convinced that it was a British Q-ship, and highly dangerous. The captain told the gunners to fire no warning shots and to aim directly for the bridge, hoping to knock the ship out of commission with a single swift blow and avoid a gun duel with a heavily armed warship.

By 5:00 A.M. *Atlantis* was well within five thousand yards of the suspect ship. At 5:30 the enemy ship's black-banded red funnel came clearly into view. Rogge decided it was time to attack. *Atlantis* turned to port, bringing more of its guns to bear on the target. At the same time the other ship sped up and turned on a course parallel to *Atlantis*. Rogge, afraid the ship was about to attack, ordered Kasch to launch a torpedo.

Within a few seconds one of *Atlantis*'s torpedoes was racing toward the target. The torpedo ran astray and Captain Rogge immediately followed up with 150-mm gunfire. The guns scored three direct hits amidships. The target's bridge and mid-deck were promptly engulfed in flames, and the crew abandoned ship without ever even attempting to man the solitary defensive gun.

Rogge had been wrong. The ship was an ordinary merchant ship after all. He brought *Atlantis* to within three hundred yards of the stricken vessel and decided the fires were too intense to send a search detail or demolition party on board. He dispatched Mohr and the boarding party to assist the other crew members in the rescue effort. Picking up the survivors was a difficult task as the seas were rolling in ten- to twelve-foot swells every few seconds.

Even at a distance of three hundred yards, those aboard *Atlantis* could feel the heat of the burning merchant ship. The ship's structures began to collapse and shower the surrounding sea with smoldering debris. The scene bothered Rogge. The fortunes of war had forced him into actions that resulted in needless death and destruction for a second time. He wanted to maintain the chivalrous naval tradition of the raider *Wolf,* but the technology of his era continued to make it more difficult and risky with each passing day. The danger of wireless transmissions or gunfire from merchant ships was too great to ignore. The possibility that *Atlantis* might meet a Q-ship dictated fast, hard strikes.

The German sailors used the first light of dawn and the marker lights attached to the survivors' life vests to pluck the men from the water one by one. Rogge was very anxious to sink the ship and leave the area. It sat in the middle of a major shipping lane, burning out of control, giving life to a thick column of black smoke visible for fifty miles. Once Rogge was sure all of the survivors were safely on board *Atlantis,* he ordered Kasch to start the shelling again. Because the range was so short, the exploding shells sent fragments whizzing back over *Atlantis.*

As the shelling continued, Rogge learned the details of his sixth victim. The badly burning ship was *King City,* a 4,744-ton merchant built in 1928 for the Reardon Smith line, en route from Cardiff to Singapore with five thousand tons of coal. *King City*'s suspicious activity had been the result of mechanical problems. The ventilators had failed, and the ship could not push against the trade winds. The ship's captain, H. W. Marshall, stopped and made repairs, and was trying to nurse his ship along when the engines quit again. The crew had not even sighted *Atlantis* until three minutes prior to the attack. Six people from the crew of forty-four were killed during the initial round of shelling. Rogge disliked the fact that he had been forced to shell the last two ships without warning, but he was satisfied that his actions had been taken to protect his own ship.

The shelling had ripped great holes in *King City,* and the fiercely burning cargo of coal poured out of the gaping wounds into the sea. The hull boiled the water at the waterline and gave rise to a great cloud of hissing steam. As the men on *Atlantis*'s deck watched, *King City* quickly rolled over and exposed its keel, let out a great scream of twisting metal and collapsing bulkheads, and then slipped into the abyss. The coal fires of the burning ship did not die immediately. *King City* left behind a large patch of water that bubbled and seethed for minutes after the ship disappeared.[2]

Rogge moved his ship just slightly to the south of the spot where *King City* went down and began searching for targets once again. The stricken ship had not broadcast any wireless messages, so Rogge decided he could continue to scour the area until *King City* was listed late at its next port of call.

This most recent sinking came a full nineteen days after Rogge dispatched Waldmann and *Tirranna*, yet Rogge still had not heard a single broadcast concerning the fate of his prize ship. Rogge knew *Atlantis* had not missed any transmissions from the SKL. The ship kept a constant radio watch and had even recently received a message allotting fifty more Iron Crosses, Second Class, to the crew and an Iron Cross, First Class, to Rogge. The captain began to worry about *Tirranna* but decided the safest course of action for both *Atlantis* and its prize was to maintain radio silence. Rogge did, however, change his mind about medals for the crew and decided to award the eighty Iron Crosses while still at sea. He felt the presentations would go far to maintain the crew's fighting spirit and morale.

Kühn mustered the crew in the late morning of 1 September 1940, for *Atlantis*'s first formal awards ceremony. Rogge reminded the men that the day marked the first full year of war. He talked to them about the difficulties they had experienced while maintaining the traditions of chivalry in battle and reemphasized his commitment to fighting in a lawful and proper manner. Captain Rogge then called forward the eighty men he had selected as recipients of the Iron Cross. He presented each man with an official notification certificate that had been printed aboard the ship, shook the crewman's hand, and saluted. Rogge had no actual medals to present, but the ceremony raised spirits and reinvigorated the men. Rogge closed the proceedings by thanking the crew for their dedication during the 27,435-mile cruise over the previous five months and reminding them of the importance of their mission.

Atlantis steamed due south for two days at a steady eleven knots. By 4 September, Rogge could wait no longer to dispatch a message regarding *Tirranna*. He sent a terse message to the naval staff: "Prize number 1 sailed

4th of August." This time atmospheric conditions and the ship's location allowed the transmission to carry all the way to Germany. One hour later Berlin acknowledged receipt and replied, "Prize number 1 sailed 4th of September." The SKL had made a mistake in the date that could doom *Tirranna*. Captain Rogge was livid. Some shore-bound sailor's inattentiveness forced him to send yet another transmission to correct the first. He could not allow *Tirranna* to sail into the Bay of Biscay unannounced. He turned his ship east, sailed all day, and then broadcast: "Sent 7,230-ton ship *Tirranna* ETA Saint-Nazaire about September 10, carries gun aft and deck cargo of lorries."[3] The SKL got the message correct this time and dispatched a congratulatory reply to *Atlantis*. Rogge turned north again and continued the search for another Allied merchant ship.

The tedium ended at 6:30 A.M. on 9 September when a lookout spotted a yellow funnel fourteen miles away. The weather was still, and visibility reached up to forty miles at times. Rogge easily recognized the silhouette of a tanker as he increased speed and turned *Atlantis* to an intercept course. *Atlantis* closed the range quickly by steaming up toward the tanker at fourteen knots. Mohr noted the telltale British aft-mounted defensive gun just as a squall moved between the two ships and blocked visibility. Rogge increased speed to seventeen knots and tried to run up on the enemy ship under the cover of the rain.

When the rain lifted thirty minutes later, the range between the two ships was eighty-five hundred yards and the tanker had its gun manned and pointing at *Atlantis*. Rogge turned his ship away. The tanker followed suit and then turned to match *Atlantis*'s move. The two ships ran a nearly parallel course for seven minutes until the tanker's master decided his suspicions had been wrong. The British ship altered course and resumed its original heading. Rogge was ready to launch his attack, but the international distress call period was active, so he had to wait. The enemy ship raised a British ensign and then quickly pulled it down, a gentle request for *Atlantis* to raise its own ensign. The British captain surely did not expect to see a Kriegsmarine battle flag go up the mast in reply, but that is what he got.

At 8:01 A.M., when open broadcast time for SOS transmissions had passed, *Atlantis* immediately opened fire at a range of sixty-eight hundred yards. The first shots dropped short. The second salvo followed immediately after the first and straddled the tanker. In response to the shelling, the British tanker began to beat out a constant QQQ message giving its position and the circumstances of the attack.

Two minutes into the attack, *Atlantis* lost its electric steering and swung around, locked into a starboard turn. The raider's guns had yet to score a hit. The British ship noticed the attacker's predicament, stopped transmitting, and began to sail away. Rogge sent men to the aft emergency steering station and soon had *Atlantis* back under control and heading toward the target once again.

As *Atlantis* narrowed the range, the tanker began transmitting another SOS message and fired three shots at its attacker. The defensive shots missed *Atlantis* but quickly got the attention of the gun crews. Kasch's gunners found their mark and pounded the tanker with direct hits. The enemy gun crew abandoned their post, the QQQ messages stopped, and the ship hove to and raised the flag for "I require medical care."

Atlantis sailed up close and responded, "I am coming to your aid." A radioman broke the short silence when he yelled into the bridge, "Ship transmitting!" At once, all available guns opened up and devastated the British ship with a close-range salvo of high-explosive shells. Rogge quickly ordered a cease-fire and sent a boarding party to inspect the tanker. The boarding party found the English ship in a shambles. The tanker's bilges and engine rooms were leaking, and the cargo of volatile fuel was flowing everywhere. *Atlantis* would not even have the opportunity to refuel from this ship. Rogge ordered the boarding party back to *Atlantis*.

The Germans returned with two boats containing the thirty-seven survivors from the tanker's crew. Three men, including the ship's master, Capt. A. E. Tomkins, had been killed by the second close-range gun barrage from *Atlantis*. The ship was the 9,557-ton *Athelking*, a fourteen-year-old steamer owned by the United Molasses Company. Captain Rogge asked the prisoners why a radio message had been transmitted after the ship had stopped and requested medical assistance. *Athelking*'s radio operators insisted that they had transmitted no messages after the ship surrendered. Perhaps, they suggested, the ship's master had gone to the radio shack and started the second series of SOS broadcasts himself. Rogge responded that Captain Tomkins must have been a very dedicated patriot. He had to have known that his decision to initiate another radio message would surely bring more shells down on his ship—yet he did it anyway.

Ready now to move on, Rogge ordered the tanker's destruction. The 150-mm guns opened up again, tearing immense holes in the motionless, unmanned target. The badly beaten *Athelking* sank in thirty-seven minutes. John Creagh later described what he saw firsthand: "She sank by the stern, standing vertically on her stern for over half an hour, this being due to the buoyancy of the empty tanks. She then disappeared to the fo'c'sle head, stood in that position for a few minutes and then slid out of sight."[4] The ship disappeared stern first, extinguishing the fires and leaving behind only a few small wisps of white smoke and a large patch of floating fuel oil. In all, *Atlantis* fired ninety-one 150-mm shells during the effort to sink *Athelking*. Rogge was disappointed with the circumstances of the attack. His ship experienced a mechanical breakdown at a crucial moment, the gunners expended too many shells, and the raider was not able to salvage one usable thing from the tanker before it sank.

Soon after *Athelking* disappeared, the radio officer, Leutnant Wenzel, approached his commander with more bad news. Wenzel reported that messages to British warships were filling the airwaves and also that he believed the second series of SOS broadcasts had not come from *Athelking* after all, but from another ship so close that it was probably within earshot of the gunfire. The destruction of the tanker and the death of its captain had been unnecessary.

This, the third mistake in the same number of encounters, bothered Rogge greatly. The confusion of battle and the need to protect the safety and secrecy of *Atlantis* had again brought about undue destruction and death. Try though he might, he could not fight a bloodless war or avoid all of the possible errors that imprecise information could spawn. Rogge realized that his attempts to adhere to the traditions of the past were simply not practical. The use of modern high-speed transmitters and receivers forced *Atlantis* either to attack without warning or to risk being sunk itself. Rogge was nevertheless determined to maintain as much of the old honor code of the sea as possible while safely accomplishing his mission.

Later that day, the SKL sent *Atlantis* a transmission informing Rogge that the Admiralty had extended *Pinguin*'s operating area to overlap that of *Atlantis*. Rogge was not particularly happy with this decision. The territory shift could allow the two ships to get dangerously close to one another. Two raiders operating so close together could increase the chance of discovery or even lead to an exchange of gunfire as a result of mistaken identification. Both, after all, were pretending to be Allied ships.

To counter the encroachment, Captain Rogge moved *Atlantis* off toward the northeast. At noon the very next day the masthead lookouts spotted another ship off the port quarter at a range of about eighteen miles. The two ships sailed on slightly converging courses for the next thirty minutes until the ship spotted *Atlantis* and turned away to the north. Rogge, trying to imply that his ship wanted no contact either, turned *Atlantis* away to the south. In a short while, the enemy noticed Rogge's move and turned back to its original heading.

When *Atlantis* tried to turn back to a converging course again, the enemy ship countered and turned off to the northeast. The enemy captain was following the British Admiralty's orders to the letter. Rogge knew it was impossible to approach the enemy ship without eliciting a stream of SOS messages, so he called Pilot Officer Bulla to the bridge.

When the excited Bulla reported, Rogge asked him if he was prepared to attack a real target from the air. Bulla replied that he was more than ready. The captain instructed the pilot to attack the radio antenna first. If he were successful, *Atlantis* would be able to close the range without the threat of an SOS broadcast. Rogge told Bulla to use the trailing hook to swoop down and grab the main radio antenna strung between the masts, just as he had practiced on *Talleyrand*. If that failed, Bulla was to silence the radio with his machine guns.

Rogge also recalled overhearing the prisoners talk about the tendency of the lascar stokers to panic at the sound of gunfire or loud noises. Acting on that bit of information, the captain also told Bulla to shoot up the funnel and bridge. Such an attack might create enough draft within the steam system to stop the ship, or perhaps even produce sufficient terror to scare the stokers into abandoning their posts. Bulla acknowledged his orders, saluted, and left the bridge.

Bulla and Stabsfeldwebel Borchert prepared their attack plan as the armorers loaded the Heinkel floatplane with two 110-pound bombs, machine-gun ammunition belts, a grappling hook, and sixty gallons of fuel. Rogge put *Atlantis* into a hard turn to port. The course change made it appear as though *Atlantis* was following British instructions to turn away from all unknown ships. In actuality, the hard turn created a protected area of calm water behind the ship that permitted launching of the seaplane. Within a few moments Bulla put the seaplane under power, cruised away from the ship, lifted off, and slowly disappeared from view.

A large rainstorm moved between *Atlantis* and the target ship and entirely blocked visibility between the two vessels. Rogge ordered the ship brought up to full speed and turned back on a closing course with the target, hoping to dash into effective gun range while Bulla kept the enemy's attention focused on the sky.

Within ten minutes of the seaplane's departure Oberleutnant Wenzel reported that his radio operators had picked up an SOS message emanating from the enemy ship. Fortunately, he continued, the enemy radioman had transmitted in such haste that he mistakenly reported his ship in a position more than sixty miles away from its actual location. Rogge was disturbed by the fact that the ship was able to broadcast an announcement of the air attack, but relieved to learn the wrong coordinates had been sent.

Bulla soon radioed *Atlantis* and reported that his twenty-two-minute attack was successful. He also provided the target ship's location, direction, and speed. Bulla and Borchert returned and landed next to *Atlantis*, expecting to be immediately picked up. To their surprise, *Atlantis* continued to cruise hard toward the British ship, leaving them floating on the water with no ammunition and scarcely any fuel. Rogge could not stop; he had to use the limited period of blocked visibility to close in on the target.

Atlantis burst out of the rain cloud at a full seventeen knots only five miles away from the enemy ship. The crew ran up the Kriegsmarine war ensign and signal flags instructing the ship to heave to. When the Allied ship did not react, Rogge ordered the forward guns shown. When the display of arms caused no reply, Captain Rogge uncovered the aft guns, again with no response from the other ship. At a range of thirty-four hundred yards Rogge gave Kasch the order to fire a warning shot. The forward 150-mm guns put two rounds in front of the target ship, which appeared not to notice. The next series of warning shots went directly over the bridge of the British ship, which began to lose way at once. The enemy ship came to a complete stop in less than ten minutes.

The boarding party was on its way when a radioman leaned into the bridge and screamed, "Ship transmitting: QQQ SS *Benarty* bombed by plane from ship . . ."[5] Kasch ordered the forward starboard gun into action. The rounds landed on the number-three hatch cover, immediately abaft the bridge. The hatch cover broke apart and rode the force of a giant fireball high into the air, showering the ship and sea with burning debris. The shelling set the cargo on fire, and it began to burn furiously. Those on the bridge of *Atlantis* could plainly see the flames beginning to climb out of the deep hold. Rogge's plan had called for taking this ship without shelling it, but the British Admiralty's insistence that all ships under attack attempt radio broadcasts regardless of the situation had once again forced *Atlantis* to shoot.

Benarty's crewmen began to lower boats and abandon ship just as *Atlantis*'s boarding party arrived. The Germans ordered the Allied sailors back to their burning ship and followed them on board. The boarding party realized at once that they would need assistance to extinguish the furious blaze. The leading petty officer signaled *Atlantis* with a request for help. First Officer Kühn immediately formed a work detail and sent it over to *Benarty* to help extinguish the fire. The fire-fighting crew went to work while the boarding party searched the ship.

Benarty was carrying an important cargo that included a thousand tons of lead, four hundred tons of wolfram, one hundred tons of zinc, a large portion of paraffin, and, most important to Rogge, thirty bags of mail. Mohr collected all of the official documents from the captain's quarters, the bridge, and trash cans, and then arranged to transfer all of the fresh food, the documents, two large boats, and the mail back to *Atlantis*. When that had been accomplished, the Germans began to shuttle *Benarty*'s crew of twenty-seven Chinese workers, one naval gunner, and twenty-one English officers and deckhands to the raider. Rogge was happy to learn that not one of the forty-nine-man crew had been injured during the shelling.

Benarty was a 5,800-ton coal burner built in Glasgow in 1926 and owned by the Ben line of W. Thomsen and Company of Leith, sailing from Rangoon to Liverpool under Captain Watt. Mohr reported that the Chinese stokers had indeed left their posts when the plane attacked with its guns. He had taken note that the engine telegraphs on *Benarty*'s bridge remained at the full speed ahead setting, yet the hungry boilers had no fuel to answer the command because the stokers had abandoned them.

With all of their work complete, the boarding party set demolition charges, lit the fuses, and took to their boats. The search, transfer of all materials and prisoners, and placement of the explosives had been accomplished in less than three hours. Fehler's three scuttling charges went off in rapid succession, and the eighth victim of the German raider *Atlantis* slid beneath the sea, stern first, in twelve minutes with only a few muffled pops and gasping whiffs of steam.[6]

Atlantis swung around and headed back to pick up Bulla and Borchert, who sat patiently on the wing of their drifting seaplane. On the bridge, Rogge charted *Atlantis*'s track, location, and progress on a large wall map. As he plotted the locations of the last three attacks, he realized that they painted a fairly clear picture of *Atlantis*'s course and intentions. The last attacks were all directly in line with the approach to the Sunda Strait. Rogge decided to head due south and run out of the shipping routes as soon as the crew had the floatplane loaded back on board.

As the ship sailed south out of harm's way, Mohr began to search through the official mail and documents the search party had found on *Benarty*. The adjutant discovered that *Athelking*'s SOS message was, in fact, repeated by another ship. This confirmed that the second round of shelling on that ship had been avoidable. In mid-July the British had changed their code tables, ending Rogge's ability to read their message traffic. Adjutant Mohr restored his captain's tactical advantage when he found a copy of the new British code table crumpled up in the bag from *Benarty*'s trash can.

When Rogge spoke with *Benarty*'s captain, he learned that the ship's master had thought *Atlantis* was an Allied ship based on its appearance. His belief was reinforced when *Atlantis* turned away from *Benarty* as if it were operating under British Admiralty orders to turn away from all other ships. He had not been warned about any German raiders in the area, he told Rogge, but he had been told that *Kemmendine* was overdue and that one of its lifeboats was found adrift. The information gleaned from *Benarty*'s captain and the official mail the captured ship carried were invaluable to Rogge.

On 12 September, Captain Rogge assembled his crew on the lower deck and summarized the lessons of their most recent encounter. Their disguise had fooled *Benarty*'s master, he told the men. No one was expecting a raider disguised as an Allied ship. Henceforth, Rogge told the crew, they would feign innocence and slowly approach Allied ships. This tactic meant they would sometimes turn away before having the opportunity to rush in and attack. The only glaring deficiency in their disguise was the lack of a stern-mounted self-defense gun. Rogge ordered Kühn to uncover the stern 150-mm gun and modify it to look like a standard British 4.7-inch gun. The British had placed all of their merchant captains on guard and instructed them to take quick evasive actions, send SOS messages, and repeat those from other ships, Rogge continued. The new British tactics narrowed the raider's escape time and margin. Rogge concluded by telling the crew that their mission remained the same, but the British were now certain of their existence and had mounted an active effort to locate and sink all of the raiders. Their mission had become decidedly more dangerous.

Atlantis sailed on a south-southeast course toward the Australian route at a steady nine knots until noon on Wednesday, 18 September, when the engines were shut down to save fuel. At 10:33 the next evening the port bridge lookout spotted a thick cloud of smoke. The unknown ship was sailing westward, away from Australia. Rogge ordered Kielhorn to start the engines and bring the ship up to twelve knots. Since *Atlantis* had been drifting, Rogge could not ask for any more speed than that until the engines had fully warmed up. Cold engines could not burn all of the fuel supplied for full speed; the unburned fuel would go up the funnel and come down in a bright red shower of glowing embers. Rogge turned his ship toward the unknown smoke cloud and approached it slowly for thirty minutes, until the fireboxes were hot enough to consume all of the oil required for full speed.

Captain Rogge was able to make out the ship's outline within an hour. What he saw was a large ship with several funnels. The captain discussed the attack options with his gunnery officer. The two men decided the attack should come from the stern. With the attack plan set, Kühn put *Atlantis* into a maneuver that allowed the ship to circle around and come up astern of the target ship.

At eight minutes past midnight on 20 September, *Atlantis* opened the gun flaps, ran up the war flag, and closed in tightly on the new target at a steady ten knots. When the range was under thirty-four hundred yards, a signalman on the bridge flashed a message to the English merchant ship: "Heave to or I will fire. Do not use your radio."

The reply came quickly, "Understood."

Atlantis asked, "What ship?"

"*Commissaire Ramel*," was the response.

A searchlight from *Atlantis* illuminated *Commissaire Ramel*'s black hull and yellow upper works, and the German signalman sent, "Wait my boat."

Commissaire Ramel blew off steam, switched on its lights, and replied, "Understood."[7]

Rogge was very anxious to capture this large ship intact because he wanted to use it as a prisoner ship. Just as he started to tell the watch officer to have the prisoners begin packing, a radioman yelled into the bridge, "Enemy transmitting six-hundred-meter band! RRR RRR, *Commissaire Ramel* . . ." Rogge unleashed his guns. They scored hit after hit, yet William Brown, Ramel's radio operator, kept broadcasting. The Sydney-born Brown dispatched two complete messages on his main transmitting gear before German shells knocked out his power supply. The men on *Atlantis* worked feverishly to jam the SOS messages, but the pleas for assistance got through and were picked up and relayed by Mauritius and other shore stations.

After a short pause while Brown and his second operator, Dick Chapman, rigged emergency gear, *Commissaire Ramel* broadcast half of yet another SOS message. Finally, a shell struck the radio shack and destroyed the last bit of radio gear. Brown and Chapman fled the collapsing radio room and the broadcasts ended.

The fifty-six high-explosive shells had reduced the ship to a useless hulk. The forecastle was engulfed in flames, and fire was plainly visible through the portholes along the side. The crew of *Commissaire Ramel* signaled for *Atlantis* to send help and then began to abandon ship. The German boarding party took on the difficult task of rounding up the prisoners in the high seas.

Cutters from *Atlantis* gathered up all of the lifeboats and towed them back to the raider. From the original crew of sixty-six, *Atlantis* picked up sixty-three survivors.

Once the survivors were out of the water, Rogge ordered the 10,061-ton *Ramel*, a former French passenger ship, sunk with gunfire. Rogge found the master and asked him why he had broadcast an SOS after the ship had stopped. The sixty-four-year-old captain, a Scot named Mackenzie, told Rogge he had stopped at the radio room and ordered the operator to begin sending before he continued on to the bridge. Only after Mackenzie reached his bridge did he learn that the first officer had already surrendered. Rogge accepted this answer and closed the matter.

Captain Rogge stood on the bridge of *Atlantis* and watched shells pound the red-hot, hissing hull of Messageries Maritimes's *Commissaire Ramel* until the ship sank in a great, steaming roar.[8] Germany lost the cargo of steel, wheat, and leather, and Rogge lost another potential prisoner ship.

Atlantis sailed away from the scene slightly north of due east at fifteen knots. The captain was anxious to depart the area as quickly as possible because *Commissaire Ramel*'s wireless broadcasts had alerted the entire British defense network of *Atlantis*'s approximate location. Rogge's wall chart plotting the latest sinkings indicated *Atlantis*'s course as southwesterly. He moved in the opposite direction of the indicated route, hoping *Pinguin* would capture a ship somewhere to the southwest to assist in throwing the British off his tracks.

Once the ship departed what Rogge considered the immediate danger area, Chief Engineer Kielhorn requested permission to recondition the overworked engines again. He wanted Rogge to allow him to shut down one large diesel at a time for maintenance. Rogge agreed, and Kielhorn immediately began work on one engine. During the next few days, *Atlantis* either drifted quietly or ran slowly on the one assembled diesel engine.

While the work was being conducted on the engines, the ship's combat capability was limited and Rogge kept his raider far from the heavily traveled shipping lanes. The days went by slowly, but the men seemed to enjoy the break in the action. Kühn had some work crews touching up the paint and correcting minor flaws in the disguise, but for the most part the men were allowed to lounge around and take it easy. Adjutant Mohr became the center of attention each night as he reported events from the land war gleaned from the BBC, American broadcasts, and the news from Berlin. From these sources Mohr could gather a clear idea of the actual progress of the war.

The idle days went on until 27 September, when the ship received a bulletin from the SKL with news of *Tirranna*. The men were jubilant to hear that their first prize ship had made it safely around the Cape of Good Hope, through the U-boat hunting grounds, and around the Azores, and had entered the German-controlled waters off the French coast on 22 September. At no time during the cruise had *Tirranna* been in contact with the SKL, although it was not for lack of trying. *Tirranna*'s crew monitored the radio and searched the assigned frequencies without fail, but the SKL never came on the air to issue sailing instructions. In fact, German Naval Command did try to reach *Tirranna* on several occasions, but due to yet another oversight, the Admiralty broadcast the messages on the wrong frequency band each time. *Tirranna* made it to port regardless, sailing through the U-boat hunting grounds unaided and sighting eight other ships, including a British cruiser, during the voyage.

The crew's happiness was soon shattered by a second wireless transmission from the SKL giving word that *Tirranna* had been sunk by a British submarine while awaiting an escort into port. Waldmann had anchored the prize ship off Cap Le Ferret on the French coast expecting German patrol craft to come out and question his intent. When no one came to investigate, Waldmann stopped some local fishermen and tried to ask them to send out the German port authorities. When Waldmann could not get his point across to the French fishermen, he released them and dispatched Leutnant Mund ashore to secure sailing instructions from Berlin and a local harbor pilot.

German Naval Command did not return any instructions to Mund until the following day. When he finally received his orders, Leutnant Mund immediately took them back to the ship. Berlin instructed Waldmann to remain in place and wait for some minesweepers to escort *Tirranna* into port at Bordeaux. *Tirranna* was still waiting for the escort ships when, just after mid-day on 23 September, three torpedoes from the British Trident-class submarine *Tuna* struck in rapid succession.[9] The ship sank within two minutes. Eighty-seven people were killed in the attack on *Tirranna*: seventy-one Indian prisoners, nine British prisoners, three of *Tirranna*'s original crew, three of *Talleyrand*'s crew, and one German prize crewman, Obermaschinenmaat Karl Seeger. *Atlantis* had sustained the first casualty from among its crew in the attack.

Word of the loss deeply affected each crewman on *Atlantis*. The sinking took the lives of people the crew had come to know and respect over their many weeks aboard *Atlantis*. The raider's hard-earned prize, a sturdy merchant ship loaded with valuable cargo and captured documents, was lost. The personal mail sent by the crew, their first communications with home in nearly six months, was lost as well.[10]

The loss had a terrible impact on the morale of *Atlantis*'s crew. The disaster was entirely preventable and stemmed from errors and inattentiveness on the part of the High Command and naval shore units. Rogge penned a bitter note about the German Naval High Command's lack of leadership in the official log of *Atlantis* and decided to sail to an isolated area to allow his crew to get over the loss of *Tirranna* and the deaths of their friends.

6

Hell Ship *Durmitor*

For the next few days *Atlantis* maintained its position in one small deserted area of the sea, drifting with the current and then steaming back over its tracks again and again. The lookouts sighted no other ships, which was exactly what Rogge wanted. The crew needed a break from action after the terrible news of *Tirranna*'s loss.

Rogge deliberately kept *Atlantis* out of the shipping lanes until 1 October 1940, when he decided it was again time to begin an active search for enemy shipping. The captain entered his standard daily information into the ship's war log, the *Kriegstagebuch,* and then closed out that day's report with a statement that he planned to make a sortie into the Sunda Strait. Rogge ordered Kamenz to set a direct course for the strait.

Atlantis arrived in an ambush position where the main shipping routes exited the strait just a few days later. Like a spider in the middle of her web, the ship sat at the point where several shipping lanes converged. Every man on board was keyed up with the tension and anxiety of waiting for combat. Despite the active search for targets, however, *Atlantis* could not find any contacts. Apparently, most British shipping had been diverted into safer routes. The crew's renewed enthusiasm and excitement began to wear off within a few days. As the days lapsed into weeks, the men endured the tedium or tried to entertain themselves by fishing for sharks, lounging in the hot sun, or practicing battle routines, but the lack of action became ever more burdensome. All the while, *Atlantis* crisscrossed the shipping lanes in a vain attempt to locate another victim.

Bulla was able to take his seaplane up for a reconnaissance flight only once during the entire time. A problem with the plane's engine prevented him from dropping the engine's RPMs and forced him to make a high-speed landing. Flight Officer Bulla managed to bring himself and his crewman back safely, but the high-power landing snapped off a strut and an engine mount. *Atlantis* carried no more spares for the plane, so the disabled aircraft was hoisted on board and stowed away. The incident ended Bulla's flying career until *Atlantis*'s machinists could fabricate the necessary parts and securely remount the engine.

Other concerns plagued Rogge at this time as well. Complaints from the crew and especially from the prisoners began to increase. Prisoner disobedience and infractions of the rules started to become commonplace, until finally Rogge was forced to throw an English sailor into the brig for failure to obey his own English captain. Rogge knew the solution was to find an enemy ship to engage. A battle would restore his men's fighting spirit and a prize would relieve his ship of the problematic prisoners.

Relief came on 22 October 1940. As a stiflingly hot night began to give way to dawn, the white upper works of a ship appeared on the distant horizon. Rogge called the men to action stations, and on a sea as smooth as a sheet of glass brought *Atlantis* onto a direct intercept course. The range quickly decreased to just over five thousand yards, and Rogge could plainly see the Yugoslavian flag painted on the side of the ship. Yugoslavia was still neutral at that time, but Rogge decided to stop the ship and check its cargo just the same. If the ship was carrying no contraband, he would release it. If the ship carried cargo to support the Allies, Rogge planned to capture it and use it as a prison ship. The months of maintaining so many prisoners on *Atlantis* had placed a terrible strain on his ship and crew.

At three thousand yards Rogge gave the command to raise the signal flags. A signalman ran up the flags to spell out "Heave to" and "Do not use your wireless." The merchant ship did not acknowledge the flags in any way and started to transmit a wireless message. *Atlantis* responded by raising the Kriegsmarine battle flag and unmasking its guns. The transmission stopped.

As Mohr prepared his boarding party to climb into their motor launches,

Rogge noted that a pajama-clad figure had appeared on the bridge, and then the Yugoslavian ship broadcast two SOS messages. The messages were useless, however, because the Yugoslavian radioman neglected to report his ship's position. This error allowed Kasch to hold his fire. Rogge was determined not to fire on the ship because he desperately needed it to off-load his cargo of prisoners.

The ship then radioed directly to *Atlantis:* "What ship? This is *Durmitor.* Who is calling me? Please answer."

Atlantis did not answer.

Durmitor continued: "SS *Durmitor,* Lourenço Marques for Japan via Batavia. Who are you?"[1]

Again *Atlantis* did not respond. Rogge waited for the boarding party to arrive at the ship and explain the details.

The German crewmen clambered up the sides of the rusty ship and easily took command. After a quick survey the boarding party relayed to Rogge the information that *Durmitor* was a 5,623-ton tramp from Dubrovnik's Ragusa Steam Navigation Company carrying a crew of thirty-seven and a nearly worthless cargo of eighty-two hundred tons of salt.

Captain Rogge decided to declare the ship a prize. He based his decision on Prize Regulation Articles 23, 28, 39, and 40, which applied because *Durmitor* had visited an enemy port and used its radio after being instructed not to do so. Rogge put Leutnant Emil Dehnel and a prize crew of twelve Germans aboard the ship and sent it to a rendezvous point about two hundred miles south of Christmas Island.

The men of *Atlantis* were still somewhat restless despite the action, and grumblings of discontent filtered up to Rogge. His men had been at sea for more than seven months, and their sense of adventure had run thin. On 25 October, Captain Rogge called the men together on the deck and told them he was aware of their unhappiness and displeasure. Rogge first told the crew that he would accept no mutinous behavior and that grumbling and failure to follow orders would be dealt with swiftly and severely. A breakdown in discipline could end their cruise and ultimately hurt the German war effort. The captain then announced some duty changes to ease the burden on the men. Specifically, Rogge declared two new policies designed to reenergize and motivate the men.

The first new order gave members of the crew not standing an active watch certain afternoons off when demands were low. Rogge borrowed the second new policy from Captain Karl Nerger of World War I fame. Captain Rogge ordered First Officer Kühn to institute a policy of "leave-on board" wherein four men from each division would be relieved of any and all duties, excepting battle stations, for one uninterrupted week. The men "on leave" would live in the empty quarantine area of the aft sick bay and were free of all formations and morning reveilles, although they were still required to wear their uniforms and to salute all officers.[2] Rogge concluded his briefing by reinforcing his stand on discipline and then finally announcing that he planned to sail the ship to a remote area where the crew could spend a peaceful Christmas. The men responded well to their captain's talk, and duty performance returned to a very high level almost immediately.

The following morning *Atlantis* sighted *Durmitor* at the meeting point as planned. Captain Rogge assembled all of the captive merchant captains and officers and explained that the conditions on board the planned prisoner ship, *Durmitor*, were very bad. Rogge wanted each of the merchant captains to have the opportunity to protest the move.

All of the captured officers decided to leave *Atlantis*, preferring to endure the spartan conditions on the barnacled, rusted tub than be locked in the sweltering, foul-smelling, cramped prisoners' quarters of *Atlantis*—especially while it conducted dangerous raiding operations. Rogge agreed to allow the prisoners to transfer if each captain would give his word of honor that none of his men would attempt a mutiny or sabotage. Each of the captured merchant captains gave his word, and the prisoner transfer began soon afterward.

Leutnant Dehnel and his twelve-man prize crew shoveled enough salt over the sides of the Yugoslavian tramp to allow the prisoners to fit into holds number one and number two. There were not enough mattresses for everyone, and most of the prisoners had to sleep on tarpaulins placed directly on top of the cargo of salt. Only the prisoners over fifty years of age had the pleasure of a mattress.

The transfer of the nearly three hundred prisoners took the entire day of Sunday, 26 October 1940. Dehnel had the captives herded behind a barbed-wire barrier on the forepart of the ship. They had free access to the foredeck and the two holds, but they were blocked from entering the rest of the ship by a continually manned machine-gun post set high on the bridge. The Germans put on a demonstration of the weapon's firing capabilities to reinforce the point when Leutnant Dehnel told the Allied prisoners not to try any mutinous acts.

Atlantis's officers calculated that the trip to Italian-held Somalia would take about nineteen days, but they told the prisoners that it would take only fourteen. The Germans figured out exactly how much coal, bread, and water Dehnel would need to reach his destination of Mogadishu, then compared their figures with *Durmitor*'s inventory. Leutnant Dehnel calculated that he had enough coal to reach the Italian port at a comfortable speed of seven knots, but food and drinking water were a problem; both were in very short supply. Captain Rogge transferred only the absolutely necessary amounts of bread and drinking water to *Durmitor*. He could spare little, if any, of his precious supplies, yet he had to relieve his ship of the mass of prisoners. Rogge gave Dehnel two weeks' worth of bread and enough water for each man to have one quart a day. Rogge noted in the log entry for that day that the war effort had forced him to overlook certain human considerations and comforts that would normally be expected. As those aboard *Durmitor* soon discovered, Rogge's log entry was an understatement of major proportions.

Atlantis rested on the water as *Durmitor* slowly sailed away.[3] As soon as Dehnel had taken his ship over the horizon from *Atlantis*, his men made a terrible discovery. Under the crusted-over top layer of coal was a large pocket of air! The officers had included the hidden hollow space in the fuel calculation. Clearly, the ship did not have enough fuel to reach Mogadishu.

Leutnant Dehnel faced an agonizing dilemma. If he slowed the ship to save fuel, he would run out of food before reaching port. If he maintained speed, he would run out of coal far from any port. Dehnel decided to reduce both the ship's speed and the men's daily ration. He slowed the ship to a crawl and cut the men's rations to almost nothing. To further add to the problems, the captives discovered that the holds of the prison ship were infested with rats, roaches, and other vermin that pestered and nipped at them throughout the night. The salt was nearly impossible to lie on, much less sleep on. It was rock hard and had countless sharp edges that effectively eliminated any opportunity for comfort. The salt stuck to the men's sweaty bodies, rubbing, chafing, and irritating their skin.

Within a few days Dehnel found it necessary to reduce each man's water allotment again, from one quart to one cup. The prisoners became so desperate that they began inviting death by tapping the engine steam pipes and drinking the hot, rusty water. The German guards watched, not daring to stop the men from quenching their maddening thirst.

The blessing of rain came occasionally. During the short showers the men would rush up on deck and cheer at the sky as they collected and drank as much water as they could or washed their salt-caked bodies. The relief brought by the rain showers was short-lived, however, because the rain also filled the holds with water, creating an all-invading salt soup that the prisoners could not escape. The thick, salty water wicked through the tarps and clothing, soaking the men when they tried to sleep and burning their eyes and noses. Soon, all of the prisoners had developed painful running sores accompanied by patches of severely peeling skin.

After eight days of this torture, the incarcerated men began to shout crazed threats of murder and mutiny at their captors. Leutnant Dehnel pointed to a distant smoke cloud and told the prisoners the tower of smoke was *Atlantis*. Dehnel warned the prisoners that the warship was still close enough to react quickly to quash any prisoner uprising. The prize officer had no idea what ship was on the distant horizon, but he was certain it was not *Atlantis*. The ploy worked nevertheless. The prisoners calmed down and became rational once again. Dehnel then led a delegation of the prisoners through the German living areas to show them that the German crewmen were living under the same dreadful conditions. Dehnel's actions appeased the captive men and ended the threat of a prisoner takeover.

Desperate to do anything to hurry the voyage, Dehnel ordered his prize crew to erect a tarpaulin sail between the mainmast and funnel each night to help the underfueled engines drive the ship. The makeshift sail was taken down each morning on the offhand chance that an Allied ship might catch sight of the bizarre sail. The Leutnant did not want to raise any unnecessary curiosity.

On 11 November 1940, the anniversary of the World War I Armistice, Dehnel assembled all the men aboard *Durmitor* for a ceremony to commemorate the dead from the First World War. The German lieutenant made a short address to the men and then observed two minutes of silence in remembrance. A German rifleman fired a shot to begin and end the silence. At the close of the ceremony the warring factions staggered back to their designated areas of the ship. Everyone on the ship suffered greatly from nagging hunger and constant thirst, but no one was yet gravely ill. Dehnel remained steadfast in his determination to reach the chosen destination with all hands alive.

By the thirteenth, the lack of coal had forced Dehnel to begin burning wooden items from the ship in order to maintain a head of steam. First the barrels and other useless wooden objects were burned, then the doors, furniture, paneling, and wooden stripping were all gradually removed, cut up, and consumed as fuel. The Germans used the one small handsaw on board to cut up anything that would burn. *Durmitor* slowed to a pitiful speed of just over two knots. The men continued to hack up the barren ship from the inside out. Soon even the lagging, derricks, and lifelines became fuel.

Finally, with no more wood to burn, Dehnel's men began making briquettes of fuel from a mixture of coal dust, sawdust, paint, grease, and ashes. The stench of burning garbage hung over the ship like a sickening pall, yet the men continued to push on. Using their jury-rigged sail and homemade fuel briquettes, they kept the ship under steam until a bridge lookout jubilantly reported landfall on the night of 22–23 November. The men arrived at the tiny port of Warsheik, Somalia, after twenty-nine days of torment, with almost no water, a mere 661 pounds of beans, and 400 pounds of coal remaining.

The Germans eagerly signaled their Italian allies and waited in vain for a reply. The coy shore stations ignored all attempts to establish contact. At 4:00 the following afternoon Dehnel's patience ran out and he tried to bring the ship into port. He had no charts for the area and ran *Durmitor* hard aground on a sunken coral reef. The Italians in charge of the port finally dispatched a cutter. In their haste to celebrate their "capture" of an Allied ship, the Italian military authorities arrested everyone on board. All the men were taken ashore, loaded onto trucks, and driven thirty-four miles to Mogadishu for a hastily arranged victory parade. The Italians marched the weak, exhausted men through the streets for hours before Dehnel could make them understand that some of the "prisoners" were in fact sailors of the German Kriegsmarine—and their allies. The embarrassed Italian authorities apologized and returned the men to the ship, which had been refloated and docked at Warsheik's tiny pier.

Once back on board, the Germans and the original Yugoslav crew got *Durmitor* under way again. In his hurry to leave Warsheik behind Dehnel ran the ship aground once more. This time the crew freed the ship themselves and staggered south to Mogadishu. When they tried to make port there, the Italian authorities ran them off, fearing the ship would offer an irresistible target for a British cruiser that had passed by earlier and shelled the port. The Italians ordered *Durmitor* to Kisimayu, 246 nautical miles away near the Kenyan border. Dehnel and his crew completed the cruise when they brought their ship into the port at Kisimayu.[4] There they finally washed their hands of the "Hell Ship *Durmitor*" forever.[5]

In the meantime, *Atlantis* stayed in the Sunda Strait until 1 November, when Rogge fixed course for the Bay of Bengal. Seven days later, on the night of the eighth, as *Atlantis* searched the Colombo–Singapore route slightly north of the equator, the lookouts spotted an eastbound ship. The unidentified ship was plainly visible against the moonlit background while *Atlantis*'s silhouette was shrouded by thick, dark rain clouds. Rogge used this advantage to slowly approach the long, flat ship.

Within twenty minutes the raider's crew could plainly see the unmistakable outline of a tanker. Rogge ordered the gun flaps opened and continued to close. At the point-blank gun range of five hundred yards, *Atlantis* still remained unseen. Rogge ordered a rating to illuminate the target ship with *Atlantis*'s powerful searchlight. Instantly, the brilliant light broke the inky darkness and gripped the enemy tanker in its powerful white beam. *Atlantis* began to flash out a message with its signal lamp that instructed the target ship to stop and not use its radio.

The surprised and confused tanker's bridge crew flashed back a response giving the ship's name as *Teddy* from Oslo and asking the identity and intentions of the intruder. Rogge told his signalman to respond as HMS *Antenor*, a British armed merchant cruiser of 11,174 tons that closely resembled *Atlantis*. Captain Rogge hoped to dispel the fears of *Teddy*'s crew by posing as an Allied ship on a routine search operation. *Teddy* answered with three long blasts from the siren to signal its intent to stop. *Atlantis* continued to hold the Norwegian ship in the searchlight's blinding beam, and Rogge could plainly see the tanker's deck gun, covered and unmanned, and the red-banded black funnel of the Klavensee Company line.

As soon as *Teddy* came to a stop on the long, slow swells of the tropical sea, Mohr rushed his men to their boats and raced off toward the tanker. The Norwegian crew stood on deck armed with rifles and offered the boarding boats no lines or assistance. The Germans came alongside *Teddy*, timed the rise of a swell, and raced up the ladders just as the wave raised them to its highest point. The Norwegians, blinded by the light from *Atlantis*, were taken completely by surprise. Adjutant Mohr ripped open his Royal Navy jacket to expose his Kriegsmarine uniform, put on his German naval officer's cap, drew his weapon, and told *Teddy*'s captain, "I am an officer of the German navy. You are my prisoners!"[6] *Atlantis* captured the 6,748-ton tanker without firing a shot. Rogge put a prize crew under the command of Leutnant Breuers on *Teddy* and brought Capt. Thor Lütken and his thirty-one-man crew to *Atlantis*. Lütken informed Rogge that the ship had been sailing from Ābādān to Singapore with ten thousand tons of fuel oil and five hundred tons of diesel fuel. Rogge badly wanted the diesel fuel—it would extend his endurance limits two more months—but he could not afford to attempt a refueling operation in the Bay of Bengal, where he might be surprised at any moment by an English patrol. Rogge sent *Teddy* five hundred miles south to a position in open water below the equator designated "Point Mangrove" to wait while he studied his options and decided what he wanted to do with the tanker. Breuers and his crew quickly got *Teddy* under way and sailed south out of sight.

Flight Officer Bulla and *Atlantis*'s mechanics had by then completed the makeshift repairs on the seaplane, giving their ship the advantage of aerial reconnaissance once again. Shortly after the new engine struts were in place, Bulla was aloft. He took off from the calm water surrounding *Atlantis* on the afternoon of 10 November and quickly returned to report the sighting of another eastbound enemy ship just to the north of *Atlantis*.

As the crew recovered the floatplane, the officers calculated a course and speed that would put the raider on the enemy just after nightfall. *Atlantis* turned to the new heading and steamed into the fading light at top speed. Within a few hours, *Atlantis* came up on the stern of the ship. The bright moonlight made the long, flat deck of another tanker clearly visible from the bridge. However, the moonlight also allowed the ship to catch sight of *Atlantis*.

The tanker turned away, laid on speed, and began to radio a QQQ, QQQ distress call, broadcasting its name as *Ole Jacob* and its position as 6 degrees, 29 minutes north latitude and 90 degrees, 16 minutes east longitude. Rogge wanted to avoid using his guns if at all possible; even one high-explosive shell would destroy the tanker and waste its vital cargo. Captain Rogge allowed the broadcast to continue but ordered the signalman to flash a message to the ship telling it to stop and be prepared for a boarding inspection by HMS *Antenor*. The tanker responded with a request for *Atlantis* to stop following. Atlantis repeated the signal, continuing to pretend to be a British armed merchant cruiser (AMC) that wanted the tanker to heave to for a routine search.

Ole Jacob lost way and finally came to a stop, but it also started to broadcast another distress call; Rogge held his fire, continuing to feign the demeanor of a British AMC. The captain wanted to capture *Ole Jacob* with deception, not destruction. Rogge signaled that he was sending a boat over to conduct an interview with the tanker's captain. Mohr and Kamenz stood in the motor launch with a coxswain at the helm. They were the only three figures visible, but there were ten other sailors armed with MP-40 submachine guns and grenades hidden beneath a tarpaulin in the launch.

Atlantis switched on its powerful searchlight and illuminated *Ole Jacob* as the motor launch was between the two ships. In the bright light Mohr could see that *Ole Jacob*'s deck gun was manned and trained on *Atlantis*. He could also see that the tanker's rail was lined with men in British-style helmets looking down on them. Mohr stood tall in his British officer's coat as they pulled alongside *Ole Jacob* and waited for a swell to give them the opportunity to dash aboard.

A crewman from *Ole Jacob* yelled down to Mohr asking him if he was British. Mohr responded with a bit of unintelligible English, but his response was drowned out by the motor launch scraping against the steel of the tanker's plating. Tensions were extremely high on both sides. When a rising wave brought the motor launch up to the boarding ladder, Mohr, Kamenz, and the hidden attack party sprang over the rail and onto *Ole Jacob*. Mohr landed on deck and ripped off his British uniform coat. He charged a Norwegian rating, tore the rifle from the rating's hands, and commanded: "Hands up!"

The volatile situation could have resulted in a gun battle won by either side as the armed Norwegians faced off against the armed Germans for a terrifying moment before surrendering. Mohr, still operating on adrenalin, rushed off to the bridge, where he burst in on Capt. Leif Christian Krogh. Captain Krogh, who had seen everything that happened on deck, immediately surrendered his ship.

Atlantis had successfully captured another ship without having to fire a single shot. Rogge was not as happy with the capture of *Ole Jacob* as he had expected to be. The two-year-old, 8,306-ton tanker of the Johs Hansen Tankrederi line carried eleven thousand barrels of high-octane aviation fuel, an extremely valuable cargo, but not the diesel fuel Rogge had been hoping to capture.

Rogge took most of the thirty-two prisoners off the captured ship and replaced them with a prize crew led by Kapitänleutnant Paul Kamenz. One of the very first responsibilities of the prize crew's signalman was to use the tanker's own distinctive key to cancel the earlier distress calls as mistakes. The British stations that received the cancellation signal were not completely appeased; the commander in chief, East Indies, dispatched a hunting group of two light cruisers, an AMC, and a heavy cruiser to inspect the area in question. The German Admiralty in Berlin, on the other hand, was completely fooled. The German Naval High Command dispatched a message to its raiders announcing that the Allied merchant ships in the Indian Ocean were so nervous that they panicked and called for help even when approached by one of their own AMCs!

By dusk on 10 November, the transfer of the prisoners and supplies was complete. Captain Rogge ordered his prize crew to take *Ole Jacob* to "Point Rattang" three hundred miles farther south. This was in the same general area off Christmas Island where *Teddy* also waited. Rogge set the rendezvous date for 15 November, and the two ships parted as the sun came down to touch the sea on the distant horizon.

British shore stations at Colombo called *Ole Jacob* over the various frequency bands in a vain attempt to raise the missing ship. Other ships in range repeated the plea for a response, yet the German radio operators on *Ole Jacob* steadfastly remained silent.

The morning of 11 November, Armistice Day, saw the raider's crew gather on deck for a commemoration ceremony to remember the war dead of the First World War. Little could they imagine the suffering those aboard *Durmitor* endured at the same moment on a distant sea while they conducted a similar memorial service.

As *Atlantis* glided on a flat ocean about 250 miles southwest of Achin Head, a lookout spotted a thin smoke cloud rising against the clear, bright blue sky. Rogge ordered *Atlantis* stopped so he could precisely calculate the newly sighted ship's heading, speed, and range. The other ship was eighteen miles distant and on a convergent course that would bring it past *Atlantis*'s starboard side. Rogge sent his men to action stations to wait for the contact and slowed his ship slightly to allow the target ship to close the distance.

Automedon, the ship overtaking *Atlantis*, had sailed on 24 September 1940, from Liverpool for the Far East by way of the Cape of Good Hope. The merchant ship's officer of the watch, the extra second mate, Mr. D. Stewart, sighted *Atlantis* ahead and three points off the port bow and called for the ship's master, Capt. W. B. Ewan. When Ewan reached the bridge, the two officers evaluated the situation and carefully considered what to do.

Captain Ewan decided to hold his course for four reasons. First, the ship off his bow appeared to be holding course from Madras for the Sunda Strait. Second, Ewan had received no warnings of enemy ships in the area. Third, *Automedon* was just about to enter the narrow Sunda Strait. If Ewan ordered a course change to avoid the other ship, he would have to make a major course adjustment and attempt to secure another accurate position fix. Finally, the ship on Ewan's bow appeared to be an ordinary Dutch merchant vessel of the type that routinely plied the routes around the Sunda Strait.

Both ships continued on their converging courses, with neither altering its direction. Rogge calculated that the two ships would meet at the bottleneck created by the strait. He soon recognized the unknown ship as a British Blue Funnel liner by the long-out-of-date smokestack. At 9:04 A.M. with the range forty-six hundred yards, Rogge ordered *Atlantis* into a tight starboard turn, unfurled the Kriegsmarine war ensign, and shot a 150-mm salvo across the British freighter's bow.

The old freighter's wireless transmitter called out the familiar raider warning, then the target ship's identity—*Automedon*—and finally began to broadcast its position. Only the first digits of the ship's location escaped into the airwaves; the rest of the transmission was cut off by *Atlantis*'s deadly pounding of the bridge and radio shack. The first salvos demolished the bridge and everything in it.

When *Atlantis* had closed to two thousand yards, Rogge could see that the first salvo had destroyed the bridge and the surrounding area. Still *Automedon* courageously tried to escape. The ship steamed on, sustaining eleven more high-explosive hits. The additional shelling shattered the entire midships area. Rogge was about to order a cease-fire when a British crewman approached *Automedon*'s stern-mounted defensive gun. The gunner's appearance brought another three salvos that rained down hell on the stern of the ship. Finally, *Automedon*, beaten into submission, blew off steam and slowed to a stop.

Twenty-one minutes after firing the first shots, Mohr's boarding party arrived at the starboard side of the forward well deck of *Automedon*'s smoldering hulk. Mohr found the carnage on the ship appalling. Every man standing on the bridge had been instantly killed in the first salvo: Captain Ewan; the second mate, T. G. Wilson; the third mate, P. L. Whitaker; the chief steward; and a passenger. A company employee, a Chinese worker traveling as a passenger, later died in the hospital aboard *Atlantis*. The dead had been blasted into ghastly positions. To add to the gut-wrenching scene, twelve horribly wounded men groaned and screamed as they lay on the riddled and smashed steel of *Automedon*'s deck.

Mohr, sickened by the bloodshed, searched through the twisted steel and swaying lines and cables that had once been *Automedon*'s bridge while the rest of the boarding party tried to comfort and prepare the wounded men for evacuation to *Atlantis*. The fact that the shells had devastated the bridge so abruptly and so completely meant that none of the ship's secret papers had been destroyed. Leutnant Mohr forced entry into *Automedon*'s strong room, the chart room, and then the safe. He found a treasure trove: sailing orders; Admiralty instructions; cipher pages; port defense layouts for the entire Far East; British operating instructions; parts 7, 8, and 9 of the merchant navy code tables; orders of battle for the Far East land and sea forces; 120 bags of mail; and even a sealed secret envelope in its green weighted emergency sink-bag. This most secret sink-bag had been sent aboard by Air Chief Marshall Sir Cyril Newell and was destined for the commander in chief of the Far East, Sir Robert Brooke Popham. Mohr gathered every bit of this priceless intelligence data and returned it to *Atlantis* for future examination.

The boarding party was busy transferring the one surviving officer (Extra Second Officer Stewart), thirty-six English crewmen, three passengers, and fifty-six Chinese workers from *Automedon* when Fehler's demolition party opened one of the hold covers and made an amazing discovery. The 7,528-ton *Automedon* carried a cargo worth millions! Fehler's men found crated airplanes, cars, machinery, medical supplies, microscopes, beer, whisky, cigarettes, and an enormous amount of food—all there for the taking.

Rogge was very nervous about stopping in an area with such a high level of enemy merchant and warship traffic. He instructed Fehler to transfer only the most-needed items and quickly sink *Automedon*. The sinking did not come as quickly as Rogge wanted. As Fehler's men dug deeper into the holds, they continued to locate stockpiles of crated treasures. Each time a new find was made, Fehler would signal Rogge and ask for permission to extend the deadline while the cargo was transshipped to *Atlantis*. It was well past noon when Rogge finally ordered Fehler to stop his clearing operation, set his scuttling charges, and return to *Atlantis*.

The now familiar dull rumblings of the exploding charges deep inside the hull signified the beginning of the end. *Automedon* sank by the stern at 3:07 P.M., just minutes after the scuttling charges detonated, *Atlantis*'s thirteenth victim.[7]

Rogge had taken three ships in the present area within four days. It was time to move on. He put *Atlantis* on a southward heading, toward the waiting prizes *Teddy* and *Ole Jacob,* and brought the ship's speed up to ten knots.

That evening, *Automedon*'s sister ship *Helenus,* under Capt. P. W. Savery, sailed near *Atlantis* calling for *Automedon* and repeating that ship's earlier distress call. Captain Rogge was sleeping when the radio operators picked up the signals. For unknown reasons the officer of the watch did not see fit to disturb his sleeping captain. This decision allowed *Helenus* to escape, but it may have saved *Atlantis* as well. A British hunter group was actively scouring the general area in close proximity to *Helenus* specifically looking for German raiders.

Two days later, when *Atlantis* sighted *Teddy*, Rogge had already decided to sink the Norwegian ship. The tanker carried fuel oil, not diesel fuel, making it worthless to *Atlantis*. The tanker's cargo could have been put to good use by other German ships, but Rogge had no way to effectively employ it without sending and receiving long clear-text messages to the other raiders and the SKL. He considered sending those messages far too dangerous and decided that sinking *Teddy* was his only option.

The Germans removed everything of value from the captured ship, including the five hundred tons of diesel fuel carried in one small storage tank, then the demolition men planted the scuttling charges and waited for the explosion. Nothing happened. Fehler and his men promptly shuttled back to *Teddy* and planted a second charge. The second charge exploded and instantly ignited the tanker's cargo of fuel oil. A huge fireball surged high into the air on the force of the explosion. The raging fire shot flames skyward and produced a thick cloud of black smoke that swirled and towered up into the cloudless blue sky. Rogge gazed with shock at the gigantic funeral pyre Fehler had built for the tanker. The fire and especially the immense column of thick, dark smoke could be seen far over the horizon. It was dangerous enough to ignite a volatile fuel tanker so that it burned like a bombed oil field, but it was pure folly to wait around such a scene. Rogge sailed *Atlantis* off toward the waiting *Ole Jacob* under a full head of steam. *Teddy* did eventually sink, leaving behind only a multicolored patch of thin fuel oil and some debris floating on the water's surface.[8]

When news of *Teddy*'s sinking reached the SKL, the High Command blasted Rogge for denying the fuel to other German ships, ignoring the fact that its own failure to coordinate such operations made *Teddy*'s cargo all but useless. Rogge accepted the SKL's criticism but defended his decision in writing: "My decision was largely influenced by the complete lack of any comprehensive Naval Staff directive or pre-arranged code groups concerning the capture of tankers, or of adequate foresight in planning mutual support between diesel-engined and oil burning raiders."[9]

Atlantis continued to sail south until 14 November, when it made contact with the other Norwegian prize, *Ole Jacob*. Rogge had decided to have the prize crew sail *Ole Jacob* to Japan. He knew that Japan sorely needed *Ole Jacob*'s precious cargo of high-grade aviation fuel and would be willing to deal for it. He wanted to dispatch the top-secret documents captured from *Automedon* to Berlin via Japan, and he also wanted to off-load his prisoners and once again relieve *Atlantis* of the additional burden of captives.[10]

Atlantis took all the diesel fuel possible from *Ole Jacob*, leaving on board just enough for the ship's journey to Japan. Kamenz dumped a pile of lumber, some oil, one of *Ole Jacob*'s lifeboats, and some rafts overboard, hoping to fool anyone who found the flotsam into thinking that the tanker had been sunk. After his prize crew had loaded both *Ole Jacob*'s and *Teddy*'s crews on board, he sailed off toward the nearest Japanese port.

Ole Jacob, under Kapitänleutnant Paul Kamenz, sailed into Kōbe, Japan, on 6 December. In a deal arranged by Admiral Wenneker, the German naval attaché in Tokyo, the Japanese authorities quietly refueled the tanker and dispatched it to Lamotrek Island in the Caroline chain. Here, moored in the deserted lagoon, *Ole Jacob* secretly met with a Japanese tanker and transferred the valuable aviation fuel into Japanese hands. The Japanese returned the favor by setting up secret fuel oil drops around the Pacific for German raiders to use.

Ole Jacob then sailed back to Kōbe. The Japanese delivered the Norwegians to their embassy in Tokyo, and Kamenz met with Japanese naval authorities and provided the Japanese government with copies of all of the secret Allied papers taken from *Automedon*. The astonished Japanese did not believe the information Kamenz delivered was authentic until they confirmed the dispatches against known and validated intelligence data. All of the information Rogge had sent proved accurate, complete, and very valuable. The exceptional importance of the information came to light a year later when Japan entered the war and launched an attack against Singapore.[11]

The German Naval High Command dispatched a message to Kamenz via the German attaché in Tokyo summoning him immediately to Berlin. It was a very long trip. The Japanese helped Kamenz get to Vladivostok. Once he arrived there, the Soviets, acting on a formal request from Berlin, secured transportation for the Kapitänleutnant to Moscow on the Trans-Siberian Railroad. From Moscow, Kamenz completed the journey on another train connecting directly to Berlin, where he was able to personally brief the German naval staff on *Ship-16*'s activities and turn over the reams of captured information, codebooks, and papers. Soon after Kamenz departed, the remaining German prize crew sailed *Ole Jacob* from Kōbe and headed for German-controlled waters. The ship, its crew, and the prisoners reached the French port city of Bordeaux safely more than seven months later on 19 July.[12]

After he sent *Ole Jacob* on its way to Japan, Rogge turned *Atlantis* and sailed southeast. The officers scoured their charts and sea guides looking for a remote island where they could secure fresh water, recondition the engines, and allow the men some time away from each other and their routine duties. Rogge rejected a proposal to go to Amsterdam and Saint Paul Islands, reasoning that the British could visit those islands very easily. Another crewman suggested Prince Edward Island, but that was vetoed because it was too foggy and blustery. After looking over the charts, Rogge decided on the Kerguelen Islands group.

The Kerguelens are located in and around latitude 49 degrees, 20 minutes south and longitude 70 degrees, 20 minutes east, midway between Antarctica, Australia, and Africa—very far off the beaten path. The desolate islands were once a stopping point for whalers and seal hunters, but those visits had ended many years ago. Rogge had an excellent survey of the area. The German ship *Gazelle* had visited the islands for scientific purposes just before the outbreak of the war. Rogge also had a special sea chart taken from *Teddy* that outlined the southern sea routes for Allied ships. This chart made it clear that the Kerguelens were isolated, which met one of his criteria. The Kerguelens also had fresh water, which *Atlantis* desperately needed, as well as many channels, inlets, and fjords where a ship could hide very successfully. *Atlantis* turned southward and headed for the safety of the islands in the middle of the stormy, inhospitable southern ocean.

The journey south was uneventful until a radioman reported to his captain with the text of two messages on 1 December. The first message announced the safe arrival of *Durmitor*. This happy news gave the men a fresh topic for their discussions. The second message was from *Ship-33*, *Pinguin*, to the SKL. The message informed the High Command that *Pinguin* was about to dispatch the captured tanker *Storstadt* back to Germany with four hundred prisoners and ten thousand tons of diesel fuel!

Rogge felt that his need for fuel far outweighed the risk of sending a signal. He dispatched a request to have the tanker refuel *Atlantis* before sailing on to Germany. Berlin sent a very quick response ordering *Atlantis* to meet *Pinguin* and *Storstadt* at grid square "Tulip." Rogge immediately turned his boat around and steamed northwest toward the meeting position of 34 degrees, 47 minutes south latitude and 59 degrees, 55 minutes east longitude.

Atlantis arrived at the designated location on Sunday morning, 8 December. The lookout soon spotted another large ship looming on the horizon. The two ships approached each other while the signalmen used their flags to exchange previously agreed upon code groups. Captain Krüder had his men standing in strict formation along the decks and rails wearing their white summer dress uniforms, but as the two ships drew near one another, the formation lost its military bearing and became a rowdy crowd of waving and cheering men. The two raider ships stopped very close to one another, and Captain Krüder took a small launch over to *Atlantis*.

Soon the crewmen of *Pinguin* and *Atlantis* were also shuttling back and forth between the two ships in a great celebration of camaraderie. This was the first time another German had set foot on board *Atlantis* in more than three hundred days. The crews brought out their best food and beer to share with their fellow sailors as they sang songs, swapped stories, and enjoyed the novelty of new faces.

Storstadt arrived that evening. The refueling began at once and lasted all night. The next morning Captain Rogge returned the courtesy and visited *Pinguin*. Just as Rogge was about to return to his own ship, a signal came in. The SKL was sending a message to all ships on the Hydra code cipher, the general surface warship and U-boat code.[13] The SKL used Hydra when it had a general message destined for as many Kriegsmarine ships as possible.

The message announced that Kapitän-zur-See Bernhard Rogge had become the forty-eighth naval officer to receive the Knight's Cross. The message informing him of the award read: "To *Atlantis*. Commanding Officer has been awarded Knight's Cross of the Iron Cross. I offer captain and crew my warmest congratulations on this recognition of the outstanding success achieved by the ship. Signed Commander-in-Chief."[14] When word of the award reached the crews of the two raiders, another celebration began immediately. The festivities lasted a full day until Krüder signaled a good luck wish and final word of congratulations to Rogge and sailed *Ship-33* away.

Atlantis put 124 prisoners on *Storstadt*, retaining only three badly wounded British sailors who could not be moved because they required continued medical care. In exchange for the fuel, the raider moved tons of food and water to the tanker, extending *Storstadt*'s endurance by two months. Rogge also detailed two of his sailors to augment *Pinguin*'s prize crew on the tanker. The two additional sailors were to assist in managing the tanker during the cruise back to German-occupied territory.

With a wail from its siren and its propeller churning up a great white knuckle of seawater, *Atlantis* quickly sailed away from *Storstadt*.[15] Rogge maintained a false course until the ship was well out of sight of the prisoners, who might pass *Atlantis*'s last known bearing to Allied intelligence agents. As soon as *Atlantis* was well over the horizon from the tanker, Rogge brought his ship around to the true course, nearly straight southeast. *Atlantis* steamed hard toward the Kerguelens for fresh water, mechanical repairs, and respite for the crew.

On 11 December, the SKL dispatched a message awarding more Iron Crosses to *Atlantis*. The captain called a ceremony that afternoon and awarded decoration certificates to the deserving men. This award presentation differed from the previous ones; gone now were the short sleeves and pith helmets, replaced by pea jackets and windbreakers.

In two short days of sailing due south the temperature had dropped nearly fifty degrees, forcing the men to unpack their long-stored cold-weather gear. The seas became heavy and the skies changed from bright azure to a foreboding, gloomy gray. Adjutant Mohr looked through the ship's library for information about the Kerguelen Islands and posted it on bulletin boards throughout the ship to pique the men's interest. Mohr's postings included facts about the islands' history, geology, geography, and interesting sights. The crew crowded around the boards to learn about their upcoming port of call, eager to make landfall again.

Kapitän-zur-See Bernhard Rogge, commanding officer of *Atlantis*
Joseph P. Slavick

Atlantis being converted from merchant ship to warship in the Weser shipyard
Horst Bredow, U-Boot-Archiv

Atlantis fighting heavy seas in its breakout attempt
Horst Bredow, U-Boot-Archiv

Atlantis at rest in Gazelle Bay, Kerguelen Islands
Horst Bredow, U-Boot-Archiv

Left to right: Matrosenobergefreiter Gerhard Schütze, Signal-Gefreiter Hans Bartholomay, Signal-Obergefreiter Eduard Grembowski, and Matrose Walter Mehlhorn enjoying a break on the boat deck of *Atlantis* on 16 September 1941
Hans Bartholomay

Rogge requesting "permission" from Captain Lueders for his crew to board *Python*
John R. Angolia

The conning tower of *U-129* with a mixed lot of *Atlantis* and *Python* survivors aboard. Oberleutnant Siegfried Lüdden and Kapitän Lueders of *Python* are visible in the foreground.
Johann Meyer

The shipwreck survivors approach *U-129*.
Johann Meyer

U-129 prepares to receive and assist the survivors.
Johann Meyer

U-68 laden with survivors, as seen from the conning tower of *U-129*
Johann Meyer

Lifeboats in tow behind the motor launch under the command of Oberleutnant Fehler
Johann Meyer

Atlantis crewman Hans
Bartholomay in late 1944
as an Obersignalmann
Hans Bartholomay

The Auxiliary Cruiser War Badge
with Diamonds (Kriegsabzeichen
für Hilfskreuzer mit Brilliants)
awarded to Kapitän-zur-See
Bernhard Rogge
Dan Frailey

7

A Nearly Fatal Landfall

THE DRIVE SOUTH was for a very precious commodity at sea: fresh water. Normally water would not have been a problem. *Atlantis* was equipped with a fully functional water distillation plant that could have more than kept up with the ship's demands. Unfortunately, the distillation plant operated on coal, and the coal supply was also critically low.

Atlantis steamed south, leaving behind the relatively calm waters of the Tropics for the heavy seas of the South Atlantic. The ship's plates once again had to endure the strain of pounding through white-capped, icy seas. The crew fought the waves crashing over the bow and the wind howling through the rigging for three days. Then, in the late morning of 14 December 1940, a lookout sang out: "Land ho! Land ho!" *Atlantis* was in sight of land for the first time since the men had mined Cape Agulhas eight months earlier. The crew was so excited that they crowded the rails, braving the cold rain and spray, just to catch an intermittent glimpse of the desolate islands through the blanketing stormy skies.

The Kerguelens group, which extends over an area about seventy miles wide and seventy miles long, includes many islands. Capt. James Cook is credited with first charting the islands when his expedition's ships *Discovery* and *Resolution* stopped there on Christmas Day 1776. Cook wanted to name the island group the "Islands of Despair" but opted instead to recognize their first known visitor, Yves de Kerguélen-Trémarec, a Frenchman who had stopped there twice, on 12 February and 14 December 1772.

Cook's expedition explored and charted the islands' deeply indented coasts, inlets, bays, coves, and channels, but he did not enjoy the stopover. In his log, he described the harsh land as "naked and desolate in the highest degree."[1] It is made up mainly of treeless, ice-capped mountains and deep ravines filled with thick, marshy bogs. The vegetation is a mix of sparse woody bushes and thick-leafed, barely edible cabbage plants. Only an occasional sheathbill bird or cormorant accompanies the plentiful penguins, seals, and sea lions.

The men scattered from the ship's rails when Captain Rogge ordered action stations at 9:00 A.M. Rogge did not know if the islands were occupied by Allied forces and decided not to take unnecessary risks. Before proceeding any further, the captain dispatched Adjutant Mohr with a party of eight well-armed ratings in a motor launch to conduct a survey. Mohr's party disguised themselves as whalers by covering their uniforms and weapons with skins and furs captured from an earlier prize. The landing party launched one of the larger whaleboats and set a course for the only known remains of a settlement on the island group.

The rough seas and low-hanging gray rain clouds reduced visibility. Mohr's men scanned the shore for movement as they approached a small cluster of houses and wooden shacks. When one of the men spotted a figure moving on the beach, Mohr quickly outlined a plan of attack to surprise and subdue the island's occupants. The adjutant stressed to his men the significance of rapidly securing or destroying any communications equipment the island's garrison might have. The enemy must not get the opportunity to send a message reporting *Atlantis*'s location. A crewman who had been monitoring the figure flopping along the beach observed that the man must be either drunk or insane. The chief coxswain eased the tension with a burst of laughter when he realized that the "drunken man" was really a sea lion. The men in the boat all breathed a sigh of relief when the threat of a beachfront confrontation evaporated.

The shore party beached their boat and immediately jumped over the sides to begin their inspection. It was the first time they had set foot on land since leaving Germany nearly a year before. At first, legs long accustomed to walking on rolling decks had difficulty making progress on the firm ground. In a few moments, however, the search party was able to spread out and begin looking for signs of life. The creaking hinges on the wooden doors, the smells of dust and earth, all brought on waves of nostalgia and a longing for home.

The men found no one on the island. In the large shack they found a stale, but still edible, half-eaten loaf of bread that had sat untouched for many years. The harsh environment and extreme cold precluded even the growth of mold. Mohr noted the calendar on the wall. The days marked off ended at 18 November 1936. The small room was neatly arranged and maintained. The bed was smartly made, and the cupboards held rows of unopened tins of food.

Outside, the men found the preserved bodies of two pigs abandoned in their pen, mummified by the dry, cold air. The search party wondered if the occupants had perished somewhere on the island or rushed off to board a boat leaving everything behind, including the animals in their pens. It seemed likely that 18 November 1936, more than four years ago, was the last day a living human had walked on the islands. Mohr used his low-powered radio transmitter to notify Rogge that the island was unoccupied and quickly received a response ordering the shore party back to the ship.

Rogge brought *Atlantis* slowly into a large cove along the shore. His destination was Gazelle Bay, an inland body of deep water named after the German survey ship that had recently charted the islands. Rogge's manuals provided enough information to safely enter the large outlying bays and open inlets, but not to navigate the more secluded inland waters. The captain wanted to anchor in the safe inner harbor off the Foundry Branch entrance to Gazelle Bay, which would effectively hide his ship and put his men close to a source of fresh water—a waterfall. As *Atlantis* approached the narrow entrance to the inner bay, Rogge stopped and anchored, unable to proceed further until his men had charted and marked a clear, safe channel of deep water for *Atlantis*.

The crewmen accomplished the soundings within a day, and Rogge was ready to move *Atlantis* through Foundry Branch. A crewman switched on *Atlantis*'s echo-sounder and began calling out depths as Rogge moved the ship ahead dead slow. The ship crept past two of the floating markers that made a chain of reference points outlining a safe passage. In a low-pitched voice, the man at the echo-sounder recited a repetitious stream of readings of "Six and a half fathoms." *Atlantis* slid astray and missed the third marker buoy because the ship was not under enough power to provide the required steering force on the rudder. Rogge ordered an increase in speed, and the ship came back under the helmsman's hand. The man at the echo-sounder raised his voice and called out, "Six fathoms," then raised his voice even more and shouted, "Five fathoms!" Rogge gave an immediate order for "All stop!" The engines stopped, but *Atlantis* was still making forward progress when a resounding grinding noise echoed through the ship, which came to a sudden, jarring stop. The ship had struck some unseen and uncharted underwater obstacle. Rogge ordered the engines to full astern. The ship did not move, even though the propeller was driving full reverse revolutions. *Atlantis* was grounded and immobile.

First Officer Kühn ordered damage reports from all of the division chiefs. Damage control teams searched every area of the ship and finally returned with a complete report. The oil stores and holds were intact, but one water tank holding eighty-two tons of fresh water had become salty, which indicated a breach to the sea.

The captain dispatched men all around the ship with lead lines to determine the depth. All returned with identical reports: forty to sixty feet on all sides. The puzzled Rogge ordered a diver into the icy water to determine what was under his ship. After several hours of preparation and a short time under water, the diver surfaced to report that *Atlantis* was skewered on an immense granite pinnacle that jutted out from the depths like a needle. The teams that had surveyed the channel had no way of detecting the solitary granite finger in the surrounding deep water. The diver indicated that the damage to *Atlantis*'s hull was very bad indeed—in fact, hopeless.

Rogge refused to believe the damage was as bad as the man had reported. Although untrained, he donned the diving apparatus and submerged into the icy water to examine *Atlantis*'s nearly five-hundred-foot-long hull for himself. When the captain surfaced, he confirmed that the pinnacle had punctured the ship's double hull; however, he minimized the extent of the damage as "repairable."

Rogge quickly devised a plan to free his ship. The first thing to do was to relieve the pressure on the bow. He decided to lighten the load on the bow area by moving everything possible to the stern. He ordered the thirty tons of ballast sand, the thirty tons of munitions, and hundreds of tons of oil, fresh water, cables, chains, supplies, and all other movable items carried aft. Kühn put the men to work at once on the immense task, reprising his performance as Captain Bligh.

The men sweated and cursed as they passed items down the line in long human chains. They worked nonstop through the night and late into the next morning moving the material to the stern. Kühn drove his tired men for nearly twenty hours until the last piece of equipment had been sent aft. The agonizing hard work paid off as *Atlantis* went down eight and a half degrees in the stern.

Rogge then ordered the thirty-ton anchors switched to the rear. When the exhausted crew finally set the rerigged anchors at the stern, Captain Rogge was ready to try to free his ship. He sent all of the crewmen to the rear of the ship, started the capstan to pull the ship against the rear-set anchors, and put his engines in full reverse. The ship did not move.

The captain then ordered his fatigued men to line up along one side of the ship and instructed them to run from one side of *Atlantis* to the other in time to the piping of the boatswain. As *Atlantis* rocked under the force of the crewmen, Rogge attempted once again to pull his ship free. Despite thirty-six hours of backbreaking effort, the granite spike continued to hold *Atlantis* firmly.

Rogge released the crew to their quarters for some much-needed rest while he remained on the bridge to discuss possible escape options with his officers. He did not seriously consider Fehler's offer to dynamite the ship free. Some of the other suggestions seemed more promising. Rogge said he would consider them in his cabin and left the bridge for a brief nap.

On the morning of 16 December, Mohr had just completed running the engines in full reverse for fifty-three minutes in the fourth attempt at freedom when a large wave came rolling into the channel, swept under the ship, and in a single grinding, rasping motion lifted *Atlantis* off the spike and swung the ship around to freedom. Mohr put the ship under control and alerted Rogge of the situation via the bridge speaking tube that went straight into the captain's quarters.

Within moments Rogge was on the bridge next to Mohr asking for an update. Once again Rogge launched the sounding party to guide the ship to a safe anchorage. This time the men surveyed the entire area in front of the ship and marked questionable spots with marker buoys. *Atlantis* slowly followed, picking a careful path through Foundry Branch at dead slow speed. After a few tense hours of slow going, *Atlantis* had traversed the six-hundred-foot-wide entrance to the channel and entered Gazelle Bay. *Atlantis* anchored in eight fathoms of water in a location that was surrounded on three sides by the three-hundred-foot cliffs of the Jachmann Peninsula. A large waterfall on the western side of the anchorage offered fresh water, and the surrounding cliffs almost totally hid the ship from the seaward side.

As soon as the ship stopped, Kielhorn put his sailors to work reconditioning and refurbishing the engines. Rogge, Mohr, and Fehler went ashore to survey the waterfall. They needed to take on one thousand tons of water to fill *Atlantis*'s tanks. The waterfall was seven hundred yards inland from the shore, and *Atlantis* was three hundred yards out in the water. Somehow, a method of transporting the water over the one thousand yards separating the source and the ship had to be devised. Rogge decided that it would be nearly impossible to have the men restock the water one pail at a time, so he never even considered that option. He left the technically complicated problem to his officers to solve and returned to the ship.

The captain had promised the men some rest and relaxation, but the safety and repair of the ship had to be the first priority. To ensure safety, Gunnery Officer Kasch posted a regular watch on the seaward cliff to watch for approaching ships. Kasch then marked the cliffs with numbers to correspond with the ship's artillery charts. The gunners precalculated a series of ranges, angles, wind speeds, and air pressure deviations that gave *Atlantis* the ability to shell any approaching ship effectively without being seen. The spotters on the cliff line could readily give the ship's gunners fire control orders and corrections without exposing *Atlantis* to any danger. Pleased and impressed with Kasch's defensive fire plan, Rogge turned his attention to the next problem at hand, repairing the ship's hull.

The hole in the number one water tank, although a challenge, proved not too difficult to fix. Rogge learned that two members of the crew were highly experienced in industrial construction techniques. These two men volunteered to seal themselves inside the water tank and overpressurize it with compressed air to force out the water. Once that was done, they could repair the hole by constructing a concrete slab and shoring it up within the tank. Rogge told them to go ahead with their plan.

The two ratings were lowered into the tank along with their equipment and a large food basket and then were sealed inside. By the end of the first day, they had the water pumped out and the concrete patch poured over the hole. The two remained locked in the water tank for two more days while the concrete hardened and set into place. At the end of the third day, the men shored up the patch with stout timbers and signaled that they were ready to exit the water tank. Crewmen waiting outside relieved the air pressure and opened the tank's hatch, releasing the two men. Tensions ran high as teams monitored the patched forepeak for leaks. After many hours of scrutiny, however, the patch still held firm. Rogge was one step closer to having his ship back in fighting shape.

While repairs were being conducted in the water tank, Fehler had devised a plan for catching the water at the top of the waterfall and using the force of gravity from the three-hundred-foot drop to transfer it to *Atlantis* under pressure. Fehler's plan called for lowering a barrel into the onrushing water to catch it and forcibly funnel it through a hose connected to the bottom of the barrel. Fehler's men struggled for three hours to carry a large barrel up the slippery volcanic rocks to the top of the waterfall. It took another three hours for the men to set the barrel with rigging and guy wires spanning the waterfall's twenty-five-foot width. Once the barrel was completely rigged, Fehler tested his system and lowered the barrel into the water. It held fast and appeared to catch the water as planned. The men raised the barrel and tied it off until they could lay the hoses between the barrel and the ship.

By the time darkness settled over the first day's work, the men already had two hundred yards of fire hoses and pipes laid out and secured in place. Their progress far exceeded Captain Rogge's expectations. At noon the following day the detail reached the beach with the hose. As the second day drew to a close, the workers finished the pipeline crossing the three hundred yards of open water out to *Atlantis,* floating it on a bed of life preservers. When the two-day task was complete, the hose stretched from the raised barrel to the open hatch of one of *Atlantis*'s empty water tanks.

Rogge stood on the quarterdeck and watched the end of the hose as

Fehler signaled that he had lowered the barrel into the rushing stream. Rogge fully expected the barrel to be torn loose by the force of the water and later admitted that he was quite surprised to see the slack hose stiffen and then emit a steady three-inch stream of glacier water into *Atlantis*'s water hold. The system carried water down to the ship constantly for two days until all of the water holds were full and many of the empty beer barrels were completely filled and capped.

So far the crew had solved four of Rogge's critical problems: Kasch had ensured the ship's safety during the stop; Kielhorn had completely reconditioned and tuned the diesel engines; Fehler had managed to fill the ship with more than one thousand tons of water; and the leaking forepeak had been repaired. Two critical problems remained to be overcome before Rogge could allow the men to rest and then continue with his raiding: the ship's outer hull had to be repaired, and *Atlantis* had to be given a new identity.

The repair of the outer hull should have been reasonably easy to complete. All that was needed was a diver with an oxyacetylene torch to cut off the jagged, ripped steel and replace the damaged area with steel plates taken from within the ship. Unfortunately, the only diver trained to operate the torch underwater had left the ship as part of *Tirranna*'s prize crew. The other trained divers did not possess the specific expertise required to keep the torch lit underwater.

The men reported to Rogge that there was no way to repair the outer hull without a torch. Rogge did not relish the idea of spending the rest of the war stranded on a deserted island eleven thousand miles behind enemy lines; nor did he like the idea of living out the war as an Allied prisoner of war. There had to be some way to repair his ship. He sent Kielhorn on a dive to inspect the damage and then went down himself for another inspection. The two officers devised a plan that called for men to dive to the damaged area and perforate the weakened spots by drilling holes near the damage. The damaged steel could then be ripped off piece by piece using a shackle and the anchor winches, and patches could be placed over the holes.

The tedious job of repairing the hull inch by inch began at once. Within a few days the diving crews began to show the strain of the constant underwater work in the near freezing temperatures. Rogge periodically dove to personally monitor the progress of the slow and extremely arduous repair work, and to provide on-the-spot support for the weary men. After seven days of constant diving, the divers earned a break as the repair work stopped for a short Christmas celebration. Fehler had spent a great deal of time and effort organizing committees to build artificial Christmas trees, make decorations, and wrap presents for each member of the crew. The trees were broomsticks and rope painted green and decorated to look like evergreens. The presents were delicacies and items such as socks, ties, and tobacco taken from the holds of captured ships.

Christmas Eve was beginning to look bright and festive when a tragedy shattered the happy mood. A young leading seaman named Bernhard Herrmann was working around the rim of the funnel on a rope platform. As he worked, one of the support ropes holding up his platform crossed directly over a diesel exhaust pipe just at the exact instant that the engine was started for a routine inspection. The hot gases instantly cut the rope, and Seaman Herrmann was thrown to the deck below. He was rushed to the sick bay with two severely shattered femurs.

The next day, the crew dressed in their best uniforms to sing carols and celebrate Christmas together. The captain handed each man a carefully wrapped present, told the story of the Nativity, and bestowed another fifteen Iron Crosses, Second Class, on deserving crewmen. Despite the officers' attempts to make it a festive occasion, the men could not forget the unfortunate accident of young Seaman Herrmann. They looked at the blanket of snow covering *Atlantis* and longed for home.

The day following Christmas, the repair work resumed anew. Rogge finally allowed men ashore at two-hour intervals for a small bit of relief and solitude. He knew that two hours was not enough of a break for the men, but it was all the time he could spare. The repair effort did not allow most of the crewmen any leave time at all. During the first day of the shore break, only thirty-seven men received the brief leave of absence.

Within three more days the divers had completely removed the damaged metal from the hull. Before the patch could be applied, however, the repair work paused for a sorrowful occasion. *Atlantis* had suffered its second casualty. On 29 December Seaman Herrmann died from his massive injuries.[2] The crew wrapped the dead sailor in his country's naval ensign and brought him to the island. Rogge presided over the military funeral, and Bernhard

Herrmann, a young husband and father, was laid to rest under a cross fashioned from oak taken from *Atlantis*. He was buried near the abandoned settlement on a desolate and storm-ravaged shore in the Kerguelen Islands.[3]

The glamour and excitement of the cruise had long ago worn thin for the men. Some were fed up with the pressure of living with the never-ending threat of sinking; some missed home and their families; others began to fear a long, bitter war; and others were just desperately tired. Whatever the reason, the crew thought more and more of ending the cruise and going home. Rogge and the other officers continued to try to motivate and inspire the men, but the task of leadership was becoming more difficult with each passing day.

Rogge realized that his crew had to have a break from the dull, grinding routine. Despite the repair work's extremely intense labor requirements, the captain ensured that each crewman was allowed at least one two-hour period of solace on the island. The men used their short time ashore to stroll around and get away from one another for the first time in nearly a year. They hunted ducks, collected seashells, harassed the sea lions, watched the penguins, picked cabbage, or did whatever else they pleased. Even Ferry got to go ashore, albeit for only a short stay. The small Scottie excitedly yelped and jumped about on the beach, trying to take in all the new scents flooding his nose. His antics attracted the attention of a flock of seagulls, which flew in to protect their territory from the intruder. The birds' aggressive swoops and loud screeches so effectively terrorized the poor dog that his escort had to return him to the ship.

Rogge ordered a seaplane launch each day, fearing that a warship might approach from beyond his spotters' line of sight. Bulla patrolled the seaward exposed side of *Atlantis* and remapped the islands, correcting the mistakes of the earthbound cartographers. New Year's Day came and went with a small celebration. The captain did not slacken the repair work, and he also ran drills to ensure that the crew remained battle-ready. Finally, just as they were nearing collapse, the divers completed the patch work and framing on the ship's outer hull.

The hull repair work concluded just in time to begin another labor-intensive task. *Atlantis* needed a new identity. The British disguise had brought *Atlantis* safely through several perilous situations, but it had also seen a great deal of exposure and had outlived its usefulness. Rogge considered it more of a liability now than an asset. The captain chose the brand-new 7,256-ton Norwegian motor vessel *Tamesis* as the new cover. Built by the Schichan works less than a year earlier, *Tamesis* would not yet show up in the international registers, giving Rogge an added bit of security against discovery.

Once again the men set out with their saws, scaffolds, and paintbrushes to put a new face on *Atlantis*. Work crews removed the roof of the upper superstructure and widened the funnel to give the ship a low, squat appearance. They also moved the ventilators, shortened the masts, and applied a new coat of paint. Rogge inspected his new command and was pleased with its resemblance to the Wilhelmsen line's ship.

On 10 January 1941, after twenty-six days in Gazelle Bay, *Atlantis* slowly pulled its anchors out of the icy water. The men had completed all of the repairs, stopped all the leaks, reconditioned the engines, changed the ship's disguise, and filled the water tanks with a fresh supply of pure glacier water. Within a few hours the disguised warship successfully regained the open ocean. The "Islands of Despair" faded astern into the horizon's gray, smothering arms. Rogge steered north and ordered the speed brought up to seven knots.

The men waited tensely as Rogge increased the ship's speed to nine knots. The ship took the pounding waves without leaking. Concern for the patched hull kept nerves taut as the captain began to put the ship into hard maneuvers and performance tests. If the repair failed, *Atlantis* would sink before being able to return to the Kerguelens. The men would be left to drift in the icy waters of the South Atlantic until rescue came—if it ever did. The crew maintained a constant watch on the repaired areas looking for any sign of a weakening repair or patch. The ship held tight! Rogge fired a full broadside while the ship was under way. The thunderous guns jolted the ship, but the hull maintained its integrity. The tests convinced Rogge and the crew that *Atlantis* was back in fighting shape.

Rogge sent a short dispatch to the SKL requesting orders back to his old hunting grounds. The High Command's reply came quickly, denying Rogge's request. That area was already in another raider's territory. Lacking further guidance from the SKL, Captain Rogge decided to look toward the Arabian Sea as his new area of operation. The navigator shaped course for the Australian shipping routes between the Mozambique Channel and Singapore, and the captain ordered *Atlantis* up to cruising speed. As the hours slowly passed, the ship sailed away from the cold southern waters and the air temperature began to warm. Within days the frigid Antarctic air was just a memory. The raider was once again beneath the blistering blaze of the tropical sun patrolling the most frequently traveled British merchant routes. Rogge had detailed charts, captured from *Automedon,* showing the shipping lanes and trade routes in the area. He knew exactly where the Allied merchant ships would be.

As soon as the raider hit the sea lanes, Rogge started dispatching Bulla to conduct long-range, over-the-horizon reconnaissance. The air searches proved worthwhile on 23 January 1940, halfway between Madagascar and southern India, when Bulla spotted a ship nearby. Bulla returned to his ship with the details of the sighting. Even before landing, he signaled Rogge that an unidentified ship was running a parallel course about sixty miles north of *Atlantis*. Bulla quickly brought his plane down and taxied in close; within an hour the aircraft had been recovered and *Atlantis* was steaming north toward the new target.

The British were finding it difficult to pinpoint where the German raiders were moving and operating. This was due mainly to the fact that *Atlantis* and *Pinguin* were operating in the same general geographic area with slightly overlapping hunting grounds. The British Admiralty believed the combined actions of the two ships were the work of a lone raider. The two ships helped support that conclusion by conducting operations that combined to paint a confusing and extremely unpredictable picture of a single ship's actions. As the British would narrow the scope and close in on the general area of one of the raiders, the other would strike outside the British hunting grounds and throw the Royal Navy off the trail of both raiders.

Atlantis steamed north after the target Bulla had spotted, approaching the Australia–Gulf of Aden shipping route. On entering the shipping lane Rogge noted a dense black cloud of sooty smoke rising up from the horizon. The soot told Rogge that the ship was a coal-burner, an old ship, not a newer diesel-powered armed merchant cruiser. He told his helmsman to turn *Atlantis* around and allow the unknown vessel to get ahead. *Atlantis* conducted a large, sweeping turn using the column of smoke as a point of reference. Several hours later, with his ship almost directly astern of the target, Rogge issued orders to begin slowly to overtake the old coal burner. Just as

Rogge was able to begin to make out the faint outlines of his target's mainmasts, the target sighted *Atlantis* and made an evasive turn to starboard. Rogge immediately turned his ship hard to port, directly away from the target ship, hoping to convince the captain that he too was under Allied orders to avoid all contact with other ships at sea. The trick seemed to work. When the other ship noticed that *Atlantis* had turned off course, it returned to its original heading. At a range of eighteen miles *Atlantis* turned back to its imaginary original course also. Rogge decided to wait for dark and rush in on a directly converging course at top speed. The days of leisurely steaming up on another ship and raising his battle ensign were gone. All of the British merchants now knew that raiders existed and were extremely wary of any vessel that came anywhere near them. The approach of any ship elicited an endless stream of SOS messages.

Rogge kept the other ship right on the edge of visibility until nightfall. When the black tropical night replaced the sun, he made his move. He called his crew to action stations, came up to flank speed, and steamed along an interception course toward the target—only to arrive at the intercept point alone. He searched the general area and found nothing. The target ship had made an unforeseen course change. Knowing there was nothing more he could do that night, Rogge stood down half of the crew and allowed all except those on watch to retire for the evening. He steamed *Atlantis* in large zigzags covering as much area as possible while his combat watch remained vigilant for the target ship.

At first light, Rogge called Bulla to the bridge and asked him to locate the target again. Bulla responded with his usual enthusiasm and went to prepare his aircraft for flight. Within a short time, the crane swung out and set the floatplane on the water. Bulla cranked the engine, taxied straight away from *Atlantis,* and was aloft in minutes. He quickly returned, landed, and reported to his captain. The Allied merchant ship was just outside the range of visibility, twenty-five miles to the north. Rogge realized he had to act fast or risk entering the range of enemy patrol aircraft operating out of South Africa, so he decided to storm up on the enemy ship while Bulla distracted it with an attack from the air.

Rogge's plan called for Bulla to gain a very high altitude and attack the enemy ship from out of the sun. On Bulla's first pass, he was to rip out the enemy's radio aerial and cause general confusion by machine-gunning the deckhouses. Captain Rogge put four men in a motor launch with spare fuel and ammunition for Bulla. The motor launch would stay behind to provide logistical support to Bulla's aircraft should the plane return and need to rearm or refuel. Once again, Bulla lifted off from the water, this time loaded with ammunition and two 110-pound gravity bombs and trailing a wire with a grappling hook. As he climbed high out of sight, *Atlantis* turned north and came up to full speed. The attack had begun.

Bulla maneuvered his craft between the rising sun and his target and swooped down in a complete surprise attack. His approach had been perfect. The hook caught the radio aerial, ripped it from its mountings, and cast it into the sea. The ship's crew had not even realized what was happening as Bulla wheeled around for another attack. During the second run, Bulla released his bombs. They straddled the ship with two great explosions that peppered the deckhouses with flying metal and showered the decks with seawater. *Atlantis* steamed over the horizon on a direct collision course with the English ship while Pilot Officer Bulla prepared for his next pass.

On board the Allied ship, Capt. A. Hill brought his old vessel up to flank speed and initiated evasive maneuvers. He had his men string an emergency aerial while his second officer brought out machine guns to defend the ship against any further air attacks.

Bulla brought his plane across the merchant ship for the third time. During this pass he machine-gunned the structures and deckhouses. The English returned fire, but their antiaircraft attempt proved ineffective as most of the gunners took cover while the German Heinkel-114 passed overhead.

Atlantis was still out of visual range. As his ship closed the distance, the captain ordered the Kriegsmarine battle ensign unfurled and the gun ports opened. There was nothing more to gain from concealment.

Bulla, out of ammunition, retired from the attack and plotted the twenty-five-mile return course to his support boat. *Atlantis* was continuing to close the target when the radio room reported that the target ship was transmitting a message. Captain Hill had succeeded in rigging an emergency aerial.

Rogge could do nothing to stop the broadcasts. Bulla had left the area, and *Atlantis* was still out of gun range. The English merchant sent out a request for help and continually repeated it: "QQQ *Mandasor* bombed by raider, position ... QQQ *Mandasor* chased and bombed by merchant raider ship."[4] *Mandasor* continued to transmit distress calls while the raider's radiomen tried to jam them or fake the British Admiralty's acknowledgment of the broadcasts. As noon approached on 24 January, *Atlantis* finally came within gun range. At a distance of about eighty-five hundred yards, *Atlantis* turned hard to starboard, bringing maximum gun exposure to bear, and fired on the zigzagging *Mandasor*.

The first salvo missed, and *Mandasor* continued to try to escape, all the while sending out a stream of distress calls. The raider's second salvo struck the ship solidly amidships and silenced the radio. *Atlantis* continued pursuing and firing on *Mandasor* until the ship hove to, beaten into submission by eight direct hits from the sixty-one shells expended in the attack.

Mandasor lay dead in the water, burning furiously amidships, as its British crew used the relatively intact bow and stern sections to abandon ship. The German boarding parties en route to the captured ship had to stop and assist the men in the water. Johann-Heinrich Fehler, who was in one of the German launches, later described what happened next. "As Mohr, engaged on his scholarly task of boarding the ship for intelligence purposes, approached the British survivors he suddenly spotted a series of menacing black fins whipping swiftly towards some swimmers near the stern. Immediately he opened fire with machine guns, driving the sharks away."[5] *Atlantis*'s crewmen fished the Allied merchantmen from the water while a German boarding party motored over to the stricken ship.

From Captain Hill, Rogge learned that *Mandasor* was a twenty-year-old, 5,144-ton motor ship owned by the Brocklebank Company from Liverpool carrying a cargo of two thousand tons of pig iron, eighteen hundred tons of tea, and a smaller load of jute fiber. The ship had sailed from Calcutta and was bound for England via Durban. The eighty-two-man crew consisted of nineteen Britons and sixty-three Indians. Two of the British and four Indians had been killed in the shelling. The English captain explained to Rogge that he knew raiders were operating in the area and had even heard of *Automedon*'s disappearance while he was in Calcutta, but had not really worried that he might meet a raider himself. His suspicions had been eased when he watched *Atlantis* turn away from *Mandasor* just as *Mandasor* turned away from *Atlantis*. This was not the first time an English captain had revealed this fact to Captain Rogge. Rogge made a note to continue this practice as a standard deception tactic in future engagements.

The boarding party signaled that *Mandasor* carried a large quantity of foodstuffs and important papers. Rogge ordered the crew to transfer the useful and important items before Fehler's men ignited the scuttling charges. The boarding parties quickly began to ferry the reams of important papers, charts, fresh foods, canned foods, and machine guns from the burning ship to the raider.

After several hours, only Fehler's demolition crew remained on board. Shortly after 4:00 P.M. the scuttling party lit the fuses on the charges and quickly left *Mandasor*. At 4:20 the explosives went off deep within the ship, and within six minutes the burning hulk slid bow-first under the water, leaving behind only a large patch of debris and floating tea.[6]

Rogge put *Atlantis* under power and turned back to search for his waiting boat and seaplane. Dusk was closing in when a lookout spotted the boat and seaplane on the near horizon. Rogge, who had feared that he might be unable to locate them once darkness cloaked the sea, was relieved. The captain was not happy, however, when he reached the scene and found a capsized "attack" plane, a motor launch with a ruined engine, and some very seasick crewmen.

Pilot Officer Bulla had landed his craft some distance from the motor launch only to learn that the men in the small boat could not start its engine. Bulla attempted to taxi his aircraft to the motor launch over the rough seas, and during the process the port float submerged under a large wave top and broke off at its struts. The unsupported aircraft heeled over and plunged headlong into the water with the propeller still spinning. Bulla and his crewman escaped the capsized aircraft unharmed and swam to the motor launch. Once everyone was safely in the motor launch they could do nothing but wait and hope for *Atlantis* to return before the rapidly advancing nightfall swept over them. The drifting sailors found the wait agonizing as their small boat bobbed like a cork on the huge rollers. Just as it seemed that nightfall would arrive before *Atlantis* did, the ship appeared on the horizon.

Atlantis took the men aboard, and Rogge ordered the now worthless plane sunk with gunfire. The loss of the plane was significant. The craft had proved invaluable in the capture or sinking of three enemy ships. *Atlantis* was again bound to the visibility limits of a ship resting on the ocean's surface.

Seychelles Radio had picked up *Mandasor*'s SOS but had not been able to understand it. The Seychelles station was still very suspicious, however, and ordered the steamer *Tantalus* to change course away from the area. The British Admiralty dispatched four cruisers to search for the source of the mysterious broadcasts. Rogge did not wait for trouble to arrive. He steamed *Atlantis* northward to get away from the immediate threat and at the same time intersect the tanker routes out of the Persian Gulf.

Four days later, Rogge brought the ship to action stations once again. The lookouts had spotted a distant smoke cloud on the horizon. As *Atlantis* closed in, Captain Rogge made out a very distinctive three-funneled silhouette which he assumed to be that of the 83,000-ton passenger liner turned troop ship *Queen Mary*. The crew were jubilant at the sight of this enormous prize. Much to their chagrin, Rogge ordered his ship to turn away. As *Atlantis* ran from the large liner at fifteen knots, the captain explained to his men that the huge ship could make more than twice the top speed of *Atlantis,* was much more heavily armored, and was probably protected by a sizable escort. Given the likely situation, the men agreed with their captain's decision to avoid combat with that particular ship.[7]

Rogge searched in long, lazy zigzags as *Atlantis* closed in on the tanker routes out of the Persian Gulf. The men whiled away the hours with little to do, always waiting for the next call to action stations. The quiet ended about six hundred miles north of Madagascar at 6:11 P.M. on 31 January 1941, when Matrose Willi Freiwald spotted the two thin vertical lines of a ship's mastheads peeking above the horizon. The watch officer called the ship to action stations, bringing Rogge and Oberleutnant Kasch rushing to the bridge.

As soon as Captain Rogge reached the bridge, he ordered the gun flaps opened and the battle flag raised. Kasch worked out the course and speed of the target vessel as 240 degrees at ten and a half knots. While Matrosenobergefreiter Georg Straußberger called out the decreasing range every couple of seconds, Rogge and Kasch dead-reckoned the intercept course as 219 degrees at fourteen knots. By 7:20 it was far too dark to see if they were coming up on the unknown ship. Rogge's only option was to wait and see if the calculations were correct.

The anticipation ended at 9:30 when the moon came out from behind a cloud bank and illuminated a ship less than two miles ahead of *Atlantis*. On board the target ship, two gunners spotted the German vessel closing on them and immediately notified their captain. The poor visibility prevented the English gunners from seeing that the approaching ship had large-caliber cannons aimed at them, so no alarm was raised. The English captain altered course to get his ship off what appeared to be a collision course.

Rogge knew the other ship had seen *Atlantis* when he saw it turn sharply and alter speed. Rogge now expected the other ship to begin broadcasting distress messages at any moment. The airwaves remained silent. At 9:50 the target broke into evasive action, turning hard to port attempting to come stern-on to its pursuer while opening up the distance between the two ships.

Atlantis continued to trail the English ship for three more minutes until Rogge gave the order to open fire. The four 150-mm guns boomed almost in unison and lit up the sky with their great orange flashes. The shells flew over the target and landed in the sea beyond, sending great geysers of water skyward and filling the night air with the smell of propellant and red-hot metal. Rogge ordered the target illuminated with the raider's large searchlight, and Kasch pushed the firing buttons again. The bright light clearly picked out the 100-pound shells landing astride a typical medium-sized British merchant ship.

After Kasch's third salvo, the target ship lost way and Rogge blew the cease-fire siren. Rogge ordered a signalman on the bridge to flash out a message telling the ship to stop, not to use its wireless, and to identify itself. As soon as the signalman finished flashing out his message, the other ship responded to *Atlantis* with only one word: "S-P-E-Y-B-A-N-K."

Adjutant Mohr, Stabsobermechaniker Willi Lender, and ten other armed men crossed the short stretch of water between the boats and boarded *Speybank*. Mohr came up on deck as his men were spreading out to round up the prisoners. He approached an English officer and issued his standard order to have the captain brought to him at once. The third officer went to the bridge to deliver the message and returned with one of his own: "Captain Morrow says that if you want the Master, he is on the bridge of his own ship."[8] Mohr decided to allow common sense to prevail. Instead of becoming angry, he calmly proceeded to the ship's bridge to meet Captain Morrow.

Rogge decided to keep *Speybank* as a prize. The English ship had been taken without a fight or utterance of a distress call, and it was extremely well provisioned, having sailed from Cochin for New York only a week before. The 5,154-ton merchant ship carried a cargo with items valuable to the German war industry, including teak, ilesite, manganese, and monazite. Furthermore, *Speybank* belonged to a line with sixteen other nearly identical sister ships, making it very easy to disguise.

Rogge placed Leutnant Breuers in command and allotted him a prize crew of ten men. The German boarding party transferred seventeen members of *Speybank*'s crew to *Atlantis* and left the ship's second officer, both the chief and second engineers, and forty Indian sailors aboard. This transfer brought the prize ship's combined German, British, and Indian complement to fifty-four men.

In Rogge's quarters, the Belfast-born Captain Morrow explained that he had not realized that *Atlantis* was a hostile ship. He had assumed the ship approaching *Speybank* was simply a passenger ship with an inattentive navigator. His evasive actions were taken only to ensure that the two ships did not collide. He was just about to order his second officer, C. R. Eaddy, to send a stern message to *Atlantis* telling the navigator to pay attention to his course when the raider opened fire. Morrow then realized that resistance was futile and decided to surrender immediately.

The two ships parted company at five minutes past midnight on 1 February 1941. Breuers set off to a position on the Saya de Mahla Bank near latitude 10 degrees south and longitude 60 degrees east, where he would wait for *Atlantis*. Rogge sailed in search of new targets in the waters off the East African coast.

The next day, one of *Atlantis*'s lookouts spotted another ship heading westward. Rogge put his ship on a parallel course so he could hide just over the horizon while he worked out an attack plan. The other ship spotted *Atlantis* while the raider was still more than sixteen miles distant, turned away, and began to broadcast: "03°26'S, 52°35'E *Troilus* suspicious."[9] The radiomen of *Atlantis* attempted in vain to jam the broadcasts. Rogge and the other officers on the bridge noted in the registry books that *Troilus* was a 7,421-ton ship of the Blue Funnel line and a sister ship to *Automedon*.

The master of *Troilus*, R. S. Braddon, had trained his lookouts to remain alert and keep a sharp watch on all sides of the ship. The lookouts' vigilance gave him advance notice that most of the other, less vigilant English ships were not afforded. *Troilus* used the extra time to turn away and lose its pursuer, and also managed to successfully broadcast an alert to Colombo nine times.

Rogge decided not to pursue *Troilus* because it would be virtually impossible for him to close to the close range required to employ Kasch's guns. That decision proved to be extremely fortunate. On receiving *Troilus*'s warning, the British Admiralty office at Colombo initiated a major search by dispatching HMS *Formidable*, a 23,000-ton Illustrious-class aircraft carrier, and the 9,800-ton cruiser HMS *Hawkins* from the nearby Somaliland coast.

The two English warships, code-named Force K, quickly reached *Troilus*. On finding the merchant ship unmolested and safe, Force K turned and went back to the coast. Had the warships continued on and investigated, they might have easily located and destroyed *Atlantis*. It was the closest *Atlantis* had come to getting caught since breaking through the blockade. Only after the war, when the Royal Navy and Kriegsmarine records were compared, did anyone realize just how close *Atlantis* had come to being discovered.

Rogge sailed *Atlantis* east, away from *Troilus*, and then turned south to keep a comfortable distance from the African coast. As the raider continued south on 2 February, a lookout spotted the outline of a tanker just above the curve of the horizon. *Atlantis*'s officers tracked the tanker, plotted its course, and worked up a heading that would bring the raider and the target together after nightfall. Rogge wanted to take the ship without loss of life if he could.

Seizing a tanker without casualties was a difficult proposition because an errant shell could cause a massive explosion. Rogge expressed his concern to the men on the bridge, and within hours they came up with a plan to take the tanker without firing a single shell into the ship itself. The men made a large sign with the English words "STOP. DON'T USE RADIO" printed boldly across the width of the banner. On Rogge's command, crewmen would unfurl the Kriegsmarine ensign and uncover the guns, and at the same time drape the banner over the side of the ship and illuminate it with floodlights. Kasch's gunners would then send a 150-mm warning shot over the heads of the men on the tanker. The men were certain that together, the banner, the war flag, and the ranged warning shot would compel the tanker's master to surrender his ship. Rogge listened to the plan, thought about it for a bit, and then agreed to try it. He knew that the men on the tanker would be just as concerned as he was about explosive shells landing in their volatile cargo, and it seemed likely that the plan might work.

Under cover of the night *Atlantis* closed the distance while the crew rigged the banner and floodlights. At the proper range, Rogge gave the order to drop *Atlantis*'s disguise, run up the war flag, and display the banner. With a loud pop, the floodlights came on and illuminated the sign draped over the side of the German ship. Rogge then told Kasch to fire a warning salvo over the tanker.

The gun crew fired off a salvo and promptly hit the tanker's funnel, which vented a great cloud of steam and smoke. Kasch cursed at the rotten luck and the poor aim of his gun crew. Rogge had the searchlight turned to illuminate the tanker's decks just as the ship's running lights came on and it began to lose way. The crew of *Atlantis* watched as the tanker's deck filled with the panic-stricken crew. Men were running about aimlessly; some flung themselves into the water, others tried to lower the boats in such haste that they capsized, or overloaded them until they foundered. Mohr led his boarding party up the ladder and into the rampant panic. He could not find the captain among the forty-three Chinese and nine Norwegians rushing around the deck, so he approached a Chinese stoker and asked for the ship's master. The terrified stoker immediately let out a wail, dropped his small satchel of personal belongings, and flung himself overboard.

While the Germans fished the tanker's crew out of the water, Mohr continued his search of the ship. In the radio room he found the name of the ship: *Ketty Brøvig*, from Bahrain en route to Lourenço Marques. In Captain Erling Møller's quarters Mohr made an exciting discovery. The ship's papers indicated that the 7,031-ton tanker was loaded with 4,125 tons of diesel fuel and 6,370 tons of other valuable fuels.

Mohr went topside and flashed a message to *Atlantis* reporting his discovery. Rogge immediately signaled back that he would keep the ship as a prize.[10] Diesel oil was exactly what *Atlantis* needed. Rogge also knew that there were other German and Italian ships in his general area in need of the windfall to replenish their dwindling fuel stores.

When the German damage repair teams made their way over to *Ketty*

Brøvig, they found that *Atlantis*'s shells had pierced one of the main steam lines. Normally this would have been no problem for the repairmen; they would simply drain the boilers, allow the steam to escape, and then repair the pierced pipe. However, one of the Norwegian crewmen explained that *Ketty*'s boiler water pumps and fuel pumps all were driven by steam from within the boilers that they serviced. The system was entirely self-contained and interdependent. If the steam was allowed to drain off, there would be no way to restart the engines. The Norwegian added that *Ketty* required a jump-start of pressurized steam from shore each time the ship made port and the boiler pressure was allowed to drop. The Germans, puzzled by the strange design of the twenty-three-year-old ship, set out to devise a scheme to fix the line while keeping the boilers stoked up enough to run the required machinery.

After much contemplation and debate, the engineers agreed on a repair plan. They started work and informed their captain that the prize ship should be seaworthy within a day. After the war, Oberleutnant-zur-See Johann-Heinrich Fehler, the man appointed by Rogge as *Ketty*'s prize captain, described how his men overcame the problem:

> Splinters from our unlucky shell had perforated the main steam pipe. We tried to close the steam valve, but the main valve was too near the hole, and the escaping steam made it quite unapproachable. I had a conference with the Norwegian officers, and then our Chief Engineer came over from *Atlantis*, with metal bandages to place over the wrecked pipes. Not until two in the morning did we succeed in shutting the valve. It was an unpleasant job and very slow. We had to wrap ourselves in wet blankets to approach the thing, and then used an iron bar, sticking it between the rungs of the wheel, levering the valve shut inch by inch. The heat was colossal and we almost collapsed. But we got the main bandage on and the Chief returned to the raider, reporting his task done.
>
> "Will you be able to get her going?" [asked Captain Rogge.]
>
> Through the megaphone I bawled back, "Yes."
>
> "Good!" came the voice of Rogge. "We'll be back next morning at ten o'clock." Then he and his *Atlantis* disappeared into the dark.[11]

Once the flow of steam was stopped, the repair team concentrated their efforts on the critical repairs needed to get the Norwegian ship under way. The engineers had a sleeve fabricated and secured over the damaged steam pipe by the time *Atlantis* returned the next morning. Fehler had made sure the boilers remained hot enough to ignite the fuel oil by breaking up all of the wooden furniture on *Ketty* and feeding the hungry boilers. The repair team returned to *Atlantis*, and Fehler ordered the steam brought up to an operational level to test the repair work.

The mended pipe proved sufficient to contain the pressure, and Rogge ordered the second mate, three engineers, the steward, and thirty-two Chinese crewmen back to *Ketty Brøvig*. They would return to their duty posts under the supervision of a prize crew. Oberleutnant Fehler, the prize crew's captain, set off and piloted his prize to a predetermined rendezvous point while *Atlantis* hauled off to the northwest to continue hunting.

Within days of leaving the company of *Atlantis* Fehler had a very close call with an English warship. *Ketty*'s lookouts spotted warships off the tanker's starboard bow. Fehler feigned obedience to the British Admiralty orders by turning away from the ships at a right angle. One of the British cruisers nevertheless broke away from the rest and headed straight for *Ketty Brøvig*. Fehler kept turning his ship to maintain a 90-degree aft-on attitude toward the approaching British ship. Soon, the faster British cruiser was within five thousand yards of Fehler's prize ship. Fehler alerted his crew to stand by, fully intending to scuttle and abandon the ship. Just as Oberleutnant Fehler was about to give the order to sink his ship, the British cruiser turned to a full-on broadside, brandishing its impressive guns and armored shields, then continued to turn and hauled off, its white Royal Navy ensign clearly visible to those on the German prize.

On 5 February, Rogge dispatched a quick signal to Berlin telling the SKL that he had sunk or captured 111,000 tons to date. He also outlined his operational plans for *Atlantis*. Later that day, Captain Rogge decided to send the naval operations staff a more complete message. The latter signal described the two ships *Atlantis* had captured and asked for permission to send *Speybank* home as a prize. Rogge also requested a meeting with the raider *Kormoran* and the pocket battleship *Admiral Scheer*, to give the other warships the opportunity to refuel from the captured tanker, and ended with a report that *Atlantis* was fully operational and ready to carry on until ordered to do otherwise.

The SKL's reply instructed Rogge to meet *Tannenfels* and the Italian submarine *Perla* at position "Nelke." Both ships were very low on fuel and provisions, having just escaped the British ground assault on the port cities of Italian Somalia. The Naval High Command also gave permission for Rogge to rendezvous with *Kormoran* and *Admiral Scheer,* with the caveat that *Scheer* not be fueled with the diesel oil from *Ketty Brøvig.* Rogge was ordered to refuel *Scheer* from his own fuel tanks and then to refill his ship's bunkers with *Ketty Brøvig*'s lower-grade type 32.6 APL diesel fuel.

On 8 February, *Atlantis* met *Speybank* as planned. On the ninth, while Rogge replenished his ship's stores from *Speybank*'s supplies, his other prize, *Ketty Brøvig,* appeared on the horizon. The last ship of Rogge's flotilla, the 7,480-ton German supply ship *Tannenfels,* finally came into sight around noon on Monday, 10 February.[12]

Tannenfels was three days late because a crewman had plotted the wrong position and missed the rendezvous point. When the error was discovered, *Tannenfels* rushed to the correct location and found *Atlantis* and its two prize ships waiting. The late arrival sat high in the water and showed a fouled hull from its many months in port.[13] *Tannenfels* also brought a wonderful surprise for the men of *Atlantis*: Leutnant Dehnel and his *Durmitor* prize crew were on board. Dehnel and his men had managed to find refuge on the German naval ship while it was detained in the port.

Dehnel gave his captain a full report of the cruise of *Durmitor,* and for the first time Rogge learned of the hardships and events that occurred while *Durmitor* sailed for Somaliland. He praised Dehnel for his leadership under the most trying of situations and acknowledged that the prize crew and prisoners had christened *Durmitor* the "Hell Ship" with good reason.

The ships of Rogge's small fleet lay peacefully on the calm Indian Ocean awaiting resupply. Each ship was lacking supplies or operating on incomplete stores, but their individual needs varied greatly. Rogge had to first determine each ship's requirements and then prioritize them against the needs and missions of the other ships. To accomplish the allocations, Captain Rogge secured detailed inventories from each ship, then sat down with the ships' officers and compared what each ship had aboard with what it needed to meet its operational requirements.

Their goal was to equip each ship as fully as possible and still ensure a fair distribution of food, fuel, water, charts, sextants, signal equipment, supplies, lines, lifeboats, and many other items among the four. The plan ensured that each ship would be capable of operating on its own for an extended period. Ship provisioning on the required scale was a lengthy and labor-intensive process even in port; at sea, it was a logistics nightmare. The needs of each ship seemed boundless, and working out a plan for interchanging the supplies between the four ships proved quite challenging. Despite the difficulties, the men had initiated a three-phase distribution plan within twenty-four hours. The first phase called for replacing Fehler's prize crew on *Ketty Brøvig* with the recently returned Leutnant Dehnel and his crew. Dehnel and his men were more experienced with prize ship operations and better suited to sail the captured merchant. Furthermore, Fehler's demolition function on *Atlantis* was critical, and Rogge was unwilling to let him go.

Next, boats transferred the 103 prisoners *Atlantis* was carrying to *Tannenfels,* relieving Rogge and his crew of that burden. Once the prisoners had been moved, the work of transferring the provisions began. Motorboats and cutters started running between the four ships in a nearly perpetual shuttle of goods from ship to ship to ship.

Finally, on Wednesday, 12 February, each ship had all of its required supplies and equipment on board and stowed away. Rogge let the ships' crews stand down for a good night's rest, but he alerted the prize officers of his plan to set sail the following morning. The next day, after each ship's captain reported his status as functional and seaworthy, *Atlantis* and its small flotilla moved off, cutting a broad path through the calm waters as they steamed south toward a memorable rendezvous.

8

A German Battleship and an International Incident

As expected, the weather steadily worsened as the flotilla sailed south. Rogge had not told the crew that they were about to rendezvous with a German battleship. At noon on 14 February, a lookout caught a glimpse of a distant ship over the violent gray seas. Rogge gave Mohr a knowing grin but remained silent. Ten minutes later, the crewmen were openly anxious as they realized that *Atlantis* was closing on a powerful and fast warship. The lookouts called out again and again, with increasing urgency, "Warship on the port bow," and then watched Rogge for a response. Each man hoped to hear the order to turn and run. The deck crew's anxiety built as the expected order did not come and *Atlantis* continued to bear down on the capital ship.

The tension and fear turned to jubilation when a rating recognized the distinctive triple-gun turret of a German pocket battleship and the sailors realized they were about to meet with the German battleship *Admiral Scheer*.[1] The ship was a splendid sight, both beautiful and ominous. The subsequent meeting of a ship of the line, an auxiliary cruiser, a supply ship, and two captured prizes marked the largest gathering of German warships outside European waters in all of World War II.

As the somewhat weathered *Atlantis* drew near the pristine, 13,660-ton *Scheer*, the large armored ship signaled a greeting and proposed a meeting of the two captains as soon as the storm subsided. Rogge would have nothing to do with waiting. Despite the terrible weather, he prepared to make a courtesy call on *Scheer*'s captain right away. Rogge and Mohr used one of the especially seaworthy captured Norwegian cutters to fight their way through the thrashing seas and driving rain to call on Kapitän-zur-See Theodor Kranke.

This meeting was Rogge's first with a peer since his ship left port. He later wrote that he found talking frankly and freely with an officer of the same rank a refreshing respite. At their brief first meeting the two captains decided to move their ships to calmer waters before attempting a transfer of fuel and supplies. Rogge returned to the battleship's deck, carefully timed his jump into the wave-tossed cutter, and told the helmsman to depart. His smart exit was somewhat diminished when, as they fought their way back to *Atlantis*, Rogge realized that he had left his adjutant on board *Scheer*. Mohr was anything but unhappy about being forgotten. He was delighted, in fact, at the prospect of spending a night in the relative luxury of visiting officers' quarters on a spacious and gleaming warship!

As the sun began to get heavy in the sky, the five ships moved off to find calmer seas about five hundred miles northeast of Mauritius. During the night's steaming, *Ketty Brøvig* lagged behind and eventually became lost from view. The other four ships arrived without incident and waited for the slower tanker, which arrived a full two days later.

In the meantime, the men of *Atlantis* visited *Scheer*. The visits were a wonderful experience for the men from the raider. For only the second time since leaving port they were able to exchange news and learn the details of the situation at home and the progress of the war from those with firsthand experience. Not all of the news was pleasant. The code-breaker and radioman Heinrich Wesemann received official notification that his older brother had died nearly a year before, on 14 May 1940, in a battle at Sedan. When Rogge authorized mail movement and had the stacks of *Atlantis*'s unsent mail brought over to *Admiral Scheer*, the men's morale shot even higher.

With the arrival of *Ketty*, activity on the ships stepped up considerably. *Scheer*'s chief engineer inspected the oil in *Ketty Brøvig*'s bunkers and was actually quite pleased with its quality. The captains ignored the SKL's order and pumped twelve hundred tons of *Ketty*'s diesel oil directly to the battleship. When *Scheer* had topped off its fuel bunkers, *Tannenfels* refueled. Rogge had kept *Tannenfels* attached to the group in case *Scheer* had any prisoners on board. Once he had confirmed that *Scheer* had no prisoners to offload, Rogge sent *Tannenfels* off to the French coast with only five men to guard the 103 prisoners he had transferred earlier.[2]

Atlantis refueled, and Rogge met again with *Scheer*'s captain to discuss their hunting grounds and courses of action. They agreed that *Scheer* would search the area southwest of the Seychelles. *Atlantis* had already patrolled and raised the alarm in that area. It would be too dangerous for the smaller raider to return and risk an encounter with a prowling British cruiser. *Scheer* had quite a different perspective on a gun battle with a British cruiser, so Kranke agreed to patrol in that sector. *Atlantis* would enter a new patrol area to the south and east on the route toward the Chagos Archipelago. Rogge and Kranke made plans to meet again on 25 February to reevaluate their methods and strategy.

From their stock of captured goods the men of *Atlantis* presented each man on *Scheer* with a heavy fountain pen. *Scheer*'s crew responded with a gift of 150,000 fresh eggs taken from the recently captured British refrigerator ship *Duquesa*, which carried a cargo of 1 million eggs. The raider's crew, who had not seen fresh eggs for many months, could not have thought of a better gift.

With the refueling and exchanges finished, the two-day meeting ended. The ships steamed away from each other with shouted wishes of good luck, blinking lights, and siren blasts. *Atlantis* and its scouting satellite *Speybank* sailed for their new patrol area, *Ketty Brøvig* steamed away to lay low in a secluded position just off the Saya de Malha Bank, and *Admiral Scheer* went south.[3]

As the German capital ship faded from view over the horizon, so did the sense of security its radar and big guns had provided. A rating commented to Rogge that the only nights he had slept peacefully since leaving Germany were the nights *Scheer* had been next to *Atlantis*. Rogge told the young rating that he spoke for the entire complement of *Atlantis* with that statement.

Atlantis steamed off in search of new targets, with *Speybank* thirty miles away on a parallel course. The presence of the prize ship would more than double the raider's search area. A special set of signals had been arranged so that *Speybank* could report contacts to *Atlantis*.

When Leutnant Breuers, the prize captain of *Speybank*, was not busy directing the ship's operations, he experimented with trying to track ships by using the emanations from their radios as beacons to establish homing bearings. Rogge did not really believe that such direction finding was possible without highly specialized equipment, but Breuers proved him wrong. On 20 February, *Speybank* sighted a medium-sized tanker and then withdrew over the horizon and used its radio receivers to track the ship and stay in contact. Captain Rogge ordered *Speybank* to drop back to a safe distance as *Atlantis* took over the chase.

After prepping for battle and closing on the target for seven hours without incident, Rogge was confident the attack would be quick and uncomplicated. As the light of day slowly faded, the tanker suddenly switched on its lights. The lookouts also spotted two other lights low in the water near the target ship. The Germans flashed out a signal asking the ship to identify itself. The response came back immediately. The ship was the Vichy French naval tanker *Lot* accompanied by two Redoutable-class submarines, the 1,379-ton *Pégase* and the 1,384-ton *Monge*. The German Admiralty had previously advised Rogge of the French ships sailing from Diego Suarez to Dakar with the full permission of the German authorities. The captain ordered the crew to stand down from action stations but continued to move in for a closer inspection.

While *Atlantis* was cutting the distance, a lookout spotted several small, fast boats beyond the French ships. Rogge assumed they were some sort of torpedo boats approaching the French ships. The German captain wanted nothing to do with the developing situation; there were too many boats around. He flashed "Bon voyage" and "Vive la France" to *Lot* and quickly left the area to patrol elsewhere.

The next morning *Speybank* reported another contact. *Atlantis* took position once again and began to track the unknown vessel. After nine hours of plotting, graphing, and preparation, *Atlantis* finally closed into gun range. Moments before Rogge was to issue the order to unmask the guns, the target's lights came on, indicating that the ship was claiming neutral status. Rogge immediately suspended the attack preparations. The men were released from action stations when Mohr, frustrated by the wasted effort, confirmed the ship's reported identity as the SS *Africa Maru*, a 9,476-ton neutral Japanese ship from Osaka's Syosen Cargo line.

Unhappy with the patrol area, Rogge set *Atlantis* on course for the location just west of the sixtieth parallel where the second planned rendezvous with *Scheer* was to take place. *Atlantis* sailed for four uneventful days before reaching the meeting site. To everyone's surprise, *Scheer* was not waiting as expected, but its recently captured prize, the 6,994-ton tanker *British Advocate*, was. As Rogge grudgingly supplied the prize ship, he learned that *Scheer* had fled to escape a British task force searching for the pocket battleship. The force, whose whereabouts Rogge now had to worry about, comprised an aircraft carrier, five cruisers, and an armed merchant cruiser.

Rogge also learned that Captain Kranke had placed his worst men aboard *British Advocate* as the prize crew. Rogge was familiar with the practice of putting troublemakers on prize ships, but he was shocked to learn the extent of this group's misconduct. The German sailors gave the British crew free run of the ship while they lounged on deck with their pistols. When Mohr boarded *Advocate* and tried to roust the sailors into action, he was summarily ignored. Fehler fared no better when he made an attempt. Finally, Rogge intervened and threw the ringleader into the brig for three days. The captain's actions brought the prize crew up to a standard just sufficient for Rogge to allow *British Advocate* to sail for Bordeaux on 27 February. Captain Rogge told Mohr he had serious doubts that the prize would ever reach the French coast, but the ship pulled into Bordeaux without incident just over two months later, on 29 April.[4]

Atlantis and *Speybank* continued to patrol, but targets proved elusive. The men were bored with the lack of activity. Complaints about food were beginning to filter up to the bridge. The crew had eaten a constant diet of eggs since receiving the gift from *Scheer* some weeks earlier: scrambled, poached, boiled, fried, raw, and every other way imaginable. A rating calculated that each man had eaten six to eight eggs every day for two straight weeks. There was no complaint from the crew when the order came down in mid-March to throw the remaining eggs overboard!

On 21 March, Rogge signaled *Speybank* to meet *Atlantis* at a position slightly northeast of Mauritius. When the two ships converged several hours later, Rogge replaced the less-experienced Leutnant Breuers on *Speybank* with the former first mate of *Tannenfels*, the thirty-eight-year-old merchant seaman Paul Schneidewind. Rogge was no longer willing to risk losing *Speybank* and its valuable cargo, so he dispatched Schneidewind and a crew of twelve Germans (seven from *Atlantis* and five from *Tannenfels*), a Briton (the ship's original second engineer), and forty Indians to Bordeaux that evening. *Speybank* made fast to the pier at Basin 19 in the French port nearly two months later on 12 May. The German High Command quickly converted *Speybank* to a minelayer, renamed it *Doggerbank,* and pressed it into Kriegsmarine service as a warship. The SKL commissioned Schneidewind as a reserve naval officer and gave him command of *Doggerbank.* Schneidewind would prove himself an outstanding seaman and commander, completing many dangerous missions and earning distinction while commanding the ship.[5]

Rogge's command diminished even more when the German naval staff sent a signal to Rogge instructing him to send *Ketty Brøvig* to a position off the Australian coast where it was to meet the German ship *Coburg*. The Admiralty planned to use the two ships to assist the raider *Pinguin* in its mining operations around Australia. Rogge immediately dispatched *Ketty* to the area the SKL had specified.

When *Coburg* and *Ketty Brøvig* arrived at the given location, they found two cruisers waiting for them. Using captured documents and an amazing intelligence network, the British had begun cracking and reading some of the more common German naval transmission codes, including the supply ship codes. With advance knowledge of where the prize supply ships were headed, the British Admiralty dispatched HMAS *Canberra* and HMAS *Leander* to lay a trap. On 4 March, *Canberra*'s plane sighted the two German ships and brought the cruisers' guns to bear on them. *Coburg* was hit by the long-range gunfire and began to go down. The crew of *Ketty* saw that there was no escape and opened the sea cocks, scuttling the tanker.[6] Leutnant Dehnel and his men were captured.

Much to Rogge's disgust, the SKL then sent *Atlantis* on another support mission instead of a combat patrol. The High Command instructed the raider to meet and resupply the Italian submarine *Perla* as it headed home from the Red Sea. When *Atlantis* arrived at the designated area, the submarine was nowhere to be found. Rogge cruised aimlessly for hours until the submarine began broadcasting wireless messages guiding *Atlantis* to a spot some 120 miles away from the designated location. Rogge was irritated by the broadcasts, which openly announced the meeting position to all receiver stations, friend and foe alike. Any Allied warship in the general vicinity could have ambushed both ships. The debacle was the fault of the Italian naval staff, which had passed the wrong coordinates to their submarine.

When *Atlantis* rendezvoused with *Perla* on 8 March, some two hundred miles off Cape Dauphin, Rogge found the submarine in a terrible state, slowly cruising on only one barely functional engine. The only navigation map the boat possessed was a crude, handmade wall chart. The submarine was critically low on fuel and food, and the forty-one-man crew was disillusioned and completely lacking in fighting spirit.

The Italian High Command had dispatched the small, 855-ton coastal submarine to conduct operations in the Red Sea. On reaching its station, *Perla* was quickly located and pinned down in Massawa Harbor. The submarine's crew endured nearly constant air attacks from British planes, and the boat barely escaped destruction on many occasions. Rogge provisioned the submarine with seventy tons of fuel, food, proper charts, liquor, cigarettes, and many other essentials and amenities.

During the resupply the Italian commander, Tenente di Vasello Bruno Napp, confided to Rogge that he had been submerging and sailing away from every ship he spotted without even considering an attack. Rogge spoke in private with the Italian submarine commander for quite some time and managed to convince him to work in concert with *Atlantis*. The two ships would patrol the area around South Africa until 8 April, the submarine in the coastal waters and the raider in the offshore area. Rogge seriously doubted that Captain Napp would stand by the agreement, but he planned to complete his portion of the arrangement regardless. His doubts were confirmed when he received a wireless message from the SKL informing him that *Perla* had returned to a hero's welcome at the Italian submarine base in Bordeaux.[7] For his honorable and valiant service, *Perla*'s commander had been awarded the Medaglia di Bronzo al Valor Militar and a personal audience with Il Duce himself.[8] The Italian government also bestowed the award on Rogge on 25 September 1941, for the "gallant assistance and comradeship that had been extended to an Italian warship."[9]

Atlantis continued to sail the southwestern approaches to the Indian Ocean without sighting a single target. The last time the raider had seen action was 2 February, when it captured *Ketty Brøvig*. The crew enjoyed the hot sun and flat seas for a time, but soon boredom set in. The tropical heat and the lack of action began to spur petty disputes and conflicts. Rogge tried to rally and encourage his men, but even the captain and his officers were beginning to suffer from the relentless sun and the long period of inactivity.

The last day of March 1941 marked *Atlantis*'s one-year anniversary at sea. Grand Admiral Raeder sent a congratulatory message and awarded the entire ship's company Iron Cross, Second Class, medals. The signal also authorized Rogge to award a number of the more prestigious Iron Cross, First Class, medals to selected crew members.

During the first days of April, *Atlantis* cruised back and forth over the ocean just east of Durban. This area had been a high-traffic merchant shipping lane until the British diverted all of their merchant traffic into more secure out-of-the-way paths in response to German naval activity. The lookouts saw nothing until the fifth, when the sharp-eyed men posted on the masts spotted a smoke cloud crossing the raider's path.

Within a few short, hectic moments *Atlantis* altered course to assume an intercept course with the target. The vessel continued on its way and docilely allowed *Atlantis* to approach. Rogge flashed the signal for the ship to heave to. The larger ship did not respond but promptly complied with the order. Armed boarding parties went off to search the stopped ship and quickly signaled back to *Atlantis* that the vessel was the nineteen-year-old Vichy French ship *Chenonceaux*, a 14,825-ton transport of the Messageries Maritimes line carrying Senegalese troops to Madagascar. Rogge recalled his boarding party and allowed the ship to proceed.

In three consecutive instances, *Atlantis* approached a ship, unmasked itself as a merchant raider, and then allowed the ship to go on its way. This exposure greatly troubled Captain Rogge. The other ships' personnel were liable to report the incidents to the British and were sure to relate stories of their encounter with the German "pirate" ship to their friends in port.

The SKL was apparently of a like mind and signaled *Atlantis* to move its operations to the Atlantic Ocean. The raider departed the Indian Ocean on 8 April 1941. Rogge steered his ship far south around the Cape of Good Hope, hoping to avoid the ever-increasing British patrols. This southern route and the few days of cloudy weather that coincided with the passage probably combined to save *Atlantis*. The British had somehow been alerted that a suspected German raider was about to pass by the cape. Either *Atlantis*'s lookouts missed an earlier passing ship or one of the French ships Rogge had approached had already made a report regarding *Atlantis*, because the British were aware of the raider's relative location. As *Atlantis* rounded the Cape of Good Hope, the British were actively searching the area for it. Only Rogge's decision to go very far south, some luck, and the limited visibility during his transit saved the raider from almost certain destruction.

Rogge reflected on the cruise so far by summarizing the ship's actions and his perspectives of the events in the ship's log. As of the date of the log entry, *Atlantis* had captured or sunk sixteen enemy ships, captured 919 prisoners, and caused a relatively low thirty-three deaths. Rogge was satisfied with his ship's disruption of the British war plans and sea trade. *Atlantis* and the handful of similar German raider ships had sunk vital supplies and equipment; had forced the British to reroute shipping, send capital ships to remote areas, and arm and augment merchant ships' companies with sailors from the Royal Navy; had delayed shipments; had driven up shipping and insurance costs; had disrupted mail and message services; and had caused concern and fear in the merchant fleet. The captain also noted that he found it increasingly difficult to maintain the old raider tradition of "fairness." At all times *Atlantis* endeavored to cease firing as soon as possible, care for the injured, and rescue the survivors. Technology and the British insistence on resistance forced Rogge progressively to alter his attacks from shots across the bow to salvos across the ship to salvos aimed to disable without warning. Personally, the captain did not approve of the more destructive method of attack, but it was his only option if he was to continue his assigned mission without unduly risking his own ship and crew.

The SKL sent *Atlantis* to a specific grid square in the mid-Atlantic some thirteen hundred miles east of South America. Here he was to meet with the German supply ships *Alsterufer*, *Dresden*, and *Babitonga*; the U-boat supply ship *Nordmark*; and the raider *Kormoran*, Ship-41. When *Atlantis* arrived at the meeting place, only *Dresden* was waiting. As Rogge greeted Capt. Walter Jäger, the barrel-chested, bowlegged captain of the Norddeutscher Lloyd liner *Dresden*, he sensed that something was amiss. *Dresden* was due to supply *Atlantis* with fresh fruits and vegetables, which the men of *Atlantis* desperately needed. Captain Jäger apologetically told Rogge that he had no fresh food to offer.

For some reason, a German naval attaché in Brazil had ordered all of the fresh food transshipped to *Babitonga*. When both Captain Jäger and *Babitonga*'s master explained to him that *Babitonga* had no cold storage capacity to carry fresh food, the attaché ordered the two captains to comply with his directive or face the consequences. Rogge was enraged by such callous idiocy. His crew's health was deteriorating as their vitamin pills began to lose their effectiveness. They were sorely in need of fresh food, and they had been robbed by yet another example of staff incompetence and inefficiency. Rogge considered the attaché's actions nothing short of criminal and noted the incident in the ship's log.

Dresden did provide what it could: potatoes, fresh water, lubricants, and timber. Once the crews had completed the resupply, Captain Rogge ordered Jäger to remain in the area until *Atlantis* could find *Kormoran* and he could determine if that raider had any prisoners to transfer to *Dresden*. As *Atlantis* sailed away from Jäger's charge at three hours after midnight on 17 April, Rogge had no idea that he would soon be the focus of an international incident—or that it would be his own ship that would require *Dresden*'s prisoner quarters.

Atlantis spotted a fairly large ship on a southeasterly heading about an hour after parting company with *Dresden*. The ship was running completely blacked-out, but the brilliant moonlight presented a perfect silhouette of its unusual four masts. The only other time Rogge had seen such a ship was on a visit to England in 1937 as part of the team representing the German navy in the six-meter international yacht race that was part of the coronation ceremonies for King George VI. After the race, Rogge asked his British escort officer if he could perhaps visit the Royal Naval College at Dartmouth. The English officer happily obliged and gave Rogge a personal tour of the facilities. While at Dartmouth, Rogge noticed several odd-looking four-masted ships and asked his escort about them. The British officer told Rogge that the three-deckers were Bibby liners from the First World War that the Royal Navy had retained as troop transports.

Four years later, Captain Rogge was sure he was looking at one of the same English Bibby liners. The ship turned away from *Atlantis* and began to zigzag very erratically, without the precise timing characteristic of the crew of a well-trained English merchant ship. Rogge suspected the ship was a Royal Navy–crewed armed merchant cruiser trying to act like a frightened merchant vessel.

Atlantis maneuvered behind the target ship and stayed in its wake. Rogge planned to continue to close until daybreak and launch an attack without warning. He wanted to prevent the ship from fighting back if it was in fact a disguised armed cruiser. At the very least, he wanted to prevent the ship from sending any radio messages. His new Atlantic patrol area was smaller, narrower, and more heavily patrolled, and an SOS would immediately put *Atlantis* in grave danger.

As *Atlantis* closed in, the Bibby liner tuned up its radio and sent a message asking the approaching ship to identify itself. Fearing that an SOS broadcast would be next, Rogge ordered the guns uncovered and began the attack at 5:55 A.M., at a range of ninety-two hundred yards. The first shots missed, falling short of the target by only twenty yards but directly in line with the bridge. The second traveled long and bracketed the target for the gunners. The Germans fired fifty-five shells scoring nine hits. One of the first shells to strike the ship exploded in the radio room, another hit the engine spaces, two entered the ship at the waterline, and the other five exploded in the superstructure.

The ship turned broadside to *Atlantis*, turned on its lights, and blew off its remaining steam. Rogge suspected something was amiss when the lifeboats came down in a mass of haste, confusion, and error. Some boats overturned, some hung in their davits unused, and others hit the gently rolling swells with only one or two shrieking, panic-stricken crewmen in them. The best description of the evacuation was written by Charles J. V. Murphy, an American journalist who happened to be aboard the sinking ship:

> Let it be said for the crew that at least they got the boats over quickly and in good order. But let it also be said that once they themselves were safely in the boats, their behavior was abominable. They screamed and bellowed at the top of their lungs, they fought to pull away when boats were only half full, and because we couldn't understand them nor they us we had a horrible time trying to control the boats.[10]

As the sun began to come over the horizon, the liner took on a heavy list to port and then settled evenly in the water, down twelve feet from the waterline. Mohr and Fehler set out in separate boats with the intent of recovering the lifeboats and were appalled to discover the stricken ship's crewmen alone in the boats while terrified passengers pleaded for help from the ship and the surrounding water. The German crewmen launched several more motor launches to collect the screaming passengers bobbing in the calm sea and take on the abandoned passengers gathered around the sinking ship's railings.

When Mohr boarded the sinking ship he was met by William Grey Smith, the ship's master. Smith told Mohr that the ship held 202 passengers, including seventy-three women and thirty-five children. The passenger list was made up of many nationalities: 138 Americans, twenty-six Canadians, twenty-five British, five South Africans, four Belgians, two Greeks, one Italian, and one Norwegian. Many of the passengers were missionaries or clergymen; the rest were volunteer ambulance drivers, reporters, or businessmen and their families. The crew numbered another 129, mostly Egyptians and Sudanese with two Englishmen, Captain Smith and Mr. Burns, his chief engineer. Ten people had been injured during the shelling, three very seriously. Frank Vicovari, an American ambulance driver, had his right ankle shattered and his left thigh broken by collapsing beams and falling debris. Ned Laughinghouse, a tobacco buyer, received a severe head wound from a shell splinter. Dr. Robert Starling, an English chiropractor, sustained a traumatic injury to his right thigh. Leutnant Mohr immediately flashed the distressing information over to Rogge on *Atlantis*.

While the Germans expeditiously transferred the passengers over to *Atlantis* and collected the crewmen from the sea, Rogge learned the specifics about his latest victim. The 8,299-ton ship was the neutral Egyptian passenger ship *Zamzam*. In sinking it he had made a grave error.

Rogge actually had been correct in his identification of the ship. It had indeed once been the British troop ship *Leicestershire*; however, the thirty-two-year-old ship had recently been sold to Egypt and renamed *Zamzam*. Rogge looked down from the bridge to see a mass of soaking, barefoot, pajama- and nightgown-clad Belgians, Norwegians, Greeks, Canadians, and Americans standing on the foredeck. *Atlantis* looked like a crowded immigrant ship. Captain Rogge clearly understood—and dreaded—the international consequences for Germany of this attack.

In 1915, a German submarine sank the British ship *Lusitania* with Americans on board. The sinking caused an international outcry and helped push the United States into World War I. Even more neutral Americans had been on *Zamzam* than had been lost in the *Lusitania* sinking in 1915.[11] On the other hand, only three of the passengers had been seriously injured in the shelling. Captain Rogge called his officers together for a meeting. Every member of *Atlantis*'s company must be on his best behavior, he told them. The civilian passengers were to be treated with the utmost kindness, chivalry, and generosity. Rogge wanted to limit the unfavorable news coverage of the sinking, and the best way to do that was to have the prisoners speak well of both their treatment and their captors.

The Germans spent the next four hours salvaging as much of the passengers' personal belongings as possible. They went from room to room on *Zamzam* snatching armfuls of clothing and carrying back personal luggage. The Germans also cleaned out the Egyptian ship's freezers of such delicacies as lobster, duck, and goose along with the bar stock. All the while Mohr was bombarded with an array of questions ranging from "When is tea time?" and "Where is the bar?" to "Where is the baby formula stored?" He answered each question with patience and tact, always trying to make everyone as comfortable as possible.

After *Zamzam* had been picked clean, Rogge gave the order to send it down. Just after two o'clock Adjutant Mohr informed the prisoners that *Zamzam* would be sunk by scuttling charges planted by the raider's crew. Mohr went on to give an American photographer for *Life* magazine, David E. Scherman, special permission to photograph the sinking, "even showing him the best place to stand. 'Sometimes they die quite gracefully and always they are different,' remarked Lieutenant Mohr."[12] Rogge hoped that allowing Scherman to photograph life aboard the raider would ensure a favorable account of the events surrounding the sinking and the Germans' conduct.

The three charges went off in rapid succession. *Zamzam* shook violently and spewed forth great fountains of water from the ventilators, listed heavily to port, then rolled on its side, tearing off the tall stacks. Within ten minutes the ship slipped beneath the roiling sea, leaving behind a few small puffs of steam and a small amount of floating debris.

Rogge got his ship under way and made a beeline for *Dresden*. During his time aboard *Atlantis* Scherman put his photographic privileges to use. Not only did he record the sinking of *Zamzam*, he also photographed many aspects of life aboard the raider. The Germans were unaware of one photograph, however, that would have a very significant impact on *Atlantis* in the months to come. While Scherman was sitting in a lifeboat waiting to be picked up by the Germans, he snapped a full-length, three-quarters-view shot of *Atlantis* from off the starboard bow. This single photograph would contribute greatly to the raider's end.

As *Atlantis* made its way toward a rendezvous with *Dresden*, the complaints began. Many of the prisoners/passengers complained that Rogge had initiated an unprovoked attack on an unarmed, neutral passenger ship and called the Germans pirates and criminals. Rogge met with four representatives from the passengers and put an end to the unfounded accusations. He reminded the prisoners that their ship was running without lights, operating in radio silence, and sailing under British orders while transporting a three-million-dollar cargo of ammonium nitrate, aviation fuel, oil, radios, steel, and American trucks bound for British soldiers who were conducting hostile operations against Germany. "I am sorry this had to happen," Rogge told them. "I can only tell you that we shall do everything in our power to put you safely ashore but you must remember that this is war and in traveling on the ocean you have assumed many risks."[13]

The next morning *Atlantis* met *Dresden* and the 2,729-ton supply ship *Alsterufer* at the designated location. Rogge was happy to find the two ships waiting for him. *Alsterufer* carried much-needed supplies and replacements for *Atlantis*, and *Dresden* would be Rogge's prisoner ship. As soon as *Atlantis* had drawn up near the other ships and stopped, Rogge called a meeting of the three ships' commanders. Rogge repeated his instructions about the fair treatment of the prisoners to Captain Jäger of *Dresden*.

The crewmen of *Atlantis* immediately began arranging the transfer of the supplies and the prisoners between the three ships. *Alsterufer* had brought enough supplies to provision *Atlantis* up to the same level as when the raider left port more than a year ago. To his delight, Rogge discovered that the supply ship had also brought three new, all-metal Arado Ar-196a seaplanes and a shipment of personal mail for the crew of *Atlantis*—the first they had received. The morale of the crew shot up when news of the letters from home circulated through the ship.

Rogge was pleased with *Alsterufer*'s cargo but not fully pleased with the three officers the SKL had sent to him as replacements; only one fully met Rogge's strict military standards. One officer decided to show up for duty in his bathrobe and slippers. Rogge did not approve and had the man returned to *Alsterufer*. The second man, Oberleutnant-zur-See Rodig, had sustained wounds earlier in the war that damaged his hearing. He was highly motivated and wished to stay on board, but he was fairly hard of hearing. Rogge reluctantly allowed him to stay aboard. Captain Rogge fully approved of the third replacement, Leutnant-zur-See Wooge, an experienced naval professional. The replacement distribution was just another example of the High Command's inattentiveness and general second-class treatment the auxiliary cruisers received.

Once *Zamzam*'s prisoners had all been moved to *Dresden*, Rogge bid them farewell and charged Jäger with their safety. He did not, however, release *Dresden* to return to Germany. He used his senior rank to order *Dresden* to stand to in the immediate area while *Atlantis* searched once more for targets close at hand.

Dresden's crew locked all of the prisoners into the holds and kept them there until *Atlantis* was eight miles away to allow the raider to depart unseen. Once *Atlantis* was out of sight, Jäger bellowed for all the captives to come on deck. As soon as everyone was assembled, Jäger introduced himself and apologized for any inconvenience the Germans had caused them. In an article he wrote for *Life* magazine after he returned home, Charles Murphy related the gist of Captain Jäger's message to the prisoners:

> "This may be a long voyage," he said, "and you will be obliged to do a great many things for yourself. I have neither food nor quarters to support nearly 400 people including my own crew comfortably. You must expect some hardship but I promise you we will do everything we can." ... He warned us: "I will stand for no monkey tricks from behind." His crew totaled barely 60 and with nearly 230 male prisoners aboard his fear was evident that we may try to take

the ship. "My orders are to fight this ship or try to run away if an English warship should intercept us. That is for your protection. I shall let you off first in boats and when you are safely away I shall scuttle this ship. I have enough bombs already placed to sink her in two minutes. I have plenty of rifles and machine guns and grenades also. Remember that if you have any funny ideas."[14]

The prisoners did not attempt a takeover and soon fell into a routine as *Dresden* circled about for nine days waiting for *Atlantis* to return.

"On April 26," Olga Guttormson later recalled, "we approached the raider for the last time. The wife of one of the men and a few friends were permitted to go aboard and visit the wounded. But still too ill to be moved, the wounded were left aboard the vessel as it sailed out of our sight for the last time."[15]

During the short 26 April meeting *Dresden* provided two men to augment *Atlantis*'s crew. Initially identified to Rogge as Seamen Meyer and Müller, both were actually commissioned officers from the scuttled battle cruiser *Graf Spee* who had been posing as seamen aboard *Dresden* for security reasons. Meyer was Leutnant Fröhlich, who had been awarded a field commission for his outstanding service aboard *Graf Spee*. Müller, actually Leutnant Dittmann, was a former merchant sailor and a prize officer. Even though both men had been at sea since August 1939, they chose to transfer to the raider and remain at sea rather than return home to Germany aboard *Dresden*. Rogge welcomed the two experienced and capable additions to his crew.

Rogge dispatched the prison ship *Dresden* to the nearest neutral port where the detainees could be released. He suggested the Canary Islands but left the final decision to Jäger to make based on his stores, fuel, and tactical situation. *Atlantis* and *Alsterufer* set out for a rendezvous with the supply ship *Nordmark* north of Tristan da Cunha. Within two days of finally parting company with the supply ship, *Atlantis* intercepted a wireless message from the Naval High Command to *Dresden* countermanding Rogge's order and instructing *Dresden* to sail for the French coast. Jäger brought his charges safely into Saint-Jean-de-Luz on 20 May 1941, twenty-four days after parting company with *Atlantis*.[16]

The German authorities searched the prisoners and confiscated anything that might provide intelligence data to the Allies. The impounded property included many of the photographs David Scherman had been allowed by Rogge and Jäger to take while aboard their ships. The Germans missed one crucial roll of film that Scherman had hidden in a tube of toothpaste. Scherman was still carrying the hidden film when he was repatriated to New York via Biarritz, Lisbon, Horta, and Bermuda.

As the summer of 1941 began, just about every American magazine and newspaper printed the story of the Germans' "brutal" attack on the unarmed *Zamzam*. Nearly every article included some of the photographs Scherman had taken aboard the German merchant raider disguised as *Tamesis*. Despite Capt. Bernhard Rogge's superior treatment of the prisoners and his unyielding efforts to conduct operations properly and honorably, the articles defamed him and labeled him a butcher. Worse yet for his command, the incident provided the Allies with a clear bow-quarter, full-length photograph of a known German raider ship. Copies of the important photograph were soon being circulated through Allied intelligence offices and the Royal Air Force and Navy.

9

The Noose Tightens

ATLANTIS AND ALSTERUFER floated some five hundred miles north of the island of Tristan da Cunha for some time before they were finally joined by the fleet tanker *Nordmark*. The tanker normally remained on station near latitude 5 degrees north and longitude 31 degrees west and waited for other German ships to rendezvous with it.[1] In this instance, however, Captain Grau had been ordered to take *Nordmark* to the ships in need of fuel. When *Nordmark* hove to near *Atlantis* and *Alsterufer,* Rogge was pleased to learn that the ship had brought more than just supplies. His highly skilled navigator, Kapitänleutnant Paul Kamenz, was aboard.

After Kamenz completed his briefings in Berlin, he was dispatched to Lorient, France, to embark on a U-boat for the return trip to *Atlantis*. Kamenz sailed with *U-106*, under the command of Kapitänleutnant Jürgen Oesten, on 26 February 1941. During his time aboard *U-106* Kamenz was not an idle passenger; he actively participated in the ship's operation.[2] When *U-106* completed its first resupply rendezvous, Kamenz remained behind on *Nordmark* and waited for an opportunity to return to his ship.

The supply ships and the raider stayed together for nearly a week completing minor repairs and maintenance. Leutnant Bulla, Stabsfeldwebel Borchert, and four other aircrew technicians used the time to break out the crated aircraft and work on assembling them. It proved to be a very difficult task. The unmarked and mixed-up crates of parts included no instructions or assembly guidelines. While the airmen worked on the new airplanes, most of the other crewmen visited the other ships for a change of scenery.

On 27 April, *Atlantis* parted company with *Nordmark* and *Alsterufer*.[3] Rogge had recently received a message from the SKL telling him that the tanker lanes between the West Indies and Freetown and the Cape Town–Freetown routes were weakly guarded by the Allies. He decided to act on the information and take his raider eastward to search for prey.

Two days later, Rogge told Kühn that it was again time to change the ship's disguise. The prisoners from *Zamzam* were sure to report the name *Tamesis* and the home port of Tønsberg—they were painted conspicuously on the ship when it attacked the Egyptian vessel. Rogge decided that *Atlantis* would become the four-year-old, 9,246-ton Dutch motor ship *Brastagi* from the W. Ruys & Zonen Rotterdamsche Lloyd NV line. First Officer Kühn put his work details into action. Once again the crewmen labored to repaint and restructure *Atlantis*'s upper works. The brownish yellow of *Brastagi*'s Rotterdam Lloyd line soon began to cover the grays of the Wilhelmsen color scheme.

By morning on the last day of April 1941, Bulla reported that *Atlantis* was again equipped with a functional aircraft and Kühn reported that work on the ship's new disguise was complete. The paint scheme was not perfect. The hull should have been a lighter gray, but the high seas had forced the painters to leave it a darker shade. Rogge allowed the flaw under the circumstances. He was satisfied enough with the effort to allow the men some rest until the waves settled.

On 1 May, Rogge sent the airmen aloft to investigate a smoke cloud on the horizon. Borchert piloted the new craft and Bulla rode as an observer as they chased after the unknown ship. Although they supplied Rogge with accurate directions, *Atlantis* could not catch up to the target ship. When the aircraft returned to *Atlantis*, Bulla and Borchert sang their new craft's praises. The new seaplane was smaller, faster, and more nimble in the air and on the water; it had more power, was better armed, and even required a shorter takeoff run. Rogge was pleased to add the Arado to *Atlantis*'s arsenal.

On 4 May, *Atlantis* finally met *Babitonga*, the supply ship he had been scheduled to rendezvous with in mid-April. The 4,422-ton German supply ship had been sent from Santos, Brazil, specifically to assist *Atlantis* but was unable to fulfill its intended purpose because it could not carry the fresh vegetables and foodstuffs Rogge's crew really needed. Consequently, the meeting between the two ships was very short, and only a few nonperishable items were exchanged. Rogge dispatched *Babitonga* to take up position near 30 degrees south latitude and 15 degrees west longitude and await further instructions.

Atlantis continued for another three days until the lookouts sighted an unknown ship in the afternoon of Wednesday, 7 May 1941. Rogge shadowed the other vessel until nightfall and then closed in at high speed to force the target to heave to. The target ship proved to be the 5,700-ton French merchant ship *Lieutenant de la Tour*. *Atlantis* stopped the French ship and boarding parties searched for contraband cargo, but the ship was allowed to proceed when none was found. *Atlantis* secured from action stations and continued along the original heading.

On 8 May 1941, in a spot on the ocean far from *Atlantis*, an event occurred that would affect the entire German Kriegsmarine. On that day, *U-110*, commanded by Kapitänleutnant Julius Lemp, attacked the outbound convoy OB.318 south of Greenland. Lemp left his periscope up too long during the attack and was quickly pounced on by the British escort force. The 1,360-ton fleet destroyer HMS *Bulldog*, assisted by HMS *Aubretia* and the old American four-stacker destroyer HMS *Broadway*, mounted a relentless counterattack that crippled *U-110* and brought it to the surface. The German submarine crew, thinking their boat was sinking out from under them, abandoned the submarine with all its secret papers and Enigma encryption machine still aboard. The quick actions of a Royal Navy boarding party led by Sub-Lt. David Balme captured the U-boat with the secret papers, the highly prized encryption machine, and all of the code pages intact.[4]

This English intelligence coup would significantly contribute to the sinking of many German supply ships and warships. The British intelligence community at Bletchley Park used the information and code machine from *U-110* along with previously captured or derived intelligence data to crack the all-important Hydra-type cipher—the one used by all operational German submarines and their supply vessels. Within weeks of *U-110*'s capture the Kriegsmarine began to feel the effects of the captured equipment and broken codes, although the intelligence coup remained unknown to the

Germans. The British were extremely selective in applying their newly developed information against the German navy lest too many significant and coincidental successes raise suspicions and compromise the new strategic advantage.[5]

Rogge, blissfully unaware of Britain's new capabilities, sailed his ship on the same heading until 13 May, when he turned into the Cape Town–Freetown route. Several hours after the course adjustment, just after midnight on the morning of the fourteenth, the lookouts spotted a ship on the horizon. *Atlantis* had been sailing in the same general area more than a year before when *Scientist* became its first victim. Rogge quickly closed to within gun range of the intended target and told the signalman to order the unknown vessel to stop. The signalman snapped the shutters open and closed, beating out the signal. The ship continued on its way with no reaction.

Rogge ordered *Atlantis*'s searchlight operator to illuminate the target's bridge. The crew of the British merchant ship could not have been unaware of the powerful light sweeping over the bridge and superstructure, but still they did not respond or react in any way. Rogge ordered Kasch to put one round across the target's bow. The 150-mm gun's brilliant orange flash brightly lit both ships and the surrounding sea as the gun's thunderous boom broke the silence of the night. The gunfire brought a reaction from the ship, though not the one Rogge anticipated. The target started a tight turn, increased its speed, and tried to break hard away in an escape attempt.

Rogge ordered Kasch to fire for effect. The gunnery officer ordered the crews of two 150-mm cannons to fire one round each. The salvo from *Atlantis*'s guns exploded near the target's boat deck, causing mortal damage to the ship's bulkheads, demolishing the deckhouses, and cutting the steam pipes. The ship rapidly lost way and immediately began to sink. The crew took to the lifeboats and hastily abandoned the furiously burning ship. The master of the sinking ship, Captain Miller, flashed a signal to his attacker informing Rogge that all boats were away and the crew required assistance.

The boarding parties made no attempt to board the sinking English ship and instead turned their efforts to rescuing the survivors. Within thirty minutes of sustaining the hits from *Atlantis*'s guns, the brightly burning beacon drifting on the black water was extinguished. The ship went down over its stern, and the seas were dark once again.

Atlantis once again buzzed with activity as the crew processed and attended to the medical needs of the new prisoners. Through interviews with the survivors Rogge determined the identity of *Atlantis*'s victim. The ship was the 5,618-ton British steamship *Rabaul* of the W. R. Carpenter Overseas Shipping Company. *Rabaul* carried fifty-four crewmen and four passengers. Seven of the men had been killed during the attack, and nine had been wounded. The old steamer, launched in 1916, was en route from England to Cape Town with a load of coal.[6]

By the following morning the prisoners were secured and *Atlantis* was once again scouring the sea lanes. Although the fuel bunkers were full, Rogge stopped the ship's engines and allowed it to drift in the currents that ran along the shipping route. Although he had already exceeded the SKL's expectations by staying operational for more than a year, Rogge's mission was to stay at sea as long as possible and he was determined to continue his rigid conservation efforts.

Atlantis slowly drifted along the Cape Town route for two days until ten minutes after midnight on the morning of 17 May, when Steuermannsmaat Rudolf de Graff and a bridge signalman simultaneously detected two ships coming over the horizon. *Atlantis* was invisible to them against a cloudy, mottled horizon, but the two oncoming ships stood out plainly on the calm seas beneath a brilliant moon. The officer of the deck sounded action stations.

The sirens brought Rogge immediately from one of the lower decks to the bridge. Mohr jumped from his berth and ran to join his captain on the bridge. The men strained to see two blacked-out ships steaming in line and headed directly for *Atlantis*. The fact that two ships were sailing together disturbed Rogge. Either both ships were warships or one was a freighter carrying a very important cargo under escort by a warship. Neither possibility boded well for *Atlantis*. Rogge ordered the engines started, placing extreme emphasis on the word *slowly*. If the engines were started too quickly, a plume of glowing embers might shoot high into the sky and alert the approaching ships of *Atlantis*'s presence.

Within a few minutes the engines came to life without an aerial fireworks display. *Atlantis* gradually came under power, and Rogge started edging his ship off the starboard side of the approaching ships. At about that time Mohr caught sight of the unmistakable pyramidal superstructure of large capital ships. Both were British warships!

Rogge ordered the guns and torpedoes readied, hoping they would not have to be used in what would surely be a one-sided fight. As *Atlantis* slowly crept out of their direct path, the warships continued to steam at fourteen knots and close the gap. Slowly, almost imperceptibly, Rogge began to turn his ship stern-on to present the smallest possible silhouette to the enemy.

Less than two hours after the initial sighting, *Atlantis* began to slip away from the warships' path while maintaining the stern-on presentation toward the enemy. Rogge had done all he could do; now he had to wait and see what the British would do. Every man aboard the raider waited tensely. Had *Atlantis* been seen? Why hadn't the British signaled? When would the warships open fire? Were they planning a surprise attack? Rogge continued to order small course adjustments to minimize his ship's profile.

The men of *Atlantis* watched with pounding hearts as the first ship crossed behind their ship at a range of less than seven thousand yards. The ship was the 33,950-ton battleship HMS *Nelson*, armed with an arsenal that included nine 406-mm main batteries and twelve 150-mm secondary guns. Every man aboard knew that one salvo from the gigantic battleship would disintegrate *Atlantis* without a trace. The raider's men could plainly see the battleship's curling white bow wave as *Nelson* knifed a swath though the raider's wake directly perpendicular to their own seemingly tiny ship. The battleship passed by *Atlantis* and continued on its way, only to be immediately followed by an aircraft carrier!

The fleet carrier HMS *Eagle* and its armada of seventy planes passed behind *Atlantis* next. The 850-foot-long, 38,490-ton carrier's stern churned up a huge, frothy, white trail that spread out nearly all the way to *Atlantis*'s stern. The men watched spellbound as the two leviathans passed near their ship and continued on their patrol, both miraculously unaware of the close encounter. Several hours later, the two monstrous ships slipped below the horizon. The only remaining indications of their presence were the two thin smudges of their tall masts and superstructures.

Rogge announced to the crew that the English warships were fading from the view of even their strongest binoculars. The men let out a rousing cheer and then burst into nervous laughter. They were safe! Just then, *Atlantis*'s smokestack belched a huge puff of bright red flame and burning embers that shot high into the air like a distress signal calling the warships back.

Following the flames came blazing red embers. The embers slowly drifted down all over *Atlantis* and the surrounding sea, lighting up the raider like a prewar holiday cruise ship.

Rogge was furious. He immediately ordered Kielhorn to stop the engines and determine what had happened. If the English had caught sight of the fireworks display, *Atlantis* would surely have been doomed, but once again luck favored the German ship. The enemy ships had not seen the flames. *Atlantis*'s lookouts watched the horizon without blinking as the last signs of the two massive enemy warships faded from view.

Kielhorn and his men purged the fireboxes, engines, and exhausts and found the cause of the discharge. Some rust in the exhaust system had flaked off and been thrown up and out of the funnel. Kielhorn reported his finding to the captain and requested permission to restart the engines. Rogge assented, and *Atlantis* moved off on a south-southwest course away from the warships. The captain was careful not to plot a direct reciprocal course of the warships. He could not be sure that other English capital ships were not following the first two on the same heading.

The following morning was Sunday, and Rogge held a special service to give thanks for their narrow escape. The entire crew said a prayer together, and Rogge later wrote that the incident was one of the most memorable and moving events during the entire cruise.

May 21 brought another sighting. Rogge again shadowed the target and waited until nightfall before taking action. Shortly after midnight on the morning of the twenty-second, Kasch's gun crew put a round across the bow of the unknown ship. The steamship promptly hove to, and boarding parties went out to investigate. The target was *Master Elias Kulukundis,* a 5,548-ton Greek merchant ship sailing under the charter of neutral Switzerland. The boarding parties found no contraband cargo, and Rogge allowed the ship to proceed after the master signed a written promise stating that he would not use his wireless.

The lookouts reported another ship on 23 May. Captain Rogge again waited for nightfall and closed in. The unknown vessel switched on its lights and illuminated what appeared to be poorly lit neutrality markings. Despite the close range of three thousand yards, the officers on the deck had to strain their eyes to ascertain if the dim glow was in fact highlighting neutrality markings or hiding the guns of an AMC. Once the officers confirmed the ship to be a neutral, Rogge allowed it to pass without incident. Later that night *Atlantis*'s radio room intercepted a message from the vessel, the American ship *Charles H. Cramp,* calling Cape Town. The Cape Town station did not respond, and Rogge decided it was safe to remain on the Cape Town–Freetown route.

During the late morning hours of 24 May, Rogge dispatched an aircraft to scout over the horizon. It was not long before the seaplane returned wagging its wings to signify a contact. The plane was quickly recovered, and *Atlantis* set off to investigate the new sighting on a course planned to bring the raider within gun range shortly after nightfall.

Atlantis quickly closed the range and prepared to attack. The target bore the distinctive add-on stern gun of a British merchant ship. The captain instructed Kasch to aim for the radio room and unleash the first salvo. The initial series of shells struck home, splintering deckhouses, shattering the radio shack, and starting a huge deck fire amidships. The second salvo went astray as the Allied ship maneuvered and tried to run.

Kasch unleashed ten more salvos, striking the target with precision. The exploding shells started fires, broke the masts, blew away the funnel, leveled much of the upper works, and jammed the ship's rudder, locking it into a tight turn. The fires were so bright that Rogge ordered the ship sunk with torpedoes. Within seconds of Rogge's order to launch, the first torpedo splashed into the water and started its run toward the target. The merchant continued to steam on, locked in a tight turn and now on a collision course with *Atlantis*.

The first torpedo malfunctioned during its dash toward the target, turned, and drew a telltale frothy white line straight back toward the German raider. Captain Rogge later wrote in his war log that *Atlantis* "was in an unenviable position, for there was the burning ship heading for her at a speed of five knots, while the circling torpedo was coming nearer and nearer."[7]

The men launched a second torpedo, which also malfunctioned and missed wide of the target. As Kasch ordered yet another "eel" launched, the first torpedo swept past *Atlantis*'s bow. The third torpedo tracked a true course and struck home with a thunderous impact that nearly stopped the merchant in its tracks. The ship sank nine minutes after the torpedo exploded.[8] The rescue effort was slow and tedious. For security reasons, the rescue boats did not use lights. The rescuers located the thirty-three survivors by the small red lights attached to their life vests.

The ship had been the British SS *Trafalgar,* sailing from Newport and Milford Haven for Table Bay and Alexandria with a cargo of coal, two aircraft, and a mix of other goods and parcels. The 4,530-ton steamship belonged to the Glen Company of Glasgow and carried a complement of forty-five. Twelve men died in the shelling or went down with the ship, which had not transmitted a distress call only because the first salvo demolished the radio shack.

Once the prisoners were secured, Rogge ordered a course set for the area where *Babitonga* waited, hoping to make a quick rendezvous and prisoner transfer. During the cruise, Adjutant Mohr, who frequently listened to various news services to gather information on the status of the war, ship movements, and news of home, picked up three BBC announcements that had an enormous effect on *Atlantis*'s crew. The first broadcast announced that the German battleship *Bismarck* had outgunned and sunk the pride of the Royal Navy, HMS *Hood.* Only 3 of the 1,419 crewmen on board the British ship had survived.[9] The men were thrilled at the great victory, but the deaths of so many fellow sailors, regardless of their allegiance, was disturbing and disheartening.

Then came a message from the BBC reporting that *Bismarck* had been trapped and sunk by a large flotilla of English warships.[10] The news of the loss of Germany's premier battleship was hard on the men. Their country had lost a piece of its pride, the Kriegsmarine had lost one of its most powerful capital ships, and the men felt the noose of the war draw a little tighter around them.

The final bit of bad news came with another BBC announcement. The dispatch reported that HMS *Cornwall,* a County-class cruiser, had cornered and sunk the raider *Pinguin, Ship-33,* in the Indian Ocean following a fierce gun battle. This news struck each man personally. *Atlantis* had spent two days with its fellow raider only six months before, and every man on *Atlantis* had friends aboard *Pinguin.* Of *Pinguin*'s 254 enlisted men, 67 petty officers, and 18 officers, only 47 enlisted men, 10 petty officers, and 3 officers survived the attack. The commanding officer, Kapitän-zur-See Krüder, went down with his ship. It was easy for the men to imagine *Atlantis* in *Pinguin*'s place.

The three news bulletins caused each man on *Atlantis* to consider the wisdom and price of a long war. They remained loyal German sailors dedicated to following orders and serving their country, but they had begun to dread the nearly constant anxiety and stress of conflict.

The radio operators then received an intelligence message from the German Naval High Command announcing that the British had the ability to locate a ship by using its radio emanations. This was a fact Rogge had known for quite some time; Leutnant Breuers had already proved the principle to him. Breuers had used *Atlantis*'s radio signals to track its location from *Speybank* and later used the technique to locate the French naval tanker *Lot*. And the news had one good aspect; at least the naval staff would no longer pester him for lengthy status and location reports.

Atlantis met *Babitonga* at the designated rendezvous point and handed over the prisoners. *Babitonga* in turn departed to transship the prisoners to the U-boat supply ship *Esso Hamburg* before returning to continue its support of *Atlantis*.

Rogge decided to remain in place, complete the painting required to finish the ship's disguise, and perform repairs, maintenance, and overhaul work on both engines. Kühn set his men to work almost immediately. *Babitonga* returned while the work was still in progress, and Rogge sent the supply ship off to wait at another set of coordinates in the central Atlantic.

The SKL then ordered Rogge to take *Atlantis* farther north to patrol the northern end of the Cape Town–Freetown route and try to intercept ships as they turned west along the South American routes. Near the end of the month, he was to abandon the Cape Town–Freetown route and move south for a meeting with another raider. The SKL specified a position where *Atlantis* was to meet *Ship-36, Orion,* during the first week in July.

Rogge was not particularly pleased about the new orders, which put his ship closer to the hornet's nest of the North Atlantic Ocean. And things were about to get worse there. With the loss of *Bismarck* the large British flotilla was free to break into smaller groups and turn their attention to hunting other German ships. The fact that Germany had no naval bases or ports outside the North and Baltic Seas proved to be the Kriegsmarine's Achilles heel. The Germans had to rely on a highly vulnerable fleet of supply ships to keep their pocket battleships, large cruisers, raiders, and submarines stocked and fueled. Now that *Bismarck* was no longer distracting the British, the German supply lines were in grave danger.

On 11 June, the work crews completed the overhaul project and *Atlantis* started north toward the new patrol area. Five days later, on 16 June 1940, *Atlantis* broke the World War I raider *Wolf*'s record for time at sea. It had been 445 days since *Atlantis* pulled free of its moorings in Germany, and the crew now had the distinction of spending more consecutive days at sea than any other raider crew in history.

During the first weeks of June 1941, the British really put their ability to read the Hydra cipher to use, launching a series of concerted attacks against the fragile and overextended German supply lines. British Intelligence read the Germans' coded instructions to their U-boats and dispatched Royal Navy warships from nearby ports to respond. The well-coordinated attacks spelled the beginning of the end for the German U-boats, supply ships, and cruisers in the far reaches of the Atlantic and Indian Oceans. As long as the British could accurately direct overwhelming force against German warships, the German effort to disrupt the Allied sea trade was doomed. The British offensive directly resulted in the sinking of nine German supply ships, but it was accomplished in such a way that it did not raise the suspicions of the German naval staff.[11] There were always plausible excuses for the sinkings, and the Germans never questioned the security of their naval codes.

Rogge recognized that the war was changing. His mission became more dangerous and more difficult with each passing day. The difficulties and risks of sustaining the raider's operation were also increasing for reasons unrelated to the British intelligence successes. The first difficulty lay with the operations areas of the other German raiders. *Kormoran*, *Ship-41*, was sailing around the Bay of Bengal between Ceylon and Sumatra; *Komet*, *Ship-45*, was operating off the west coast of Australia; and *Orion*, *Ship-36*, was in the Coral Sea on the eastern side of Australia. This dispersal meant there was no auxiliary cruiser in the immediate area to confuse the enemy and help cover *Atlantis*'s tracks. The four raiders' operating areas were now distinct, separate, and clearly evident to the British naval staff. The Royal Navy was free to focus its attention on any one area and hunt down individual ships at any time.

Rogge's other problem was the lack of targets. Most of the merchant traffic had been reorganized into convoys that an auxiliary cruiser simply could not approach. The odds were quickly tilting against *Atlantis*. Nevertheless, solitary merchant ships sailed occasionally, and Rogge pinned his hopes on finding them. Against the odds, the pilots from *Atlantis* spotted their airplane's fifth victim while scouting on 17 June. It was just before dark when *Atlantis* fired the first shell across the bows of the enemy ship, which proved to be the one-year-old, 4,762-ton British steamship *Tottenham*. Before Rogge could prevent it, *Tottenham* successfully broadcast its position and an RRR merchant raider warning to two shore stations, Walvis Bay and Ascension Island.[12] The English ship then fired a round from its defensive gun in *Atlantis*'s general direction.

Rogge did not take pleasure in gunning down ships that were so outmatched, but he could not risk any damage to his own ship. *Atlantis* responded by shelling *Tottenham* until it lost way and sank. The Germans rescued twenty-nine men from the sea, including Captain Woodcock and the chief engineer, Edward Nolan.

As the Germans hurried the prisoners belowdecks and made preparations to depart, Captain Woodcock protested that seventeen of his men were still unaccounted for. Woodcock confronted Rogge and insisted that the Germans search for them. Captain Rogge responded that a continued search was out of the question because they were only 250 miles off Ascension Island and *Tottenham* had radioed for help. Rogge sent Captain Woodcock belowdecks, and *Atlantis* left the area without searching any further.

Nine weeks later, on 22 August 1941, Rogge was blamed for the deaths of the seventeen missing men when reports surfaced that a lifeboat from *Tottenham* had drifted into the harbor at Rio de Janeiro awash and empty. In reality, the accusations were false and the attacks against Rogge were unjust. The boat was empty and awash because the second officer of *Tottenham*, D. V. Cameron, and sixteen others had abandoned it when they were rescued. The men had decided to take their chances on the high seas and purposely avoided capture. With only a small bit of water, condensed milk, and hardtack, the sailors set out for Brazil, eleven hundred miles away, drifting on the steady equatorial current before the southeasterly trade winds. They were picked up by an English ship eleven days later.

In his book *German Raiders of World War II*, August Muggenthaler notes that the men's

> rescue on the eleventh day by *Mahronda* was most fortunate: their binnacle light had been seen during the night and the ship's master, thinking it might be a U-boat's, had stood off until dawn. Naturally, seaman Cameron pulled the boat's plug once everyone was off; as a good officer, you do not leave wreckage floating about where it might damage someone's propeller.[13]

The empty boat stayed on the surface, however, its freeboard level with the water, and drifted into Rio de Janeiro harbor, where it became the source of the unfounded accusations against Captain Rogge.

After *Tottenham* sank, Rogge turned his ship slightly southwest and sailed on until another medium-sized armed vessel rose over the horizon and into view. Rogge followed his normal tactic of standing off until well after dark and then running in for a quick attack. When the raider was only nine thousand yards away, the two-decker target ship attempted to broadcast a raider warning and plea for help. The radiomen on *Atlantis* were able to block the merchant's SOS with the message: "Hope to meet you next Friday, Love and kisses, Evelyn,"[14] which they broadcast at full power right over the Englishman's transmission. The British ship turned away, came to full speed, and began a zigzagging escape run.

Atlantis pursued the target relentlessly, and Kasch drove his gun crewmen to load and fire again and again. The Allied ship maneuvered hard at full speed to flee and evade *Atlantis*'s shells, and with some success; only four of the one hundred rounds fired by the German gunners struck home. After the fortieth salvo the barrels of the number five poop deck gun and the forward main gun had so expanded from the heat of firing that they jammed and refused to return from the recoil position. The gunners cooled their steaming cannons with seawater and manhandled them back into firing position. They got off only one or two more rounds before the guns jammed again. Rogge was about to give up the fight and depart when the British ship unexpectedly surrendered.

A German boarding party went over to gather useful information, take off the prisoners, and scuttle the vessel. The ship was Lamport & Holt's twenty-one-year-old, 5,372-ton motor vessel *Balzac*, en route from Rangoon to Liverpool with forty-two hundred tons of rice. When the boarding parties returned, *Atlantis* had picked up forty-seven new prisoners from *Balzac*'s crew of fifty-one. Rogge wasted no time sending the ship to the bottom.[15] The radiomen had reported that the airwaves carried a nearly constant stream of wireless transmissions. Some were in the clear, but most were coded in the patterns used by the Royal Navy. Rogge decided the area had become too dangerous for further operations.

The failure of the guns was an indication that the ship had been at sea too long. The cruise was wearing down both the ship's men and its machinery. Captain Rogge decided to give his men and his ship a short respite from battle. He moved *Atlantis* south-southeast to an isolated area far from any shipping routes. Once there, he slowly cruised until 1 July 1941, giving the men a chance to perform maintenance and, most of all, get some well-deserved rest. After nearly a week of recuperation on a calm sea, *Atlantis* set out to meet *Orion* some three hundred miles north of the circular island of Tristan da Cunha.

Orion, under Kapitän-zur-See Kurt Weyher, had left the Indian Ocean and had not seen action for eight months. At 7:07 A.M. *Orion* appeared to the lookouts as a shadow on the horizon. Rogge dared not draw nearer until both ships had exchanged the correct predetermined recognition signals. Once the signalmen confirmed that the battered old ship was *Orion*, Rogge brought his ship in close. The crews lined the rails and cheered as the two warships came alongside one another. It was the first time the two ships had met since their combined gunnery exercises off the German coast some seventeen months earlier.

The German High Command had ordered Rogge to give *Orion* seven hundred tons of fuel oil, enough for the trip home. Weyher, frustrated and angry at his lack of success, wanted to stay at sea and hunt, and asked Rogge for much more fuel. Captain Rogge would not comply. *Orion*'s inefficient engines used as much fuel in one week as *Atlantis* used in two months. Despite Weyher's strong desire to make up for the long period with no action, Rogge held firm and agreed to provide only the seven hundred tons of fuel *Orion* needed to return home. It was a waste of fuel to give him more, Rogge explained to Weyher, when *Atlantis* could patrol much longer on the same amount. Rogge was also reluctant to limit his own ship's options by significantly reducing its fuel stores, but he did not tell Weyher that.

As the two ships sat alongside one another, *Atlantis* received a wireless from the SKL giving him the authority to make port in Dakar if he wished. Rumors soon began to drift through the hopeful crew that Captain Rogge was considering a visit to a port of call or even a return to Germany.

The two ships parted company on 6 July. *Orion*, provisioned with food, 150 rounds of ammunition, and fuel, sailed westerly toward the South American coast. *Atlantis* sailed south, its new destination the Pacific Ocean. Rogge knew his decision to remain at sea would disappoint the crew, and he called the men together to explain. He told them *Atlantis* had more than 60 percent of its ammunition stores, plenty of fuel, and supplies of food at higher levels than it had carried in most of the preceding months; their duty was to stay and fight. His plan was to enter the Pacific and continue operations until mid-winter. Then, when the conditions in the North Atlantic became cold and stormy, *Atlantis* would turn for home, break through the British blockade, and return to German territory.

As Rogge expected, the men were extremely disappointed. Mohr recorded his own feelings after Rogge's announcement: "A bitter blow for the men, and a bitter blow for me. [But] it's our duty to save the ship and to worry the English as best we can."[16] The crew nevertheless accepted their commanding officer's decision without complaint. Their lack of objection was so conspicuous, in fact, that Rogge even noted it in his war log. He was pleased that the crew's conduct remained exemplary even in the face of such disheartening and disappointing news.

10

Pacific Waters

On the heels of the *Zamzam* disaster and faced with the increasingly dangerous conditions in the South Atlantic and Indian Oceans, Rogge decided to take his ship into the Pacific Ocean, a fairly new hunting ground for German raiders. Rogge hoped the move to the Pacific would provide him with a better chance of finding unescorted merchants while at the same time decreasing his chance of detection. So once again, *Atlantis* steamed south.

Three days after parting company with *Orion*, and just after the navigator remarked that the ship had crossed south of the 40-degree line, gulls and other seabirds began to circle the ship. The birds streaking and swooping overhead reminded the men of land and home and were a welcome interruption to the dull routine of shipboard life. Soon afterward the volcanic outcroppings of Gough Island came into view. *Atlantis* sailed steadily along until the islets passed astern. The birds stayed behind with the land, leaving *Atlantis* alone again with only the sea and the sky for company.

The men broke out their thick protective oilskins once more as *Atlantis* plunged headlong into the stormy seas of the Roaring Forties, an area infamous for its almost constant tempests. Holding true to its reputation, the Forties pelted the raider with powerful winds, frigid sea spray, and towering rollers. The tremendous whitecaps that crashed over the bow every few seconds flung *Atlantis* around like a toy ship in a bathtub.

Once again the integrity of their repair work became a concern for the crew as *Atlantis* was repeatedly tipped fore and aft by the force of the waves. The violent rolling and steep pitching took a physical toll on the crew as well as the ship. The ship's unpredictable and violent movements shifted equipment, slammed hatches, and caused falls without warning. The sick bay filled with men. The two doctors had not seen patients on such a scale since the terrible weather encountered during the initial breakout. The doctors treated everything from smashed fingers and broken bones to minor cuts and abrasions.

Atlantis was safe from enemy action in the stormy southern waters. No merchant vessel would ply this route, and no warships patrolled the area without a specific reason. Rogge determined that he could safely send a message to the German Admiralty to update the command staff on the status of his cruise. The radiomen tried more than one hundred times to send the SKL a short, coded burst of information but received no acknowledgment. The SKL did not receive the transmissions, but Radio South Africa did. The British could not decode the message, but they knew it was German code and they knew it was in Special Cipher 100, which was used exclusively by merchant raiders and their supply ships. The British Admiralty followed up the receipt of *Atlantis*'s message with an open-air broadcast to all ships in the south Indian Ocean warning of a German raider in the Kerguelen Islands area. The British wireless message reaffirmed Rogge's belief that the British radio detection and finding capabilities were at least as good as he had initially suspected. He decided to limit future radio transmissions to those critical to his mission and to keep them as brief as possible.

Atlantis passed the Cape of Good Hope for the third time, going even farther south than during the previous passage—some three hundred miles south of the landfall of Good Hope. After passing the southern tip of Africa, Rogge kept his ship far south but turned to the east, into the Pacific. As *Atlantis* passed just north of Prince Edward Island, the weather began to worsen significantly.

The ship fought increasingly higher waves as the cold, buffeting winds reached force 11 on the Beaufort Scale—a full-blown hurricane. Rogge ordered the ship hove to. Stopping was his only option. The ship could make no headway against the raging winds and seas. The crew could only ride along and hope the ship remained seaworthy until the storm released them. Rogge relieved them from lookout and other nonessential duties, and they remained in their uncomfortable, stuffy berthing areas cursing the wretched weather. The men tried to escape the tortuous rolling and rocking by grabbing bits of sleep whenever they could, but rest was rarely possible. The sudden and extreme movements kept the men awake until only sheer exhaustion allowed them to escape into short spells of fitful sleep. *Atlantis*'s engines stayed nearly idle for several days as the ship rode out the fury of the hurricane.

The storm finally ran out, and Rogge immediately ordered a complete assessment of the ship. All of the damage reports came back negative. The ship was sound and entirely seaworthy. Kielhorn once again stoked the fireboxes and brought the ship up to speed, and *Atlantis* continued on into the Pacific Ocean.

The crew of *Atlantis* celebrated their five hundredth day at sea off the Crozet Islands. Rogge made a short congratulatory statement to the men and then told First Officer Kühn to prepare the ship for a formal inspection. The men complained as they polished and tidied every bit of the ship, unable to understand why Captain Rogge maintained the strict inspection regime on an already seasoned and proven crew. Rogge, however, knew that inspections were a vital part of maintaining good order and discipline aboard his ship. Inspections, he later wrote, "helped to promote the individual's regard for his inherent dignity and to foster a healthy self-confidence just as much as keeping the ship and the quarters shining. Actually the dress and carriage of a man always reflected his mental attitude."[1]

At the given time, the watch officer gave the order to clear the lower deck and the inspection began. The men stood in formation in their dress uniforms. Rogge and Mohr stepped out in their own pressed and bemedaled dress uniforms, Rogge first, followed by Mohr, who recorded any discrepancies noted by the captain. On completing the inspection of the personnel, Rogge dismissed the crew to stand at their posts while he scrutinized the ship's equipment, engines, and machinery. When the thorough inspection was over, Rogge announced that he was pleased with the appearance and maintenance of both his crew and his ship. Despite their time at sea, both still presented a neat, orderly, and strictly military image. Their appearance was remarkable, in fact, after five hundred days at sea.

Atlantis continued on its Pacific sojourn for the next month. Rogge took his ship farther south for a while and then turned north into the South Pacific, making a wide detour around Australia and New Zealand. One day during the transit the crew caught sight of an albatross soaring high above them. The arrival of the enormous bird created quite a stir. Most of the men came up on deck to watch the bird sail effortlessly over the ship on nearly motionless wings. Soon the albatross began circling *Atlantis*'s masts and funnel. The men watched in wonder as the bird glided closer and closer until it was making passes just above the deck. During one of these passes some energetic crewmen grabbed the seabird and brought it down on the deck. Several men held the bird still while others measured it and took photographs of its amazing ten-foot wingspan. The excitement ended when the men realized that the bird was uncomfortable on the ship. They released the albatross, which flew off unharmed, circled the ship, and glided away.

Atlantis reached the Pacific steamer routes on 25 August 1941. The lookouts kept a sharp-eyed vigil while *Atlantis* plied the waters where merchants normally traveled, yet they saw no other ships. Eighty days after *Atlantis* had taken its last victim and sixty-six days after parting company with *Orion* the raider finally caught sight of another vessel.

Two hours after sunset on 10 September 1941, the lookouts spotted a poorly blacked-out ship emerging from a squall. *Atlantis* was sailing well east and about seven hundred miles north of Kermadec Island, approximately halfway between New Zealand and the Society Islands. The target ship's lights revealed the unmistakable silhouette of an English merchant ship located abeam of *Atlantis* and headed on an opposing course. Rogge called the ship to action stations, swung his ship about, ordered an increase in speed, and initiated a pursuit of the merchant.

As *Atlantis* approached, the Allied ship started to broadcast a raider warning, beating out a steady stream of uninterrupted QQQs. The merchant ship identified itself as *Silvaplana*, reported that it was being approached by an unknown ship, and broadcast its correct position. The radio operators aboard *Atlantis* reacted at once to jam the broadcasts but discovered that some of their equipment had been wired incorrectly. All of *Silvaplana*'s reports went out in the clear. Despite the merchant ship's radio messages,

Rogge still wanted to take it without using force. He told Kasch to hold his fire and instructed the signalman to flash a message to *Silvaplana* with orders to stop its engines and cease broadcasting. *Silvaplana* immediately complied with the order and hove to, allowing Rogge to capture another victim without firing a shot.[2]

The German boarding party went over to *Silvaplana* and used the ship's own key to cancel the raider report. The shore stations acknowledged the cancellation, but somewhat reluctantly, which caused Rogge some concern. Twelve hours later, the British shore stations asked *Silvaplana* to send another message canceling its raider warning. This time, however, they requested the reply in code. The German crew could not respond because *Silvaplana*'s captain, Niels Stange Nielson, had followed proper procedures and destroyed all of the code pages before the Germans came on board.

The single-deck, 4,793-ton Norwegian motor ship belonged to the Henry Tschudi & Eitzen Tankreederei line. It had sailed from Singapore for New York with a cargo of four hundred tons of crude rubber; 100,000 pounds of coffee; fifty cases of wooden decorative idols from Bali; an assortment of hides, spices, wax, and vanilla; and a full load of teak stored on deck. Mohr discovered a valuable bit of information when he searched the captain's cabin: a chart that plotted the ship's most recent voyage.

Rogge elected to keep his most recent capture as a prize. *Silvaplana* was just over two years old, fast, undamaged, and carried a cargo of valuable products. He wanted to refuel the ship and send it to France, but *Atlantis*'s stores could not supply provisions for both ships. Instead, Captain Rogge sent his new prize ship to a rendezvous point some four hundred miles south of Tubusi Island to wait while Rogge went northeastward with *Atlantis* in hope of capturing a ship that could provide the necessary fuel and stores.

After a few days of futile searching, Rogge took his raider south to rendezvous with *Silvaplana* at the site specified for the meeting. Captain Rogge's first order of business was to replace a portion of his ship's sand ballast with the valuable crude rubber from *Silvaplana*'s hold. The crew cleared a portion of the ballast area and transferred 120 tons of the crude rubber by boat. It was an excruciatingly slow and tedious task, but the rubber was a valuable commodity. And with the scarce rubber in its holds, *Atlantis*'s eventual return to port would be all the more triumphant.

Rogge was expecting resupply near the end of September from the German supply ship *Münsterland,* which had been ordered to cross paths with *Atlantis* because the two ships were operating relatively close together. *Münsterland* had left Yokohama, Japan, on 25 August and was located somewhere in the raider's general operating area. Rogge planned to meet *Münsterland* and fully provision both his ship and *Silvaplana.* With that done, he could dispatch the prize ship to France and continue his own raiding with no worries about fuel and food. Rogge sent *Silvaplana* to another waiting position off the Orne Bank and steamed *Atlantis* eastward toward the rendezvous with *Münsterland.*

Resupplying *Silvaplana* would have been easier had Rogge kept the ship in *Atlantis*'s company. The prize ship could have taken fuel and supplies directly from *Münsterland* at the meeting point and then gone on its way; but Rogge opted for the more secure course of action. A British patrol was far more likely to stumble on a large group of German ships than a small one.

Rogge guided his ship in close zigzags back and forth over the New Zealand–Panama shipping route until 21 September 1941, then proceeded to the rendezvous. When *Atlantis* arrived at the designated location, Rogge was surprised to find another German raider waiting there. *Komet, Ship-45,* had left its operating area off the Pacific entrance to the Panama Canal and was waiting at the rendezvous point with its Dutch prize ship, the ten-year-old *Kota Nopan,* with the same resupply intentions as *Atlantis. Münsterland,* the ship Rogge had steamed to the area to meet, was not present. The supply ship had been rerouted and delayed by a typhoon.

As *Atlantis* closed on the two other ships, Mohr reminded his captain that *Komet*'s commander was a flag officer. Rogge thanked his adjutant for preventing a serious faux pas in naval etiquette and then asked him to ready the ship to properly greet an admiral. When *Atlantis* finally pulled up near the other ships and hove to, the ship was fully prepared to meet an admiral. Konteradmiral Robert Eyssen's party received a gun salute and was piped aboard with the appropriate pomp and circumstance. The German warship *Atlantis* conducted a reception befitting a ship docked at a German naval yard, a fantastic event in a war zone in the middle of the Pacific Ocean.

The meetings between Rogge and Konteradmiral Eyssen were cordial and even friendly until *Münsterland,* under Captain Uebel, joined the party two days later. When the supply ship arrived, Konteradmiral Eyssen insisted that his ship receive a share of the stores earmarked for *Atlantis*. Rogge, a captain, could not countermand Admiral Eyssen's wishes, so he set about convincing the admiral to change his decision using hard facts and an unbiased comparison of the two raider ships.

To argue his point, Rogge had his medical officers draw up charts that outlined the daily requirements of vitamins, minerals, and essential foods for a typical crewman. Rogge then compared the supply statistics against the doctor's daily requirement charts and began his arguments. In 540 days at sea, *Atlantis* had never received a resupply of fresh vegetables. *Komet*, on the other hand, had received at least five separate shipments of fresh vegetables during its shorter 430-day cruise. Rogge went even further and analyzed the frequency with which the two crews were served particular items. One example Rogge used was potatoes, a staple in most German meals. Rogge's men had eaten a potato dish only sixteen times, the most recent being four months previous. *Komet*'s crew had been served potatoes forty-five times, the most recent being only three days earlier.

Rogge's facts and statistics combined with the doctor's reports were indisputable. The admiral acquiesced and allowed Rogge to fill his ship's stores without interference, with one exception. When it came to the division of the beer ration, the admiral asserted his rank and ordered *Münsterland* to give his ship a share of *Atlantis*'s beer supply. Rogge could not argue that beer was a critical ration for his crew. It was a luxury that was not needed to sustain his men. Moreover, *Komet* was about to sail for Germany, and Konteradmiral Eyssen wanted to ensure an ample beer supply for the crew's well-deserved celebrations on the long return cruise home.[3]

Once the two commanders had agreed on the provisioning plan, Rogge initiated the work to restock his ship. He found *Münsterland* stocked with everything a ship operating on the high seas required. The naval attaché in Tokyo, Vice Adm. Paul Wenneker, was responsible for that. Wenneker, the former commander of the 609-foot, 12,500-ton battleship *Lützow*, understood what type of supplies warships needed to sustain long patrols on the high seas.

In a short while the crews had *Atlantis* fully stocked with all of the supplies, fresh vegetables, and fuel required. Rogge next transferred all but one of the sixty-four prisoners still remaining on *Atlantis* to the other ships. *Komet* took the Allied officers on board; the crewmen and native workers went to *Kota Nopan*.

While the supplies were being transferred, Rogge discussed his plan to return to Germany that winter with Konteradmiral Eyssen. The newly reprovisioned *Atlantis* could, in theory, stay out for another year. Rogge, however, knew that neither his men nor his ship could endure another year at sea. He told the admiral that the ship and crew, despite being fit to carry on, could not continue raiding without respite. The only true relief Rogge could offer his crew was to take them home. Captain Rogge decided he would return *Atlantis* to Germany before Christmas 1941.

The plan he devised called for *Atlantis* to operate in the Pacific until 19 October, and then return to the South Atlantic. On reaching a remote area of the South Atlantic, *Atlantis* would stop for ten days to recondition the ship's engines and then hunt in the South Atlantic for ten more days before turning north and sailing for home, arriving at Kiel near the new moon of 20 December. Rogge called for Adjutant Mohr and briefed him on the plan, and then released him to spread the good news to the crew.

On 24 September, the three ships parted company. *Komet* sailed off with *Kota Nopan* for Europe; *Atlantis* and *Münsterland* sailed south to meet and restock *Silvaplana*. Spirits were high, and the men were glowing with thoughts of the return trip to Germany. "Home by Christmas!" was their catchphrase no matter what subject they were discussing.

Atlantis and its tag-along supply ship met *Silvaplana* at the rendezvous location, where the Norwegian prize was waiting according to Rogge's instructions. As soon as the ships had drawn up close together and stopped, Rogge got the crews working to move the necessary supplies over to the Norwegian ship. The newly motivated and reinvigorated crewmen completed the transfer of the goods quickly and without a single complaint.

Rogge dispatched the refueled and fully provisioned prize ship to Bordeaux on 27 September. The next day he released *Münsterland* and sent it back to Japan to wait for other German ships in need of supplies. *Silvaplana*'s return cruise to Europe was delayed by engine trouble and an encounter with a hurricane off the Cape of Good Hope, but the ship, its prize crew under the command of Leutnant Dittmann, and the thirty-two prisoners arrived safe in Bordeaux on 17 November 1941.[4]

Rogge shaped course for a shipping track marked on the chart captured from *Silvaplana*, believing it to be a new course on which the British Admiralty had ordered Allied merchant ships to sail. Perhaps the chart was intended to show merchant captains a way to avoid commerce raiders. If so, he would prove it wrong!

Atlantis sailed in slow, loose zigzags searching along *Silvaplana*'s course for two weeks without seeing even a hint of another ship. Rogge was disappointed. On the mornings when the seas allowed, he dispatched Bulla aloft to conduct long-range searches. The results of the lookouts' vigil and the aerial searches were the same: nothing sighted. Each day, the rising sun brought only another day of unrelenting heat and boredom. The doldrums were broken only by an occasional flying fish or manta ray sighting or by a passing thunderstorm.

Rogge decided to end the torment. "At last," he later wrote, "I decided to come under the lee of one of the islands where, sheltered from the heavy swell, we could launch the plane more frequently and thus enlarge our radius of search."[5] Rogge summoned Mohr to his quarters and told his adjutant that he wanted to sail to a small island where he could drop anchor, conduct extensive air reconnaissance, and at the same time give the men a shore leave on a warm tropical island. Mohr wholeheartedly agreed with his captain's plan and eagerly began to search his maps for a suitable atoll.

After searching the charts for nearby islands, Mohr suggested a nearly uninhabited coral atoll named Vana Vana located at 20 degrees, 72 minutes south latitude and 139 degrees, 82 minutes west longitude. Mohr and Rogge discussed the attributes of the small coral outcropping in the Tuamotu Archipelago. The chosen atoll was actually a small, semicircular ring of sand and palm trees rather than a lush tropical island, the least inhabited and the least frequented of the entire island group. Vana Vana was also one of the only atolls that had not been settled by European missionaries. These factors made the island the most logical and secure location for the stop. Rogge told Mohr to prepare the ship to call at the island. Leutnant Mohr notified the crew that their new short-term destination was a sandy beach on a warm tropical island, and *Atlantis* set course for the island accompanied by the cheers of the crew. They would be home for Christmas. But first they were going to stop on an idyllic isle in the South Pacific!

When *Atlantis* came within visual range of their destination, Rogge dispatched the seaplane on an initial scouting run. Bulla and Borchert launched from the ship and flew a short reconnaissance flight over the small circle of palm-studded coral and sand, then returned to the raider with a detailed report. The flyers had noted only one small village of several thatched huts and a church on the sandy beach. The bright white shoreline marked a distinct line between the blue sea and the dark greens of the small island's vegetation. The ring of sand and reef also created a naturally protected anchorage for the ship by nearly encircling a deep anchorage and creating a safe, calm lagoon.

After receiving the aviators' report, Rogge dispatched Mohr and Fehler to the island to investigate. Mohr later wrote that if every man wishing to join the landing party had come along, not a man would have been left aboard the ship. The two officers took a small rubber raft through a break in the protective reef line. The surge of the thundering surf and the cyclic push-pull of currents created by the wave action tossed the raft about like a cork. The men paddled frantically and succeeded in making a somewhat undignified stern-first passage through the cut in the reef.

The landing party surveyed the beach and investigated the huts, where they found only some yelping puppies and a pot of still-warm food. Surmising that the local inhabitants had fled into hiding places when the landing party beached their raft, the Germans decided to leave some gifts as a gesture of their good will. The men left behind a few knives and several packs of cigarettes and returned to *Atlantis* to brief the captain on their findings.

From the two reports Rogge determined that he could safely anchor and land his crew at the island. On Thursday, 10 October 1941, Captain Rogge slowly brought *Atlantis* through an opening in the reef and into the lagoon. The pristine, protected waters of the lagoon were deep enough to allow the ship to get within fifty yards of the shore before dropping anchor. Once the ship was firmly moored, Rogge ordered most of the crew to stand down and announced a shore leave rotation schedule. He placed 50 percent of the crew off duty at a time. Every post and position was to be maintained at the minimum posting level. The only exceptions were the personnel assigned to the flying section. The captain instructed Bulla and Borchert to fly three reconnaissance missions a day. The crew used the time for relaxing while the airmen spent the time maintaining and flying the aircraft.

The captain made one strict stipulation regarding the shore leave. All men going ashore were required to wear a complete and proper Kriegsmarine white tropical uniform and pith helmet. Rogge wanted the crew to maintain the honor and proper image required of the German navy. The men quickly broke out their uniforms and began preparing themselves for their first shore leave in ten months.

The gifts left behind by the boarding party had made a good impression on the island's native inhabitants. When the first leave party beached their boat and stepped ashore in their smartly pressed whites and shorts, the village chief and his twenty smiling subjects greeted them warmly. A line was quickly rigged between the ship and the shore to guide and steady the small rubber rafts ferrying the men from the raider to the beach and back. Each man enjoyed a chance to walk on firm ground. Ten months had passed since they had last had that pleasure, and that landing had been on cold and inhospitable Kerguelen Island.

The friendly natives of Vana Vana readily accepted the visitors at their meals and other activities. The crewmen relaxed, swam, lounged in the white sand, and ate coconuts and other tropical delicacies, welcoming the change in their diet. The crew even arranged to trade some of the ship's flour for five hundred coconuts. The natives were as impressed with bread as the ship's crew was with the coconuts. During their short stay, the German doctors treated the islanders for a terrible eye infection that afflicted nearly every one of them.

Bulla conducted six searches during the forty-eight hours the ship was anchored but saw nothing worth reporting. Reluctantly, Rogge decided to move on after only two days. He had other business to tend to.

Atlantis weighed anchor and moved out into the heaving Pacific Ocean once again. Sailing east and slightly south, the raider came to Pitcairn Island, where Fletcher Christian and the other mutineers from HMS *Bounty* landed in 1790. Pitcairn and its three neighboring islands of Oeno, Ducie, and Henderson all possessed a certain mystique that attracted Rogge. He set aside his interest in Pitcairn's history and his urge to visit the famous island, however, and continued to sail southeast. After nearly one hundred miles Henderson Island came into view directly in *Atlantis*'s path. Captain Rogge could not ignore this opportunity; he decided to stop and investigate the island.

Rogge once again brought *Atlantis* to anchor and sent a scouting party ashore. Henderson Island, an inhospitable volcanic outcropping barely three miles in circumference, consists of a small, nearly nonexistent beach; dense jungle; and steep, sharp cliffs rising straight up all around. The small boarding party found no signs of animal life. Mohr would later write that he would have been surprised to find even an insect there. The dense, nearly impenetrable plant growth impressed the men. At one point, Leutnant Mohr walked twenty paces into the thick jungle undergrowth and had to climb a tree to locate the beach and find his way out. The landing party did find evidence of previous visitors to the island. One such clue was a faded, weather-beaten old board that boldly stated: "This island belongs to King George V." A later addendum had been scratched on the old marker by the crew of a British cruiser. The inscription, dated 1931, reaffirmed England's claim to the island. Neither message was a source of concern for *Atlantis;* the most recent was a decade old. Finding neither swashbuckling intrigue nor anything else of value at Henderson Island, Rogge determined it was time to head for home.

On Saturday, 18 October 1941, *Atlantis* weighed anchor and set off for what the crew envisioned as an unharried return trip to Germany. *Atlantis* sailed southeast toward Cape Horn and sighted no other vessels despite sending up the seaplane on a routine basis. The men were not disappointed by the lack of action. At this point, their overriding concern was a safe return to Germany. Rogge, however, was determined to conduct raiding operations until the ship crossed into German waters and continued the daily search for victims. If the men silently hoped that no other ships would cross paths with *Atlantis,* they kept it to themselves.

On 29 October, the ship rounded the Horn for the last time. Traveling around the tip of South America through the very southern part of the Drake Passage, a route Rogge had selected to avoid Royal Navy patrols, *Atlantis* passed slightly north of the South Shetlands in the cold, foggy

Antarctic waters. In an article written after the war, Rogge described the event: "We sailed round Cape Horn at a distance of ninety-five miles from the coast; the weather was extraordinarily calm, snow alternating with fog, and there was no sign of the roaring seas so vividly described in many books."[6] Once beyond the South Shetlands, Captain Rogge turned his ship north and brought it up to flank speed. The race for Germany and home had begun!

The South Atlantic was a very dangerous area for *Atlantis*. The comparatively narrow stretch of ocean between South America and Africa was heavily patrolled by British warships. The turn to the north meant increased danger, but it also meant the ship was on the home stretch. Captain Rogge notified the SKL that his ship had a significant surplus of fuel oil that he would make available to nearby U-boats as he proceeded north.

On the last day of October, the crew of *Atlantis* marked their six hundredth consecutive day at sea with a small celebration, but for the most part it was just another day. Around 8 November, about the same time that *Atlantis* completed its circumnavigation of the earth, Rogge received an order from the SKL. The operational staff had taken Rogge up on his offer to share his excess fuel with U-boats in need. The wireless instructed Rogge to meet and refuel *U-68* at a coded location referred to as "Flower Point Daffodil," and then, later in the month, to meet and refuel *U-126* at "Flower Point Lily Ten." Rogge's willingness to share his excess supplies was going to delay his ship's return to Germany. The news was disappointing for the crew, but they understood that the operational needs of other warships superseded their need to go home. By doling out surplus fuel and other supplies among the U-boats, Atlantis could make a further contribution to the German war effort.

Rogge checked the map with the navigator, Kamenz, and worked up the plot of the SKL's first rendezvous location. The captain was shocked and angry to learn that the German Admiralty had chosen the crowded traffic lane between Freetown and the Cape of Good Hope as the refueling location! He did not want to stop his ship in that well-patrolled and heavily traversed area. The captain dispatched a terse message back to the naval operations staff: "It is suicide to send us to this position."[7] Korvettenkapitän Karl-Friedrich Merten, *U-68*'s commanding officer and a longtime friend of Rogge, sent an unprompted rider to Rogge's transmission. The one-word message said simply, "Agreed."[8] The Naval High Command adjusted the designated rendezvous to a point about 530 miles southwest of Saint Helena. The new location was still dangerous but not as foolhardy as the previously identified meeting site.

When the 1,540-ton, type IXC *U-68* encountered *Atlantis* on 13 November, the weather was far too stormy to allow any type of refueling operation to occur. Rogge and Merten decide to delay the resupply and move eighty miles north in an effort to find clearer skies and calmer seas. When the two ships met again later, Kamenz noted that the revised meeting spot was the same location where *Atlantis* had met *Dresden* and *Nordmark* just six months ago. The transfer of oil, food, and fresh water from *Atlantis* to *U-68* began without delay. Korvettenkapitän Merten came aboard *Atlantis* to pay a courtesy call on his senior officer—and personal friend—Kapitän-zur-See Rogge.

Rogge and Merten had sailed together in the yacht races before the war. The two friends met in *Atlantis*'s wardroom for a drink and some frank discussion. Rogge confided to the submarine commander that the SKL's orders instructing *Atlantis* to act as a U-boat refueler went beyond what he thought was safe. When Rogge had volunteered *Atlantis* to supply submarines, he assumed it would be an isolated event or two; he did not envision the SKL turning his ship into a sub tender. He told Merten that he was unsure of the security of the U-boat codes and worried about *Atlantis* being caught by Allied warships with a surfaced U-boat at its side. Furthermore, the captain told Merten, he knew very well that the German supply ship *Python* was near the general area and could have been assigned to replenish the submarines. Merten replied that he had read the wireless traffic and agreed with his friend.

The crew completed the transfer of the stores in record time. Every available hand from *Atlantis* assisted in the quick restocking of the U-boat. Rogge suspected that his men were either worried about the danger of the resupply operation or extremely happy to finish any task that slowed their progress toward Germany. Either way, the result was the expedient transfer of the goods.

When 16 November dawned, *U-68* pulled away from *Atlantis* almost fully provisioned and fueled. The submarine went to operate off the Angolan coast near the mouth of the Congo River while *Atlantis* went west. The following morning Captain Rogge ordered Kühn to change the disguise of the ship to that of the Dutch motor ship *Polyphemus*. The men complained about the additional labor so near the journey's end, but as the day faded to night the raider once again changed its shape, colors, and flags.

Rogge had several days to wait before taking *Atlantis* to the next meeting point. The captain gave Kielhorn a day to perform some required engine service and then launched Bulla to initiate an over-the-horizon search of the surrounding seas. After one day of fruitless searching, Bulla and Borchert returned on the second day and waggled the seaplane's wings to signal a contact.

Rogge called *Atlantis* to action stations and set off at flank speed after the unknown ship. The raider's lookouts soon spotted the break on the horizon made by the thin lines of the target ship's masts. Rogge adjusted course and speed to come within gun range shortly after nightfall. By sunset the raider was closing on the target vessel as planned when the unknown ship switched on all of its lights. Once again Rogge found that he had tracked and followed a neutral vessel. He immediately gave up the chase, secured his men from actions stations, and turned away to look elsewhere.

Rogge ordered the scout plane launched once again at first light. The Ar-196a returned within an hour with the now-familiar wag of the wings signaling a contact. Bulla circled and positioned his craft for a landing while *Atlantis* made a hard turn and created the smooth, protected "pond" that normally allowed Bulla to put the plane down safely. The plane came in on a textbook approach, but the water was still uncharacteristically rough. The waves caught the pontoons and brought the floatplane to a short and very abrupt stop, damaging the engine's supercharger in the process. Rogge hurried his men to get the damaged craft hoisted aboard the raider so they could pursue the new contact.

As soon as the crane had the plane out of the water, *Atlantis* was steaming in the direction of the unknown ship at full speed. By mid-day the lookouts had sighted the ship hovering on the limits of visibility. Rogge maneuvered *Atlantis* onto a convergent course and called to Kielhorn for every ounce of available steam. The gun crews prepared their weapons as *Atlantis* cut away at the remaining distance.

Just as Rogge began to close for the attack, the unknown ship laid on more speed and began to outpace its pursuer. Rogge tried various course refinements in a vain attempt to cut the distance. The unknown enemy ship continued to pull away and increase the range until Rogge concluded that the chase was fruitless. The ship was simply too fast for *Atlantis* to catch. Rogge broke off the chase and turned his ship north, reflecting that the target's ability to outrun his ship was just another example of how effectively new technology was putting an end to surface raider operations.

Atlantis continued the search the entire following day while the aircraft technicians removed the plane's engine and replaced the supercharger. The repair work continued into the next day when the weather became too sour to launch the plane. The strong winds and high seas lasted until the early morning of 21 November, when the plane finally flew again. Bulla lifted off and disappeared on another search for an unescorted Allied merchant vessel. He returned low on fuel and with nothing to report. This time, Bulla set the plane down so hard that he ruptured a float. The float quickly filled with water and capsized the plane. Bulla had flown his last mission from *Atlantis*.

The crane operators saved the swamped plane, and a motor launch plucked Bulla and his observer out of the water, but *Atlantis* had to move on without a functional scout plane. The loss of the plane was a critical blow to the raider's security. Rogge had wanted to use it for long-range threat detection during U-boat refueling operations, and *Atlantis* had such a meeting scheduled for the following day. There was no possible way for the aircraft mechanics to uncrate and assemble the remaining aircraft in just one night.

Airplane or not, Rogge had to set course for "Flower Point Lily Ten." The captain asked his navigator to plot the meeting point on the map, and Kamenz hunkered down over his protractor and ruler and made his calculations. Within a few moments he had determined the location of their destination: a point near 4 degrees south latitude and 18 degrees west longitude, dangerously close to a busy sea lane and in a very narrow part of the Atlantic.

The position was northeast of Ascension Island, almost due north of where *Atlantis* had sunk *Tottenham* five months earlier. Kapitänleutnant Paul Kamenz had no idea that when he took his pencil and neatly put a small black cross on his navigation chart to mark the rendezvous point, he was also marking the spot of *Atlantis*'s grave.

11

Atlantis Is Lost

THE ORDERS INSTRUCTING *Atlantis* to act as a U-boat supply ship turned out to be a death warrant. The British navy was acutely aware of the orders and intentions of the German submarine force. Each day the Royal Navy received timely and meaningful information from the broken German naval codes; sometimes the British decoders were faster than the Germans. In his book *Very Special Intelligence* Patrick Beesly notes that "by the middle of May, the hoard of material captured from U-110 had reached B.P. [Bletchley Park] and had been put to speedy use. A flood of decrypted and translated signals concerning the operational U-boats began to pour into OIC [the Operational Intelligence Center]."[1]

The British South Atlantic shore commander, Adm. Algernon Willis, responded to the intelligence by assigning a hunter group called Task Force 3, commanded by Capt. A. W. S. Agar on the County-class heavy cruiser HMS *Dorsetshire*, to respond to direction-finding reports and search out and destroy the U-boat supply vessels. Admiral Willis reasoned that the supply ships would be much easier to find than the submarines, and sinking them would have virtually the same effect as sinking the subs. Without supplies, the U-boats would ultimately have to cease operations so far from home.

The British also had a good idea of where to look. Not only did they have Ultra decrypts providing intelligence from the deciphered German naval codes and messages, they also knew the South Atlantic very well. Their patrols were centered on the areas of calm seas where the Germans were expected to rendezvous and seek sanctuary. Captain Agar later wrote:

> It so happens that there are certain areas in this vast ocean where weather conditions are relatively calm compared with others. This knowledge, compiled from years of meteorological data, is of course well known on Oceanic charts, anticipating that they would be chosen for refueling rendezvous we were especially vigilant in these particular localities.[2]

Agar and Rogge would not meet at this time and place, but their paths were destined to cross in the future.

The dawn of 22 November 1941, brought calm seas and very clear skies. *Atlantis* lay stopped at the designated position awaiting the arrival of its expected companion. No one on board the raider noticed the speck in the sky that passed high overhead on the horizon. That speck was a Walrus seaplane launched from a nearby British warship. The pilot recorded the stopped ship's position as 4 degrees, 21 minutes south latitude and 18 degrees, 50 minutes west longitude and returned to his ship with the information. The plane's host ship, a British cruiser, turned and steamed at twenty-five knots along an intercept track to investigate the unknown ship laying to just forty miles away.

Shortly after the rising sun burned off what remained of the morning haze, a lookout aboard *Atlantis* broke the silence with an excited report. *U-126* had arrived. Before long the 1,540-ton, type IXC submarine was within hailing distance and the raider's crewmen were exchanging shouts and waves with the bearded men on the sub's cramped conning tower. *U-126* pulled up close and hove to near *Atlantis*'s stern. *Atlantis*'s men dropped the refueling lines over the stern and launched a motor boat to deliver the pipes and hawsers to the submarine. The U-boat's deck crew took on the hoses, connected the two ships together, and signaled *Atlantis* to begin pumping. The two ships rode the swells in unison as the fuel lines delivered the oil to the submarine.

Adjutant Mohr stood on deck and noted the contrast between the two warships. *Atlantis*, immense and broad-beamed, rose majestically from the water and cast a long, solid shadow. The submarine, in comparison, sat barely above the surface. Its thin, cylindrical hull seemed to be a part of the smoothly rolling waves, rolling with them and not on them. The submarine's diminutive island, its conning tower, cast a small, thin shadow. Mohr observed that both ships were hunters, yet they could not have been less alike.

Kapitänleutnant Ernst Bauer and seven of his submarine crewmen came over to *Atlantis* on the motor launch during one of its shuttle runs between the ships. Captain Rogge met Bauer on deck and, in his own words, "took him into my cabin where a specially prepared breakfast was waiting—white table cloth, airy cabin, peacetime ham and eggs, and a waiter dressed in the best Norddeutscher Lloyd tradition."[3]

Rogge was eager to hear firsthand news of the world, and especially of the war's progress. *U-126* had recently sailed from France, and Bauer knew all the latest news. Rogge was engrossed in the details of what he had missed when Kielhorn entered the cabin and disturbed the conversation with his report of a serious engine problem: the port-side diesel's number three piston had seized and required replacement. Kielhorn asked the captain for permission to disassemble the engine and begin repairs. Rogge agreed and instructed his chief engineer to commence the repairs immediately. Bauer and Rogge continued their discussion while the other submariners went off to arrange for hot baths, the ultimate luxury for a U-boat man.

At 8:16 A.M. on Saturday, 22 November 1941, a yell from above marked the beginning of the end for the German warship *Atlantis, Ship-16*. The excited screams of the lookouts brought everyone's eyes to bearing "red 20 degrees" and the sight of a three-funneled British warship climbing quickly over the horizon. The well-trained men acted instantly and without hesitation. The raider's crew severed and capped the fuel lines, cast them over the stern, and made a hasty dash to their action stations. The submarine initiated a crash dive.

U-126's decks cleared and began to disappear in a flurry of bubbles and foam within seconds of the alerting sirens. Captain Rogge rushed from his cabin to the bridge and ordered the operational engine to full speed ahead. He also dispatched a runner to order Kielhorn to have the port engine assembled and running as soon as possible. Kapitänleutnant Bauer made it to *Atlantis*'s deck just in time to see his submarine submerge under the command of his young first officer, Oberleutnant-zur-See Kurt Neubert. Bauer stood at the ship's rail cursing his diving ship for leaving him behind.

Rogge put *Atlantis* into a hard turn under the power of the one functioning engine. He wanted to show the approaching cruiser only his stern, both to hide the distinguishing features of his ship's profile and to present the smallest possible target to the enemy ship. The turn also placed *Atlantis* between the U-boat and the English ship.

Captain Rogge studied the approaching ship. At 8:19 he recognized it as a British London-class heavy cruiser. In 1936, the Königsberg-class German cruiser *Karlsruhe* with Oberleutnant Rogge on board had berthed next to the British County-class cruiser *Dorsetshire* in Hong Kong during a round-the-world cruise. Rogge, as the first officer on *Karlsruhe*, had been invited to visit the British ship. When Rogge examined the approaching warship he realized he was under the guns of a sister ship of *Dorsetshire*, and he was in no position to engage in a gun battle.

The ship that maneuvered at seventeen knots and stood off at a range far beyond the reach of *Atlantis*'s guns was HMS *Devonshire*. The twelve-year-old, 9,750-ton cruiser far outclassed the auxiliary raider *Atlantis* as a warship. *Devonshire* carried eight 203-mm guns and a wide array of 100-mm guns, pom-poms, machine guns, and other offensive and defensive weapons. The 203-mm guns could strike without ever coming into range of *Atlantis*'s 150-mm guns. Rogge could not run, either. The British cruiser's Parsons-geared turbines could drive it through the water at just over thirty-two knots, more than fourteen knots faster than *Atlantis*'s top speed. Captain Rogge, understanding the severity of the situation, sent around the order to confirm that all of his men were wearing their life jackets.

Rogge and the officers of the bridge watched through their binoculars as the English ship catapulted its Walrus scout plane into the air once again. Soon the pesky little craft was circling over *Atlantis*. The plane buzzed in for quick swoops and close passes, all the while inspecting and photographing the suspicious ship. In frustration, the seamen on deck began shouting threats and calling for machine guns to shoot down the plane. Rogge silenced the men and reminded them that they were not to bare a single gun. Their only chance at survival was to convince *Devonshire* that *Atlantis* was a Dutch merchant ship.

Unfortunately, the long, snakelike refueling line floating near the ship surrounded by a conspicuous patch of oil and the cigar-shaped black silhouette of a submerged submarine outlined against the blue water were dead giveaways that *Atlantis* was no merchant ship. Rogge was not surprised to see the plane flash out a signal to *Devonshire*. The plane sent "SSSS," signifying the presence of a submarine. Captain Rogge realized that his only option now was to stall and give *U-126* time to close and set up a torpedo attack.

When the airplane notified Capt. R. D. Oliver, *Devonshire*'s commanding officer, that a submarine was present, the captain decided to fire a warning salvo at the still unidentified ship. At 8:37 *Devonshire*'s 203-mm guns unleashed two shells toward the raider. The shots were fired with two purposes. First, they were a reminder to Rogge that his ship was within range of the cruiser's mighty cannons, and second, they were intended to provoke *Atlantis* to reveal its true identity by returning fire. Oliver hoped his warning shells would induce the crew to abandon their ship, eliminating any need to shell the ship directly. The British captain wished to limit the bloodshed, especially because he suspected that the ship, if it turned out to be a German auxiliary tender, might also carry British prisoners.

Rogge continued to maintain his camouflage. One shell landed short, and the second sent an exploding column of water skyward ahead of *Atlantis*'s bow. Rogge knew exactly what the exploding shells meant. He had sent the same signal many times over the past eighteen months. The shells told Rogge his ship was perfectly bracketed by the big guns. Rogge ordered his ship stopped and turned broadside to the British cruiser.

A signalman ran up the flags reading "I am stopped." Another man used a captured British signal lamp to flash out "*Polyphemus*." Captain Rogge instructed his radiomen to send a fake distress call in the standard British format. The radio operators broadcast a raider warning transmitting the message "RRR ... *Polyphemus* ... RRR ... Unidentified ship has ordered me to stop ... RRR ... *Polyphemus* ..."[4]

Rogge's tactics bought him a little more time. Captain Oliver was confused by the cry for help. He certainly did not want to shell an innocent merchant ship. The presence of the German submarine, though suspicious, did not necessarily mean that the larger ship was a German supply ship. Perhaps the U-boat had been in the process of stopping the ship. Oliver resolved to ascertain the target ship's true identity before beginning an attack aimed to hit. He requested confirmation from the British Admiralty as to the whereabouts of the Dutch merchant vessel *Polyphemus*. While the British naval authorities determined the location of *Polyphemus,* Oliver was careful to keep his ship at a range exceeding fifteen thousand yards and continually altered its course and speed, making it exceedingly difficult for a submarine to launch a torpedo attack.

Captain Rogge told his men that the English would soon discover the location of the real *Polyphemus,* and that would put an end to the waiting. Rogge's only true hope for the survival of his ship was to maintain his disguise long enough for the accompanying submarine to attack. Unfortunately, the extreme range and the cruiser's ever-changing speed had left the U-boat in no position to conduct an attack.

Meanwhile, Captain Oliver was considering his options. Despite Rogge's attempts at disguise, Oliver was not at all convinced of *Polyphemus*'s authenticity. The fact that the ship had broadcast its SOS in the three-letter group "RRR" instead of the recently changed four-letter group "RRRR" helped resolve Oliver's suspicions. The order to change the letter groups from three to four was designed to catch enemy wireless operators from tricking Allied stations with bogus transmissions. The Germans were not aware of the change, and that was a critical flaw in their Dutch camouflage.

Atlantis's time was quickly running out. *Devonshire* flashed out a message instructing *Atlantis* to stay in position, then used its large searchlight to blink out a coded message. The signalmen on *Atlantis* had no idea what type of secret call sign was required in response to the British request, so they ignored the British signal.

Throughout the standoff, the seaplane continued to badger the raider. The pilot circled while the observer compared a photograph of the known German raider *Atlantis* with the ship below. The photograph was a copy of the full-length shot of *Atlantis* posing as *Tamesis* taken by David Scherman, the American photographer who was on *Zamzam* when *Atlantis* sank it. It was this photo, published in the 23 June 1941 issue of *Life* magazine and later distributed by intelligence agencies to all the Allied services, that unmasked the German ship. The plane reported to Oliver that the unknown vessel appeared to be the same ship as the one in the photo, adding that the stern was nearly identical. He concluded his spotting report with the information that the target matched all points of a suspicious German ship as described in Weekly Intelligence Report 64.

At 9:34 A.M. the British commander in chief of Freetown replied to *Devonshire*'s query. His dispatch confirmed that the ship under Oliver's guns was an impostor. One minute later the cruiser's turrets belched great clouds of smoke and orange flame. *Devonshire* had begun firing for effect. There would be no escape for *Atlantis*.

The first two shells missed, but just barely. They showered *Atlantis* with red-hot splinters and boiling water. Oberleutnant Kasch begged his commander to unmask the guns and allow him to return fire as a matter of honor. Captain Rogge reiterated his order to keep the guns covered and maintain the disguise. He called for all-out flank speed and ordered a turn hard to starboard in one final, desperate escape attempt.

Just as the raider got under way, *Devonshire*'s shells struck home. The first shells hit the hatch covers for the hanger deck, demolishing them and starting several fires. The shells also knocked out critical electrical, mechanical, and communication systems. The electrical steering was out, but Rogge continued to order manual course changes. He twisted and turned his ship evasively, but he could not escape the shell fire of the cruiser standing off ten miles away. Rogge continued to drive his ship generally south-southwest as two more 203-mm shells came crashing down on the aft control room and torpedo room. Captain Rogge tried one last gamble by continuing to sail away, hoping to draw the cruiser into the jaws of the waiting submarine.

When the cruiser maintained its distance, Rogge ordered his ship to create a smokescreen and slow to one and a half knots. The acrid white cloud of the smokescreen mixed with the gray-black smoke of *Atlantis*'s burning structures almost obscured the ship from its attacker. Unable to see its target, *Devonshire* tried to use its radar fire-control system, with terrible results. Oliver decided to check his fire until he could again clearly discern the target.

Rogge used the slow headway of his ship to keep it under the control of the rudder and within the protection of the smokescreen. He could not risk the lives of his crew any longer. The cruiser had the range locked in, and the disabled raider's slow maneuvers were fruitless. Finally, he gave the order: "All hands to the lifeboats and leave the ship."[5] While Rogge kept *Atlantis* inside the smokescreen, the men took to the boats, each coolly waiting for his turn to leave the beloved warship. Rogge later commented that the men's conduct during this time was exemplary. His crew executed the evacuation order quickly and calmly, as if they were conducting a practice drill. If the smoke had not blocked *Devonshire*'s gunfire, the men on *Atlantis*'s crowded decks and rails would have been massacred by a rain of explosive shells.

Nearly the entire crew was off the stricken ship at 9:43 when the smoke cleared and *Devonshire* opened fire once again. The new round of exploding shells blew hatches four and five apart and demolished the boat deck and bridge area. The only men left on board were Captain Rogge, Leutnant Mohr, Stabsobersteuermann Wilhelm Pigors, and Leutnant Fehler and his small demolition party. As Fehler and his men went to plant their charges, Mohr rushed to his cabin for his camera. He wanted to get a final photograph of *Atlantis* as it sank. He raced along the twisted, smoldering wreckage that had once been deck works and passageways. Entering the ship, he slipped and fell on a section of slick, blood-covered deck plating. Continuing onward, he saw that the entire ship's upper works were in shambles. There were dozens of fires dancing around the deck and peeking out from portals. The black smoke twisted its way up and wrapped around the broken and collapsed remnants of the masts and poles. Mohr reached his cabin and grabbed his camera just as another huge shell struck home, shaking *Atlantis* with a violent explosion. Mohr made a dash for the open deck, reaching the open planking just as another explosive projectile slammed into the ship and knocked nearly every man to his knees. The pounding was taking its toll; *Atlantis* began to list heavily to port and slowly go down by the stern.

Fehler and his team emerged from a smoky doorway leading into the ship's interior. Shortly afterward, the first scuttling charge rumbled from deep within the ship. With his work aboard the ship complete, Fehler led his men into the water.

Pigors was screaming at his captain to jump, but Rogge stood firm as he solemnly surveyed his twisted and burning ship. The ravaged ship's once-hidden guns were now uncovered and turned askew, some pointing skyward, their coverings and disguises either burning or blasted off. Rogge's attention seemed focused on something far away until Pigors approached him and yelled, "My Captain, it is pointless to stay aboard and go down with the ship. You have done all you can do here." He pointed at the men in the water below and said, "There, Captain, the men, they are what still need you."[6]

Rogge told Stabsobersteuermann Pigors to jump overboard and leave him alone. The seasoned old noncommissioned officer looked at his commanding officer and refused, adding that if Rogge went down with the ship, he was going to go down with it as well. This threat brought Rogge back to reality and convinced the captain to leave the ship. His crew, now without a ship, still needed their commander.

Captain Rogge watched as Mohr stepped over the rail on the lee side and jumped. Rogge asked Pigors if anyone else was on board and was told that the rest of the crew was in the water. Rogge then told his chief petty officer that it was time for both of them to leave the ship. The two men hurried down the sloping deck of the fiery ship and jumped. After swimming to a safe distance, they watched as five more salvos poured down onto the battered ship, which slowly settled lower and lower in the water.

When the ship's boat deck hit the waterline, a figure appeared at one of the hatches. A radioman, Oberfunkgefreiter Heinz Müller, had stayed at his post until he realized the ship was sinking beneath him. Müller stumbled to the edge of the deck and stepped into the water.

The shelling stopped at 9:56 A.M. *Devonshire* had fired thirty salvos at the German ship. At 10:02, *Atlantis*'s ammunition magazine exploded with a terrific boom. The men struggling and bobbing in the water and others already in boats watched as their proud ship slowly sank deeper and deeper. Twelve minutes later there was a powerful explosion from within the bowels of the ship. *Atlantis* shuddered and began sinking rapidly over the stern.

At 10:16, the German warship's bow rose straight out of the water and exposed the ugly scar cut into the hull by the granite spike at Kerguelen Island. The bow rapidly slid down with a great hissing of steam, and the ship finally disappeared from view.[7] The German raider had neither responded to *Devonshire*'s gunfire nor run up the battle ensign. Rogge maintained his merchant ship disguise throughout the entire attack. The men gave their ship three rousing cheers and then turned their attention to the British warship, fully expecting it to approach and take them aboard.

Captain Oliver had made a sincere attempt to limit casualties during the attack. He had ordered his gunners to arm their shells with delayed fuses instead of impact fuses, which allowed the shells to penetrate into the ship before exploding. They still caused considerable damage to the target, but the shells did not explode on deck, where the men had gathered. Despite his concern for preserving life, however, Captain Oliver did not bring *Devonshire* in to pick up the survivors. Any attempt to rescue them would expose his ship to a torpedo attack from the U-boat, whose whereabouts were unknown. *Devonshire* would not repeat the tragic *Aboukir* incident of September 1914.

During the First World War, the British cruiser *Aboukir*, sailing in company with two sister ships, was torpedoed and sunk by a German U-boat. When the other two ships stopped to pick up *Aboukir*'s survivors, they were torpedoed and sunk as well. The circumstances here may have been different, but they were just similar enough to warrant caution. Consequently, Oliver decided not to rescue the survivors. *Devonshire* swung around and departed on a northwestern heading. The ship stopped at 10:40 A.M. to pick up its seaplane and then faded from view over the horizon.[8]

The shipwrecked German sailors bobbed in the water, each man thinking his own thoughts. Rogge was crushed by guilt. His decision to maintain his disguise and not fire his guns had denied *Atlantis* the glory of a final battle. He had wanted to allow his ship to fight back, but engaging the British cruiser would have meant great loss of life among his crew and no damage whatsoever to the enemy. He had chosen the only course of action that would allow his crew to survive and fight on.

12

Sunk and Rescued—Twice

AS THE BRITISH warship sailed away, the survivors—nearly 350 men—drifted in boats and rafts, swam, or clung to floating wreckage among the debris left behind by *Atlantis*. An explosive blast had split open the ship's safe, spilling secret Kriegsmarine papers all over the surface of the sea. The men spent most of their first thirty minutes in the water tearing up all the documents they could find.

Just over forty minutes after the sinking, someone began to scream "Sharks! Sharks!" Sure enough, the men could easily distinguish the dorsal fins of sharks patrolling in and around the floating debris. The fish glided in and out between the swimming and floating men, who wildly punched and kicked at them. Fortunately, the sharks restricted their attacks to the bodies of those killed in the shelling. The predators splashed and twisted in the water, mauling the floating bodies, but they left the living alone.

The survivors consisted of *Atlantis*'s officers and crewmen; Kapitänleutnant Bauer and seven other *U-126* crewmen who had been away from their submarine when the attack commenced; and the one remaining prisoner, Frank Vicovari, a neutral American. The shelling of *Zamzam* had left him with severe wounds in both legs that required continued medical care. When all of the other detainees and prisoners had been evacuated to *Dresden*, Vicovari was not fit to travel, so he remained on board *Atlantis* as the only prisoner. In a magazine article written after the war, Vicovari related that he was in the ship's hospital ward reading Joseph Conrad's *The Rescue* when the attack began. He initially planned to kill as many Germans as possible during the confusion of the shelling, but when Dr. Reil entered the ward to wish him well, shake his hand, and usher him to a lifeboat, he could not bring himself to act.[1]

The survivors began drifting farther and farther apart until Rogge clambered into a lifeboat, stood up, and began calling for the men to assemble around his boat while the boatswain piped the call to muster. Rogge's call brought organization back to his crew. The men began to paddle, row, or swim toward their captain.

While the crew was closing in around Rogge, *U-126* finally surfaced. Leutnant Neubert cranked open the submarine's hatch expecting to be received like a rescuing angel. Instead, the young officer found himself face-to-face with his furious commander. Bauer demanded to know why Neubert had not attacked the cruiser. The first officer explained that he did go to periscope depth and begin to track *Devonshire*, but massive explosions all around the submarine led him to believe that he was under attack. The young officer mistakenly assumed that *Devonshire*'s first gun salvo aimed at *Atlantis* was a depth-charge attack against his submarine. He took *U-126* down to three hundred feet and remained there, eliminating any chance of an offensive action against the British cruiser. At this point Captain Rogge came to the young man's defense. Rogge told Bauer the cruiser had maintained a highly defensive posture that made a torpedo attack unfeasible in any case.

As Rogge assembled his crew, he received one last farewell token from his sunken ship. An empty cutter came exploding through the surface of the water. The boat had gone down with *Atlantis* but broke free and rocketed toward the surface, propelled by the pocket of air trapped inside it. Rogge dispatched a boat crew to secure the newly floated metal cutter and return it to the assembly point.

It was nearly noon by the time all the men had gathered around Captain Rogge. He took stock of the assembled crew. They were grouped together on five rubber rafts, three steel cutters, two motor launches, and a mass of lashed-together debris. The captain conducted a head count and roll call.

Mohr scanned the men's faces, searching for those who served directly with him. One man was missing. Matrosenobergefreiter Willi Krooß, Mohr's helmsmen on nearly two dozen boardings, was not present.[2]

The roll call identified Krooß and three other men—Oberbootsmannmaat Anton Dettenhofer, Obermechanikersmaat Horst Gerstenhauer, and Matrosenobergefreiter Johann Schäfer—as casualties of the cruiser's guns. A fifth man was lost after the shelling. Oberfunkgefreiter Heinz Müller, the radioman Rogge had observed jumping from the ship just as it began to go down, was never seen again. There were scores more men wounded during the shelling, including Kapitänleutnant Kühn. The two doctors and four medical orderlies worked their way across the rafts, boats, and floating debris treating wounds ranging from scratches and shell splinters to concussion, trauma, and broken bones.

Captain Rogge boarded the submarine and discussed his next course of action with Bauer. Somehow, the shipwrecked men had to be taken to safety. The two officers concluded that the submarine would have to tow the lifeboats to the nearest landfall. After eliminating most of the suggestions, the officers were left with two destinations: either the closer British-controlled port of Freetown, on the West African coast, or Pernambuco, Brazil, on South America's easternmost projection, more than 950 open sea miles away.

If they went to Freetown, the men would either surrender and sit out the remainder of the war as prisoners or struggle to avoid capture and covertly return to Germany. Freetown did not appeal to Rogge in either case. He refused to simply float into a British port and surrender his men, and escape and evasion seemed impossible considering the number of men involved and the distance they would need to travel. He recalled the plight of the two officers from *Graf Spee* while they were in hiding. The two men endured several hellish months on the run with little to eat and a schedule of constant hiding, fleeing, and sneaking along the underground network before secretly boarding the supply ship *Dresden*. Rogge vetoed Freetown and decided on the long-distance journey to the Brazilian coast. He emerged from the U-boat, went to his crew, and explained his plan.

After finishing the briefing, the captain set out to put his plan into action. The scheme called for the U-boat to tow the men to Brazil on a twelve-day voyage. Within the next four hours Bauer signaled Adm. Karl Dönitz, the flag officer of U-boats at the Befehlshaber der Unterseeboote (the U-boat command center, or BdU), notifying him that *Atlantis* had been sunk by an English 10,000-ton cruiser and that *U-126* was towing the survivors to South America. Bauer's report also added that it was essential that the submarine receive replenishment.

Rogge dispersed his men evenly on the boats and had them rig towlines to the submarine. At 4:00 P.M. on 22 November 1941, *U-126* headed west for the coast of Brazil. The submarine and its motley train of boats encountered only clear skies, fine weather, and following seas as they moved along at about six or seven knots.

It was lucky for the Germans that they got themselves moving so quickly. The British Admiralty dispatched two corvettes, HMS *Aster* and HMS *Marguerite*, to *Atlantis*'s last position to pick up the shipwrecked German crew. When they arrived at the designated location, they found an empty sea.

When *U-126*'s message reached the BdU, Grand Admiral Dönitz acted quickly. "When we received the news of this incident," he later noted in his memoirs, "I at once ordered two further U-boats, *U-124* and *U-129*, which were in the central Atlantic, to proceed to the scene and give assistance in towing the *Atlantis*'s lifeboats."[3]

Although Rogge knew that help was on the way, he did not count on its arrival. He planned on making the entire trip to safety under tow from only *U-126*. He placed the wounded men and those with a valuable specialty—fifty-five men in all—aboard the submarine. Ten officers, six chief petty officers, sixteen junior petty officers, and twenty-three sailors squeezed into every spare nook and cranny, more than doubling the crew complement and severely impairing the submarine's combat capability.

Another group of men were in boats towed behind the U-boat. Their emergency instructions called for them to cast off the towlines and allow the submarine to dive freely if the need should arise. Each of the four steel cutters and five rubber rafts was overloaded almost to the foundering point, with freeboards barely above the water's surface, and put under the command of an officer. Mohr's boat, for example, was designed for forty men but carried sixty.

Fifty-two men who could not find room in a boat or a raft were given life jackets and assigned to ride on the submarine's deck. Should the U-boat need to dive, those fifty-two men were expected to jump clear of the submerging submarine and swim for the nearest boat. The remaining small group of crewmen rode in the two powered motor launches. Rogge employed these two free-sailing boats as shuttles to carry food from the U-boat to the boats under tow.

For the first time in their almost two years at sea, the men of *Atlantis* fervently hoped that no smoke clouds or mastheads would appear on the horizon. Their progress was tortuously slow. Occasionally *U-126* was able to come up to seven knots, but it was rarely able to maintain that speed for very long. The yawing and pitching of the boats routinely broke the lines, and *U-126* either had to circle back and gather the tow load again or wait while the men frantically rowed their heavily laden boats back toward the submarine. Complete stops to allow the crew time to mend the towlines were frequent.

Whether they were under tow, on the submarine's deck, or in a motor launch, most of the men sat painfully in a small, extremely cramped space. During the first day they ate only a tiny portion of the survival rations from the lifeboats. The day's meal for each man was only a small piece of hardtack and some long-stored water. As the hours went by during that first day, the sun's heat added to their tribulations. The searing rays beat down relentlessly from the cloudless skies, heating the boats' surfaces and decking to unbearable temperatures and burning any bit of exposed skin. Only a few lucky men had shoes to protect their feet. The ones without shoes ripped clothing from their bodies to insulate their feet against the hot metal of the boats. Mohr later wrote that the men tried to escape their discomfort by sleeping. But they paid for the respite on waking, when long-motionless muscles burned and cramped. Rogge established a rotation schedule that allowed the men to move from the boats to the deck of the submarine, but there was no escape from the uncomfortable, cramped, and crowded conditions.

When the daylight began at last to fade, the men welcomed the night, but only briefly. When the sun disappeared, the temperature plummeted and the sunburned men shivered in the damp chill of the night. Funkgefreiter Johann Meyer still recalls the men's misery: "Because we were close to the equator we all wore only sport clothes.... [I]n day time the sun burn[ed] and at night it was extremely cold."[4] The evening brought more bad news and heartache for the crew. Despite the continued efforts of the doctors, two more men, Oberfunkgefreiter Ernst Felchner and Oberbootsmannmaat Emil Bührle, died from the injuries they sustained in the attack.

The next morning's sunrise resumed the scorching torture. The men's eyes and lips began to swell and crack. Their clothing, roughened by dried, caked-on salt, rubbed raw spots on their skin. At noon, Rogge and Bauer calculated and dead-reckoned their position. To their delight, the two officers learned that they had covered more than 150 miles during the first day. This revelation meant the trip would only take five or six days as opposed to the original plan's twelve days.

The announcement of this little bit of good news roused a small cheer from the tired, uncomfortable men. They were further heartened by the wonderful meal provided by *U-126*'s cook. The industrious cook supplied the combined crews of *Atlantis* and *U-126*, more than four hundred men, with a terrific hot meal using only the galley's few square feet of space and two electric hot plates. The submariners loaded the meals on the motor launches, and the small, free-running boats delivered the meals to the men under tow.

The breaking towlines presented a constant challenge. The men repaired and mended the lines until they finally became unusable. The submarine carried only a limited number of towropes aboard, so Rogge ensured that each mended line was used and used again until it could be used no longer. He was obviously concerned that the supply of lines would run out before the boats reached their destination, but the evening of the second day brought news that eased Rogge's worries.

U-126 received a message from the BdU informing Bauer and Rogge that the German Admiralty had directed a German supply ship and three more U-boats to rendezvous and assist *U-126*. The sailors' spirits rose considerably on hearing that more help was on the way. The relatively huge superstructure of the 3,664-ton U-boat tender *Python* appeared on the horizon the next day. The survivors' seventy-six-hour ordeal under tow had come to an end!

Python was the perfect rescue ship, an ex–passenger liner with ample food stores, many cabins, and quite a bit of free space. Before the war, *Python* had plied the seas for the African Fruit Company of Hamburg. The rescue ship was also well stocked with fresh food and had full fuel tanks because it had sailed from France less than a month before.

Python drew up near *U-126* and hove to, then used its immense sea cranes to quickly hoist *Atlantis*'s survivors up onto the decks. When Rogge was lifted up to the deck, he climbed aboard, offered a sharp naval salute to *Python*'s commanding officer, and stated, "I report myself and the crew of the auxiliary cruiser, *Atlantis,* aboard *Python.*"[5] *Python*'s captain responded that he was glad to have the sailors as his guests. Once the shipwrecked men were aboard, they insisted on using *Python*'s cranes to lift their metal motor launches up onto the decks as well. When asked why, an old petty officer from *Atlantis* simply responded, "You never know."

An hour after *Python* arrived, the men of *Atlantis* were waving down at *U-126* from the safety and comfort of the tender's decks. The crew of the supply ship ushered *Atlantis*'s men belowdecks and allowed them to shower or bathe and then shared their extra clothing with the needy survivors. Rogge and the officers picked their accommodations from the unoccupied cabins. Rogge's cabin selection was ironic in that he chose the same berth he had occupied five years earlier when he sailed to England to attend the coronation of George VI.

When Rogge and several officers went to the forecastle to check on the crew's berthing assignments they found the forecastle area far too small and cramped to house the men comfortably. Rogge suggested that they move to an open space in the hold and dispatched an officer to make the necessary arrangements. Within a short while the crew had carried their mattresses down into an open hold, delighted at the space, a blessing to men who had been squatting or sitting on each other for the last three days. For the first time since the sinking of their warship they could lie down, stretch out, and sleep; but first their hungry stomachs drew them to the galley. The cooks aboard *Python* turned out a large and hearty meal for the hungry survivors. The men topped off their rescue with helping after helping. Rogge described it best: "We fell like wolves on our first real meal. It tasted marvelous and we washed it down with brandy and coffee."[6]

As the shipwrecked crew showered and ate, *U-126* refueled from *Python*'s tanks and replaced the food stores the 350 extra men had devoured during the three-day trek. The U-boat sailed away at dusk on Monday, 24 November, hauling for the French coast.[7] Later that evening, *Python* too set sail for France. While they made their way toward home the supply ship's radiomen overheard a battle report from a nearby U-boat. *U-124* sent a dispatch to submarine headquarters outlining the sinking of a British cruiser about nine hundred miles west of Freetown, near Saint Paul's Rocks.[8]

The crew of *Atlantis* quickly settled into the routine of being passengers. Though they had no assigned duties, some men helped out by augmenting *Python*'s lookouts. The raider's lookouts proved to be much keener-eyed than the new and untested crew of the supply ship. The balance of the raider's crew sat around, went to meals, and slept.

Rogge, a warship captain, was now a passenger on a supply ship hoping for a safe return to German-controlled waters. Although he had no official standing on *Python,* he spent much of his time on the bridge keeping tabs on the ship's position and operations. During his free time Rogge reflected on *Atlantis*'s encounter with the British warship and pondered things he could have done differently. Although he had made a conscious decision to keep his guns covered and hide his ship's identity from the British, Rogge was still not completely comfortable with his choice. On 25 November, Rogge opened *Atlantis*'s *Kriegstagebuch,* the war diary, and penned the very last entry for the warship:

> After successfully carrying out her mission and covering 102,000 miles in 622 days at sea, *Atlantis* was located and destroyed when on the point of returning home and while engaged upon a supply-operation which was not included in her operational orders.... Our bitterness at the loss of our ship has been intensified by the thought that we had to abandon her without a fight.[9]

Python received two wireless transmissions on Friday, 28 November. The first message ended Rogge's self-doubt and provided some consolation regarding the loss of his ship. The transmission contained a personal note from Grand Admiral Raeder to Rogge that read: "I approve your decision to save your crew and maintain your disguise by scuttling your ship when you had no chance of offering resistance."[10] The day's second transmission turned *Python* away from France toward a refueling spot some seventeen hundred sea miles from where *Atlantis* had been sunk. Once again, the crew of

Atlantis found themselves sailing away from Germany on orders from Naval High Command. The location charted out halfway between the coded map locations "Flower Point Rose" and "Flower Point Dandelion." The order instructed *Python* to meet and resupply four U-boats in that location on two separate dates.

First, *Python* was to meet both Merten's *U-68* and Korvettenkapitän Eckermann's *UA* on the last day of November. Then the supply ship was to wait for the arrival of Kapitänleutnant Jochen Mohr's type IXB boat *U-124* and Kapitänleutnant Nicolai Clausen's type IXC submarine *U-129* on 4 December.

Python met *U-68* as planned about seven hundred miles south of Saint Helena on Sunday, 30 November 1941, under a slow, heavy swell. Merten's patrol off the southeastern coast of Africa had been successful and he was once again in need of supplies and fuel. Scarcely two weeks had passed since the submarine commander had been a guest on *Atlantis*, but this time Rogge and Merten met as guests on another captain's ship.

The other submarine, *UA*, was delayed; it arrived just after dawn on the morning of 1 December. The officers of the three ships met and decided to remain where they were to conduct the resupply operation. The weather reports indicated that the safer areas to the north were too rough for the crews to transfer torpedoes. With the decision made to stay, the movement of supplies began. *Python*'s deck was soon abuzz with activity. Men crowded boxes of food and cases of ammunition on deck, preparing to transfer the goods to the U-boats. Long, flexible fuel lines snaked out over *Python*'s sides to the fuel-starved U-boats while the supply ship's cranes pulled torpedoes from the hold and set them into the water. The scene more resembled ships in port preparing to set sail than operational ships on the high seas. *Atlantis*'s crewmen lounged belowdecks or ambled around the boat deck as the work went on around them.

The routine activity ended abruptly at about 3:30 P.M. when one of *Atlantis*'s sharp-eyed crewmen spotted a three-funneled ship closing from nineteen miles. *Python*'s green and untested lookouts, even those in the crow's nest, did not notice the approaching mastheads until the men from the raider alerted them. The supply operation stopped with the clanging of the alarm bells. Men scampered about the deck capping fuel lines, stowing the cranes, recovering the boats, and preparing to take evasive action.

Within minutes the lookouts could plainly identify the approaching ship as a British cruiser. The two U-boats cast off the mooring lines and hoses connecting them to *Python*. Merten's boat was the first to dive, even though the crew had been loading a torpedo through an open deck hatch when the alarm sounded. The crewmen hastily crammed the torpedo inside the submarine and secured the deck hatches as the submarine began its descent. Because the boat was in the midst of receiving and stowing supplies, it was out of trim and was not prepared or properly configured to submerge. In his book *The Sea Wolves*, Wolfgang Frank writes that *U-68* "stood on her head and plunged toward the bottom like a stone."[11] The submarine plummeted past its maximum operating depth before the frantic crew was able to bring the boat under control and begin the slow ascent back toward the surface. The submarine had been saved, but any hope of an attack was spoiled. *UA*'s descent was far less dramatic. Korvettenkapitän Eckermann conducted a controlled crash dive and slowly disappeared beneath a foaming patch of sea.

Meanwhile, Korvettenkapitän Lueders ordered *Python* brought up to full speed and steered away toward the northeast. Lueders's call for flank speed caused *Python*'s cold fireboxes to puff out a huge cloud of black smoke and disgorge a shower of glowing embers. The German supply ship's maximum speed of fourteen knots was less than half of the cruiser's flank speed, making flight hopeless, but Lueders hoped to draw the enemy warship across the bows of the two submerged submarines.

The English cruiser reacted to *Python*'s attempt to run by increasing its speed and turning onto a direct intercept course with the fleeing ship. Rogge could plainly see that the approaching enemy was a British warship, specifically, a County-class heavy cruiser very similar to the ship that sank *Atlantis*. HMS *Dorsetshire*, a twelve-year-old, 9,950-ton cruiser, was a formidable opponent.

Capt. A. W. S. Agar, RN, the commanding officer of *Dorsetshire*, had seen large patches of oil in the water and several small boats running about in the target ship's vicinity. To Agar, this indicated that the ship was either an Allied ship stopped to pick up survivors from a U-boat attack or a German ship stopped to replenish U-boats. *Dorsetshire* signaled the unknown ship and requested a response.

Korvettenkapitän Lueders ordered his signalmen to ignore the cruiser's signals and directed the helmsman to continue to flee. At this point, *Python*'s only hope for survival rested with the two U-boats. The course Lueders set did draw the British ship within range of the submarines, but no torpedoes relieved *Python* from the British cruiser's guns.

U-68 was unable to engage the enemy due to the problems experienced in the crash dive. *UA* did attack the British ship. Korvettenkapitän Eckermann maneuvered his ship into a firing position and launched five torpedoes in two separate spreads, but from too great a range.[12] The extreme range and an error in the setup calculations that underestimated the cruiser's speed caused the torpedoes to go astray and miss the target.

The cruiser continued to close until it reached a range of eleven miles, then sent a warning salvo to either side of *Python*. The massive explosions to port and starboard confirmed to Lueders that his ship was within range and bracketed by the warship's main guns. Captain Lueders had no option. He turned his ship stern-on the English cruiser, hove to, and ordered the ship abandoned and scuttled.

Atlantis's motor cutters were the first boats filled with men and lowered. *Python*'s crew, who had initially balked at bringing the boats along, suddenly appreciated the foresight of the *Atlantis* crewmen who had insisted that they hoist the cutters aboard. The motor launches, which were stored on the deck, had been kept fully provisioned and ready for use. They were quickly manned and put over the sides.

Next went *Python*'s own lifeboats. In addition to their survival rations, these boats received a complete stock of food and water from the supplies earmarked for the U-boats, which had been sitting on the deck ready for transfer when the cruiser made its appearance. Additionally, *Atlantis*'s men, remembering the frigid nights under tow, rushed to the storerooms and secured warm clothing before departing the ship.

When the evacuation of *Python* was about 75 percent complete, a seaman, thinking he was protecting the crew, started the ship's smoke generators on the stern. Soon a thick white cloud of smoke covered the ship's stern. The seasoned veterans from *Atlantis* cursed and yelled for the man to stop making smoke. The smokescreen would only provoke the English into firing again. If the cruiser's officers saw the men leaving the supply ship, they most likely would continue to hold their fire. The frightened seaman switched off the machine and the smoke quickly cleared. Captain Agar on *Dorsetshire* held his fire.

The ten cutters and lifeboats towed the seven rubber rafts away from *Python*, leaving only Korvettenkapitän Lueders, Leutnant-zur-See Fehler, and a small demolition party on board. The captain destroyed the ship's secret papers while men poured gasoline around the ship's decks and lit fires. Belowdecks, Fehler's men planted and ignited the scuttling charges. When their particular duties were completed, the men all met on the foredeck and took to the last remaining lifeboat.

Agar, watching the evacuation from a range of about eight miles, recognized the efficient and orderly manner in which the crew left the ship. The procedure appeared to be a well-rehearsed and practiced naval evolution, not the helter-skelter movements of a panicky merchant crew fleeing a cargo ship. Captain Agar also noticed that the ship had an extremely large crew for a merchant ship. These two facts combined with the large patches of oil floating around his victim made him suspect a trap, and he decided against approaching to rescue the survivors. Agar assumed, correctly, that the ship under his guns was a German naval ship, perhaps a U-boat supply vessel. He also concluded that the many extra men were reserve or augmentation crewmen for U-boats operating in the area. Agar kept *Dorsetshire* at a safe standoff range and continually maneuvered his ship erratically at speeds between eighteen and twenty-eight knots to protect against U-boat counterattacks.

At 5:51 P.M., *Dorsetshire*'s watch spotted a fire on *Python*'s bridge and foredeck. The flames spread rapidly until they engulfed the entire deck and were as high as the funnel. A black-and-gray tower of thick, billowing smoke rose vertically from the ship as it sat dead in the water. At 6:05, a dull thud resonated through *Python* as the scuttling charges exploded within the holds. The ship slowly listed to port until it rolled all the way over and exposed its keel to the sky. *Python* disappeared at 6:21 P.M. on 1 December 1941, leaving 414 men floating in eleven hard-sided boats and seven rubber rafts.

The cruiser *Dorsetshire* hauled off to the south to avoid an attack by the

U-boats the British captain was certain lay in wait for him near the survivors.[13] After the warship was out of sight, the U-boats broke through the surface. *UA* was the first to appear. Eckermann drew near the boats and began at once to tell Rogge and the others of his difficulty attacking the cruiser because of its unpredictable movements and inconsistent speed.

Then *U-68* surfaced nearby. Merten had his own tale to tell. He was just beginning to recount his submarine's plunge into the abyss when one of the U-boat lookouts cried out, "Alarm! Aircraft in sight!" A Walrus seaplane was fast approaching from the south, where *Dorsetshire* had disappeared. Both U-boats quickly cleared their decks and retreated beneath the waves once again.

The men of *Atlantis* and *Python* sat in their boats shaking their fists and cursing the bothersome seaplane. The boats danced lightly on the waves as the aircraft slowly circled to observe the scene below. The men in the boats waited, expecting the plane to release bombs or begin machine-gunning the boats. The plane did not attack. It orbited the area for a few minutes and then flew away, heading back to its ship.

Once again, Rogge took charge and called for the men to close in around his boat. The crews of *Python* and *Atlantis* paddled their boats and rubber dinghies until all eighteen craft were gathered together. As the officers conducted a roll call, the U-boats' periscopes broke the surface and carefully surveyed the surrounding area to ensure that it was again safe to surface. By the time the two U-boats emerged, Rogge had determined that all of the men were present and accounted for. The crews had evacuated *Python* without losing a single man.

When *UA* and *U-68* drew close to the cluster of floating lifeboats, Rogge went over to *U-68* and called a meeting with the two U-boat captains. Korvettenkapitän Eckermann of *UA* immediately asserted his right to command the entire expedition because he was the senior officer in command of an operational warship.

Kapitän-zur-See Rogge and Korvettenkapitän Merten disagreed. Rogge reminded Eckermann that he was a full captain; regardless of who commanded what ship, he was senior by rank and thus entitled to command. Merten added that Berlin would almost certainly object to Eckermann's apparent disregard for the established rules of rank and precedence. After several more minutes of discussion, Eckermann conceded command to Captain Rogge. *U-68* became the senior ship because Rogge was embarked on that submarine.

With the issue of command settled, the three commanders then agreed that the U-boats should tow the lifeboats to safety, just as *U-126* had done when *Atlantis* was sunk. Each submarine would embark one hundred men aboard, tow five full lifeboats, and position the loaded rubber rafts on their decks. It was long after dark on the night of 1 December when the two submarines began their journey toward a friendly port more than one-quarter of a world away.

As the U-boats sailed on their northwesterly course at barely six knots, Rogge and Merten dispatched a wireless report to the SKL informing Admiral Dönitz of the most recent turn of events.[14] Shortly after the flotilla set sail, *Atlantis's* officers worked out a plan that rotated the men from the interior of the submarine to the lifeboats, and from there to the rubber rafts that rested on the decks of the submarines. The men in the rafts had to don life vests and link arms to remain stable. The men moved between the three locations at regular intervals in order to ensure that each man had to endure similar conditions.

The eleventh boat, the motor cutter, commanded by Fehler, operated under its own power and shuttled supplies between the submarines and the boats. Fehler and his small crew ran between the submarines and the lifeboats almost constantly. They carried water to the men under the relentless near-equatorial sun during the day and supplied hot food, soup, and coffee during the chilly nights. Fehler also used his motor cutter to retrieve boats when the towlines to the U-boat snapped. This allowed the tow operation to continue making headway while the stray lifeboats were rounded up and brought back under tow. If contact with an unknown ship was established, the men in the lifeboats had orders to cast off their lines so the rafts would float away if the submarines needed to submerge. The men practiced this important evolution every morning to keep their reactions sharp and ready for a real emergency.

By dawn of the following morning, German Naval Command was aware of the loss of *Python*. When the information reached Admiral Dönitz, he issued orders to *U-124* and *U-129* directing them to proceed with all haste to intercept *UA* and *U-68* and assist with the rescue of the survivors. Both U-boats changed course and made for their new destination. Now, four hunters had been ordered away from the chase and detailed as rescuers.

Rogge later wrote that whenever he looked out at the train of lifeboats, he reflected on what good forethought it had been to recover *Atlantis*'s boats and keep them fully provisioned on *Python*'s deck. They had certainly proved their usefulness for more than four hundred German sailors, one Scottie dog, and an American detainee.

At noon on 2 December 1941, Eckermann reported his position and asked *U-124* and *U-129* to monitor the Africa wavelength.[15] Both *UA* and *U-68* then began transmitting quite a bit of radio chatter. Eckermann's boat sent out a nearly constant steam of information and reported spurious positions at routine intervals. The more experienced commander, Merten in *U-68,* generated less wireless traffic but also routinely transmitted his position, and his fix was correct. Rogge worried that the many messages going back and forth would allow the British to fix the locations of the boats regardless of the positions they reported. *Atlantis*'s radiomen had often used such broadcasts to backtrack and locate ships, and Rogge knew that the British used the same methods. Captain Rogge kept his concerns to himself until Eckermann dispatched a message giving his location and asking *U-124* for its position! Fortunately, Jochen Mohr of *U-124* responded only to Dönitz's initial request, and only with the brief message "Marinequadrat F T 83. 113 cbm. Mohr."[16] Apparently, he, like Rogge, recognized the danger of radio banter. When the three other U-boat commanders reached a lull in their wireless chatter, Rogge voiced his concerns and then ordered them to limit future transmissions.

Late in the afternoon on 2 December 1941, Korvettenkapitän Merten scanned the horizon all around his boat and caught sight of an enemy merchant vessel far off on the horizon. Merten briefly considered sounding the alarm and pursuing the ship, but he realized that his primary responsibility at that time was the safety of the shipwrecked sailors. Reluctantly, Merten allowed the enemy ship to fade from view unmolested.

Korvettenkapitän Eckermann proved less considerate of his duty. The following morning he displayed yet another example of his hunger for fame and his disrespect for authority when, over Rogge's protests, he cast loose the lifeboats and rubber dinghies in order to pursue a merchant ship. When *UA* returned from the unsuccessful attack that afternoon, Rogge dressed Eckermann down for endangering so many men, but *UA*'s commander vigorously defended his actions. He was still in command of an operational warship, he explained, and as such he was duty-bound to attack enemy shipping. Rogge did not agree, especially in light of the SKL's orders, but he could not argue with Eckermann's logic.

The late afternoon of 3 December brought a very welcome sight. All hands turned to see the source of a lookout's excited announcement: a U-boat approaching off the ships' bows! The approaching boat was *U-129*, commanded by Kapitänleutnant Nico Clausen. Without delay *U-129* hove to next to the rescue flotilla and began taking on men. Clausen's boat was able to accommodate Captain Lueders and all but three men from the crew of *Python*. *U-129* was low on fuel, so Rogge ordered the submarine to remain with the other boats and accompany them to port.

The inclusion of another U-boat eased the crowding in the boats slightly, but the men were still cramped and uncomfortable. By the third day, the men were sitting and squatting in what Rogge called a "sleepless coma." Adjutant Mohr described the suffering as one who knew it well: "And all around them all the heat haze hovered, an agony to the eyes, and vanishing only when the stars came out, the clear hard stars that heralded the cold."[17]

The three U-boats continued sailing north with the flotilla of rescue craft. They had not received any word from *U-124*, leading Rogge to surmise that Mohr's submarine had probably been sunk. He decided to plan on returning to German territory with only three U-boats. Captain Rogge realized that the crew could not continue much further in the exposed boats. His men had been blessed with calm water and following seas for the first part of their journey, but as they got farther north, the weather was increasingly likely to sour. The men could not survive the icy northern seas in open boats. Acting on that worry and the constant fear that enemy warships would come upon his exposed and helpless men, Captain Rogge managed to find room inside the three U-boats for all of the men riding in the small boats. This left only three lifeboats: Fehler's motor boat and two large steel cutters, one being towed by *UA* and the other by *U-68*. The new arrangement was an improvement, but Rogge would not be happy until he got all of the men inside the submarines.

On 5 December, the boats were about 240 miles northeast of Saint Paul's Rocks off the eastern coast of Brazil and still awaiting the arrival of the fourth U-boat. The location was the approximate area where *U-124* had earlier reported sinking the British cruiser HMS *Dunedin*.[18] Captain Rogge reasoned that *U-124* was probably no farther north than this. Most likely, the submarine either had been sunk or had followed one of *UA*'s incorrect position fixes. Although he doubted the submarine would appear, he decided to remain in the area until noon the following day.[19] While the boats waited, Rogge perfected his plan to put all of the men into the three U-boats. It proved unnecessary. Just before sunrise, the fourth U-boat, Kapitänleutnant Jochen Mohr's *U-124*, arrived. *U-124* had spotted an unidentified freighter while en route to the rendezvous and had stopped and boarded it; thus the delay in meeting the other submarines.

After *U-124* hove to alongside *U-68*, Mohr pleasantly reported *U-124* present for duty as ordered and declared his ship ready to help with the rescue effort. At once, the men in the remaining lifeboats scuttled their craft and the motorboat and moved into the newly arrived submarine. Rogge gave Mohr a stern reprimand for causing his men to suffer in the open boats for two additional nights. Mohr stood at attention as Rogge admonished him and then answered with a simple, "Aye, aye, Sir," never really acknowledging any fault or regret.[20] He had had no idea that he was the subject of so much anxiety. He explained to Rogge that he had heard none of the messages and was only doing a U-boat commander's duty by sailing south as ordered while not neglecting any possible targets along the way.

Rogge assembled the four U-boat commanders to develop plans for a safe return to a friendly port. Korvettenkapitän Eckermann once again bucked Rogge's authority and refused to cooperate fully with a joint rescue effort. Although *UA* was fully provisioned with food and fuel, Eckermann declared he had none to spare for the critically low *U-124*. Furthermore, he planned to sail his ship back to France alone, and at fourteen knots. Rogge, at his wit's end with Eckermann and not really within that officer's operational chain of command, dismissed the recalcitrant Korvettenkapitän to sail on his own accord.

UA departed for France on the night of 5 December, alone and on a course dictated solely by Eckermann. *U-129* was also fairly well provisioned, so it too sailed off alone for France. *U-68* was running a bit low on fuel, but Merten nevertheless volunteered to provide *U-124* with fifty tons of fuel oil. After completing the fuel transfer during the evening of 5 December, *U-68* and *U-124* sailed together on the morning of the sixth. Shortly after midmorning on the sixth, all four U-boats were en route to occupied France, each heavily laden with the survivors of the auxiliary cruiser *Atlantis* and the supply vessel *Python*.

13

Back to Germany

ONCE AGAIN THE men of *Atlantis* had begun their journey home. Each of the submarines carrying them had more than one hundred extra men crammed within its small confines. Even under normal circumstances the crew of a German submarine experienced very crowded conditions. Usually, only one-half of the crew could eat or sleep at one time. With the additional sailors aboard, eight or nine men shared a single bunk normally occupied by two. Each man assigned to a bunk got a ninety-minute nap before being rousted out to get up and cram himself into a small standing or crouching space until it was time to move again. The surface sailors of *Atlantis* and *Python,* accustomed to the wide-open seas, hated the claustrophobic, confined conditions of the submarines.

Lack of space was not the only factor contributing to the men's discomfort. German submarines did not have heating or cooling systems in the crew spaces, so the temperature inside the boat closely approximated the temperature of the water outside. In the Tropics, temperatures sometimes reached 100 degrees Fahrenheit within the submarine; in cold waters the crew endured ice-cold steel plating and frigid temperatures.

The submariners did not appreciate the discomfort caused by the additional occupants either. The rescue operation had turned the submarines into easy targets. Many of the U-boat men resented duty that kept them from their real task of hunting Allied ships. Adjutant Mohr of *Atlantis* wrote,

"Our arrival had presented the U-boatmen with an extraordinary variety of problems and to pretend that we were always regarded by them with a comradely affection would be more than misleading."[1]

The extreme crowding virtually eliminated the submarines' fighting capabilities. The extra men barely fit into all of the available space, leaving no room for the torpedo men or gunners to function efficiently at their battle stations. The additional weight also made the boats difficult to control and maneuver, which further reduced their operational performance.

Despite all of the problems and the terrible conditions, the men and U-boats continued steadily on toward France. The surface sailors endured the confinement, and the submarine crews accomplished their duties and kept the boats operating en route to the safety of German territory.

On the first full day of sailing, the submarines intercepted an Allied radio transmission regarding their operation. "On 7th December," note Wolfgang Frank and Bernhard Rogge in *The German Raider* Atlantis,

> Slankop radio station broadcast the British Admiralty's report of the sinking of the *Python* and added the following warning to all ships: It is believed that survivors from this ship, which was sunk in position 17°53'S 3°55'W, are afloat in about fifteen boats; they may be carrying arms. They are probably close together and escorted by one or more U-boat. If sighted they should be given a wide berth and reported at once by signal.[2]

The message did not cause the U-boat commanders to change their sailing techniques, but it did force them to increase their vigilance.

Following the signal from Slankop the airwaves suddenly filled with a barrage of reports, chatter, and messages about a Japanese attack on an American naval base in Pearl Harbor, Hawaii. When word of the attack circulated around the boats, all of the men, submariners and surface sailors alike, realized that the war had drastically expanded in both scope and magnitude. The following day, the German Naval Command informed the submarines that a state of hostilities existed between Germany and the United States of America.

On *U-68*, Adjutant Mohr immediately climbed the conning tower to find Mr. Vicovari. The American survivor of the *Zamzam* attack was sitting on the conning tower's small wooden bench. It was the only location on board where he could stretch out his stiff legs, still healing from the wounds he received on *Zamzam*. Few individuals were authorized access to that area of the submarine because the tiny access hatches limited the number of men who could pass belowdecks quickly in case of a crash dive. Vicovari had been given special dispensation from Korvettenkapitän Merten because of his injuries. Adjutant Mohr regretfully approached the American and dutifully informed him that a state of war existed between their two countries. Mohr went on to advise Vicovari that his status had changed from that of a detainee to prisoner of war.

The entry of the United States into the war had no immediate effect on the men stuffed into the boats. The struggle for comfort and survival was their main concern. Completing simple tasks became monumental feats during this time. Providing the men with a complete meal each day was a mammoth undertaking. In their tiny galleys, using a single hot plate and two or three large pots designed to feed 50 to 60 men, the U-boat cooks somehow managed to prepare enough food for 150. Even more amazing, they put out a wide variety of fairly pleasing dishes such as goulash, macaroni, cooked vegetables, soups, and stews. Those meals gave the suffering men something to look forward to and contributed to their ability to get through the long days.

On 12 December 1941 the four packed submarines carrying the survivors received good news. A wireless transmission from the BdU ordered each of the U-boats to proceed to a location off the Cape Verde Islands and rendezvous with an Italian submarine. The Italian boats would take on half of each U-boat's complement of survivors. Between the thirteenth and seventeenth, the German U-boats arrived one by one and made contact with the Italian submarines. The Italian boats took between fifty and seventy men each and greatly relieved the burden on the German boats.

Fifty of the 104 extra men crammed inside *UA* moved out and embarked on *Luigi Torelli*, a twenty-three-month-old, 1,036-ton, Marconi-class Italian submarine under the command of the highly respected Capitano di Corvetta Antonio De Giacomo.[3] Seventy sailors aboard *U-68*, including Adjutant Mohr, went over to *Enrico Tazzoli*, a six-year-old, 1,365-ton, Calvi-class seagoing sub under the command of Capitano di Corvetta Fecia di Cossato.

Captain Rogge remained on board *U-68* with *Atlantis*'s official war diary. Mohr carried a copy of *Atlantis*'s log and records to ensure that *Atlantis*'s history would make it back to Germany even if *U-68* was lost on the way home.

Mohr found conditions on the Italian submarine a great improvement over those on *U-68*. It seemed to him that *Enrico Tazzoli* had been designed as much for comfort as for combat effectiveness. The very competent crew seemed devoted to their commander. Having no duties aboard the Italian submarine, Mohr spent most of his time lounging in the ship's library reading from the collection of slightly risqué books or relaxing in the wardroom with a drink from the well-stocked bar.

U-129 transferred seventy extra men to the six-year-old, Calvi-class, 1,325-ton submarine *Giuseppe Finzi,* under the command of Capitano di Corvetta Ugo Giudice. The fourth Italian submarine, *Pietro Calvi,* under the command of Capitano di Corvetta Emilio Olivieri, took on seventy excess men from *U-124*.

The 414 men scattered among eight different submarines all headed off toward German-occupied Saint-Nazaire on different courses. For the most part the submarines ran alone and submerged. This was especially true as they crossed the dangerous North Atlantic and then the heavily patrolled Bay of Biscay known as the "British Pond." Their differing courses and speeds separated them as the days passed. They were all converging on the same spot, however, and sometimes spotted one another. These meetings were cause for small celebrations and even short races.

On one occasion *UA* sighted an outbound U-boat, *U-123*.[4] The two submarines communicated by flashing signals between their conning towers. *UA* flashed: "Bad seas; no bees," meaning there were no enemy aircraft operating due to the weather. *U-123*'s commanding officer, Reinhard Hardegen, responded: "Well done. Great seamanship. Happy Christmas."[5]

In time, all of the submarines, either alone or within sight of another boat, closed in on the mouth of the Gironde River,[6] the final leg to safety because it led to the anchorage of Saint-Nazaire. The Italian *Torelli* was the first of the subs to cast mooring lines ashore safely in Saint-Nazaire. *Torelli*'s journey had not been without incident, however. While crossing the Bay of

Biscay, *Torelli* stumbled into a Gibraltar-bound convoy escort's path on 22 December. The submarine crash-dived, endured a depth-charge attack, successfully eluded its pursuers, and eventually continued on its way. *Atlantis* crewman Johann Meyer later recalled the experience: "A day before arriving at the French coast we came into the security-escort line of a convoy. After diving, we were bombed [depth-charged] but God saved our souls and we overcame."[7] *Torelli* arrived the afternoon of 23 December, damaged but still seaworthy.[8]

That same evening, action stations sounded aboard the submarine *Tazzoli*. The officers scrambled away from the wardroom, leaving Mohr alone. Not wanting to miss the action, Adjutant Mohr made his way to the bridge to see what all the fuss was about. He noticed that the slow, relaxed Italian cadences he was accustomed to had changed to rapid and terse orders and replies. Clearly the submarine was preparing for combat. Finally, an officer on the bridge whispered to Mohr that they were tracking and maneuvering to set up a torpedo attack on an unknown merchant ship.

As the Italian commander surveyed his intended target with the periscope, the ship's doctor approached Mohr with a bottle of champagne and suggested they celebrate the submarine's impending victory. Just as Mohr agreed to partake of the champagne in the early celebration, the merchant's lights came on. Capitano di Corvetta Cossato watched his target for a bit longer, then finally identified the ship as a neutral and stood down from action stations. There would be no attack; the target was a Spanish merchant ship. Cossato stepped aside and allowed Mohr to take a look through the periscope. The German officer graciously thanked his host, but later admitted that he could not identify anything he saw through the lens. Commander Cossato ordered the navigator to shape course for port once again. Mohr and the doctor decided to celebrate with the champagne just the same.

Christmas Day 1941 brought the arrival of the second, third, and fourth submarines to port. *UA* and *U-68* had raced a bit until *U-68* prevailed, arriving in Saint-Nazaire a few hours ahead of *UA*.[9] The two German submarines were soon followed by *Tazzoli*.[10] Two days later, the fifth and sixth submarines, *U-129* and *Pietro Calvi*, arrived.[11] The seventh submarine, *Giuseppe Finzi*, pulled into port on 28 December, followed on the twenty-ninth by the eighth and final boat, *U-124*.[12]

With each boat's arrival a new contingent of haggard, incredibly dirty men—shoeless, ravenous, and dressed in the tattered remnants of uniform parts—invaded the Nates Hotel, which the navy had requisitioned specifically for the men of *Atlantis* to use. The new arrivals raced for their assigned rooms and quickly lined up for bathtubs, barbers, single beds, and beer. The crewmen took their meals in the hotel's elegant main dining room at their leisure, eating huge meals on immense tables set with crystal, fine china, and pressed white linens, with, best of all, plenty of elbow room.

Rogge had brought them home. For nearly two years they had sailed against the odds, stacking up an astonishing war record in the process. The auxiliary cruiser *Atlantis* sank sixteen enemy ships and captured six others, eliminating a total of 145,697 tons of Allied shipping and war materials. The crew had been away from home for 655 consecutive days, a new German record. Under Rogge, the crew circumnavigated the globe on a voyage of 110,000 miles on *Atlantis,* survived 1,000 miles in lifeboats, and finally endured 5,000 more miles in the submarines before arriving safely on the French coast.

With the arrival of the final submarine on 29 December, the entire crew was once again complete. Rogge assembled his men in a local cathedral where he read through the ship's roll and had the naval authorities pass out the mountain of mail that had stacked up while the men were at sea. At the end of the meeting in the cathedral, Rogge gave the men free liberty at the hotel for two days.

The tired crewmen spent their two-day rest sleeping, eating, relaxing, and simply soaking up all of the goings-on around them. The firm ground, the smells of the land, the sounds of dogs and birds, footfalls on wooden floors, the feel of linens and clean clothing were all sensations to which the men had to readjust. They needed the two days of liberty to settle back into life on land. They loved the amenities of the plush surroundings, but they had been in the Tropics for so long that they found the hotel bitterly cold and harshly drafty.

When the rest period ended, Rogge ordered the men to don their new dress uniforms and assemble at the train station for a special event. That afternoon, New Year's Eve 1941, the entire ship's complement boarded a special first-class express train to Berlin. On arriving at the Berlin train station,

Rogge walked to the end of the platform where a small tree had recently been planted. The captain bent down, wiped away the frost, picked up a handful of soil, and crumpled it between his fingers. Reflecting on the moment, Rogge later wrote that he performed the symbolic act because "there had been so many times when I had never expected to see it [German soil] again."[13]

In Berlin, the crew formed up at the Hotel Kaiserhof for a stately meeting with Grand Admiral Raeder at which each man from *Atlantis* was individually decorated. Kapitän-zur-See Rogge received the addition of the Oak Leaves to his Knight's Cross to the Iron Cross. Rogge also received a special Auxiliary Cruiser War Badge, slightly larger than the ones the other crewmen were awarded. Rogge's badge, made of 90 percent pure silver, was fire-gilded and held fifteen small diamonds within the arms of the swastika that symbolized the Third Reich. The Oberbefehlshaber der Kriegsmarine, Grossadmiral Dr. Erich H. C. Raeder, specifically authorized this badge to recognize Rogge's leadership and contributions to the German war effort.[14]

After the meeting, Bernhard Rogge passed out orders to the crew. The first set of papers each received was an authorization for nearly two months' leave. The second set was an instruction to report to a specific naval barracks in Wilhelmshaven when the vacation period was over. Rogge officially disbanded his command when he gave the crew of the auxiliary cruiser *Atlantis* their final command: "Crew dismissed!" The crewmen slowly dispersed and went their separate ways to enjoy their well-earned vacation time.

When the leave period was over, the comrades reassembled in Wilhelmshaven to receive their new assignments. Prior to receiving their new postings, promotions were handed out to all. The petty officers were each increased by one grade in rank, and all of the ratings were made petty officers. When the promotions concluded, the personnel staff presented the men with their orders and sent them off to continue their naval service in the various arms of the navy.

14

After *Atlantis*

When all the decorations had been handed out and the crew dismissed, the naval staff ordered Rogge to stay in Berlin and write a comprehensive report on the procedures and methodologies of successful raider operations. Captain Rogge put to paper his personal thoughts and all of what he had learned and experienced during his extended cruise. His long and extensive report covered everything from crew selection, food, and rumor control to leadership, officership, and combat tactics. The Oberkommando der Kriegsmarine intended to use Rogge's report as a sort of training manual to prepare the officers and men of the other auxiliary cruisers and raiders it hoped eventually to put to sea. Unfortunately, the commerce raider had already seen its brightest days.

When Rogge completed his writing project, four months had passed and he was already aware of his next duty posting: a shore assignment to Kiel. He reported to his new post as chief of staff for the Marine Educational Inspector General's Office in Kiel on 15 April 1942.

Nearly a year later, on 1 March 1943, the German High Command selected Rogge for promotion to rear admiral. The new Konteradmiral took over responsibility for monitoring the selection and training of all officer candidates for the Kriegsmarine as an inspector assigned to the Training Inspectorate Department of the naval staff. Rogge stayed in this assignment until 24 September 1944.

After leaving the Naval Inspectorate Department Rogge took over command of the navy's surface fleet training programs, an assignment that also placed him in command of the 1st Naval Battle Group in the Baltic. Since there was essentially no surface training to oversee or direct, Rogge concentrated his attention on commanding the battle group. He returned to active fleet combat service on 10 February 1945. Some twenty days later, on 1 March 1945, Rogge was promoted to Vizeadmiral.

Vizeadmiral Rogge commanded "Task Force Rogge" from his flagship, the famous Blücher-class heavy cruiser *Prinz Eugen*, under the command of Kapitän-zur-See Reinicke. The task force also included the 10,600-ton pocket battleships *Lützow* and *Admiral Scheer*. This task force would have represented a significant naval force on the open seas, but the Kriegsmarine had long since been overpowered and effectively barred from conducting meaningful deep-ocean combat operations. Rogge's flotilla was instead relegated to bombarding Russian positions along the north German Baltic coast in an attempt to assist the beleaguered German army and slow the Russian advance.

The naval effort to slow the Russian onslaught had an intensity all its own. In the months of March and April, *Prinz Eugen* expended 4,871 203-mm rounds and more than 2,500 105-mm rounds in the shelling. Despite the barrage and the Wehrmacht's rear-action holding efforts, however, the Soviet army eventually overran the German army's positions. By the beginning of April, the Russian advance was so devastating that Grand Admiral Dönitz placed all German surface warships in the Baltic under Admiral Konrad Engelhardt and ordered them to forgo combat actions and actively evacuate German soldiers and refugees from the Baltic areas. Germany's mighty warships became gigantic shuttle boats; their full attention turned to saving as many evacuees as possible.

The OKM had learned through a captured command-level map that the Allies planned to use the Oder-Neisse Line as a political boundary if Germany ended the war and surrendered unconditionally. That political dividing line would place millions of German people and hundreds of thousands of German soldiers on the eastern side of the line under the terror of Soviet control. With that in mind, the German general staff decided to evacuate the German soldiers and civilians from East Prussia and Pomerania.

The SKL ordered all seaworthy ships in the Baltic to concentrate solely on evacuating as many people as possible. Every available merchant vessel, every serviceable warship, and even some U-boats shuttled evacuees from Danzig, Gdynia, Hela, Libau, Pillau, and other Baltic cities to safe ports behind German lines or on the coast of Denmark.

As April ended, Rogge and *Prinz Eugen* continued to assist in one of the largest seaborne rescues in history. The remnants of the courageous German navy shuttled more than 500,000 soldiers and nearly two million refugees out of Baltic and Lithuanian ports to safety. The Kriegsmarine's last-ditch effort continued even after word of the German surrender was announced. On 7 May, the German head of state, Karl Dönitz, announced Germany's defeat. However, the terms of the surrender allowed thousands more refugees to escape to the West. Charles W. Koberger notes that "Dönitz finally agreed to surrender unconditionally all remaining German armed forces. This included those still facing the Red Army in the East. The capitulation, however, would not come into force until 090100 eastern European time. The lift from the east could continue."[1]

Prinz Eugen was unloading yet another shipload of refugees in Copenhagen when the German surrender order came into effect. Because of imposed time constraints and rules regarding the German surrender, *Prinz Eugen* was unable to leave port and continue its evacuation efforts. At 4:00 P.M. on 7 May 1945, Rogge followed his last order of the Second World War and had Captain Reinicke lower the ship's naval battle ensign. *Prinz Eugen* remained at its mooring and waited for the Royal Navy to arrive. The British cruisers *Devonshire* and *Dido* arrived the next day to take control of the German warships.[2] At 5:00 P.M., Rogge and Reinicke formally handed over the ship to the Royal Navy.

Prinz Eugen crewman Helmut "Teddy" Raumann later recalled the surrender:

> We had fallen in on the afterdeck of the heavy cruiser *Prinz Eugen*—our commanding officer, the first officer and ourselves, the weapons control officers. Facing us stood the commanding officer and weapons control officers of the British cruiser HMS *Dido*. The ship was handed over to the Royal Navy with typical British ceremony. The German flag and pennant had been hauled down earlier on the orders of our commanding officer in the presence of the assembled

crew, who were all moved by the occasion, and had been replaced with the randomly chosen alphabet pennant for the letter "C" of the international alphabet. Our ship had lost its identity.[3]

The victors ordered Rogge to ensure that Reinicke kept *Prinz Eugen* immobilized until the Allies determined a final destination for it. Rogge and *Prinz Eugen*'s crew stayed aboard the ship, essentially under house arrest, until the British issued sailing orders. Finally, the cruiser received instructions to leave Copenhagen and sail for Germany. Under close Royal Navy escort from *Devonshire* and *Dido*, *Prinz Eugen* left Denmark on 24 May 1945, and arrived in Wilhelmshaven two days later. At Wilhelmshaven, Vizeadmiral Rogge honorably surrendered his flagship and crew to the Allied port authorities.[4] Admiral Rogge, acting under orders from the British district commander, then officially issued an order dissolving his command as of 28 May 1945.

The British occupation force politely asked Rogge to remain in the local area until a determination was made regarding his status. Rogge complied with the request and secured a barracks room for himself. He informed the occupation authorities of his whereabouts and waited for further instructions. On 7 July 1945, the British occupation forces summoned Rogge and relocated him to Heiligen-Holstein, where he entered an internment camp.

Soon after he arrived at the camp, Rogge learned that his military career had been officially terminated. Just prior to his arrival, the Allied forces issued a unilateral order that removed the authority of and ceased to recognize any and all German military force structure. This decree effectively made Germany an occupied state administered by the Allied powers. All of the interned men waited for the victors to pass judgment on their conduct and character during the war. Rogge's actions during the war were acknowledged to have been lawful and appropriate under all international law. Consequently, he was cleared by the Allied authorities and discharged from imprisonment on 14 September 1945.

Although he was no longer a naval officer, Mr. Bernhard Rogge maintained his affiliation with the sea. He worked in a variety of oceanic trade businesses as an adviser and manager for the next twelve years. When the governing powers of the North Atlantic Treaty Organization decided that

Germany should reconstitute its armed forces, Rogge was one of the first officers recalled to active German military service.

The new Konteradmiral Rogge entered the Bundesmarine of the Federal Republic of Germany on 1 June 1957. His first assignment was the command of Military District I, encompassing Schleswig-Holstein and Hamburg. Rogge's abilities quickly garnered the respect of his NATO peers and superiors, and his responsibilities were soon expanded. He became the commander of all NATO ground, air, and sea forces responsible for defending northern Germany. Rogge served in this capacity until his retirement from the military on 31 March 1962.

Bernhard Rogge and his second wife, Elsbeth, moved to a fine house on the edge of a large pond in the Hamburg suburb of Reinbek, but Rogge still could not separate himself fully from the sea. In retirement he continued to co-manage the Hamburg-Atlantik line, a merchant shipping business; served as a German government consultant for civil defense matters; and held the post of president of the German Ocean Sailing Association.

In 1955 Rogge published *Under Ten Flags,* an English-language account of his time aboard *Atlantis*. The book was very well received throughout the world and even gave rise to a successful motion picture, the Dino de Laurentiis production *Under Ten Flags,* released by Paramount. In 1968 Rogge followed up *Under Ten Flags* with a more detailed and comprehensive account of the cruise in German entitled *Schiff 16: Die Kaperfahrten das schweren Hilfskreuzers* Atlantis *auf den Sieben Weltmeeren* (Ship-16: The raids of the heavy auxiliary cruiser *Atlantis* on the seven seas). Throughout his retirement Rogge enjoyed occasional vacations sailing the oceans on private sailing ships or cruising on liners.

On 29 June 1982, Bernhard Rogge, Vizeadmiral, Retired, one of the most successful naval officers in history, the forty-fifth recipient of the Knight's Cross, and only the ninth naval recipient of the Oak Leaves to the Knight's Cross, died in Hamburg, Germany, at the age of eighty-three.

NOTES

Chapter 1. Bernhard Rogge

1. *Commentaries,* vol. I, book I, chap. 13, section 418, 1765.
2. SMS *Freya,* launched on 27 April 1897, was initially used as a coastal defense ship during the first part of World War I. In 1915 the navy ported *Freya* in Flensburg and used the old battlewagon as a training ship. The ship was stricken (i.e., all its weapons were removed and its naval functions were taken away) on 25 January 1920, and used as a police barracks until it was broken up a year later.
3. SMS *Moltke* surrendered at the end of the war. The forty-three officers and 1,010 crewmen remained interned on *Moltke* at Scapa Flow from 25 November 1918, until 1:10 P.M. on 21 June 1919, when the crew scuttled the ship. The hulk was raised and broken up in 1929.
4. SMS *Stralsund* carried a complement of eighteen officers and 336 crewmen. The ship survived the war only to be stricken on 10 March 1920. It became a French prize on 3 August 1920. *Stralsund*'s bell is now on display at the Laboe Naval Memorial in Germany.
5. *Pillau* was originally built as *Murawjw Amurski* by the Schichau shipyard in Danzig to fill a Russian navy order. In 1914, the Imperial German Navy commandeered the ship and commissioned it *Kleiner Kruezer Pillau.* During World War I the ship served as a scout with the 2d Reconnaissance Group and took part in the Battle of Jutland. The ship survived the war and was stricken on 5 November 1919. Italy took *Pillau* as a prize of war on 20 July 1920, and it became the Italian cruiser *Bari.* It was sunk by U.S. aircraft on 28 June 1943, at Livorno.
6. Abdication Proclamation of Wilhelm II:

> I herewith renounce for all time claims to the throne of Prussia and to the German Imperial throne connected therewith. At the same time I release all officials of the German Empire and of Prussia, as well as all officers, non-commissioned officers and men of the navy and of the Prussian army, as well as the troops of the federated states of Germany, from the oath of fidelity which they tendered to me as their Emperor, King and Commander-in-Chief. I expect of them that until the re-establishment of order in the German Empire they shall render assistance to those in actual power in Germany, in protecting the German people from the threatening dangers of anarchy, famine, and foreign rule. Proclaimed under our own hand and with the imperial seal attached. Amerongen, 28 November 1918.

7. Charles S. Thomas, *The German Navy in the Nazi Era* (Annapolis: Naval Institute Press, 1990), 27, quoting Ludwig von Rueter from *Scapa Flow: Das Grab der deutschen Flotte,* 2d rev. ed. (Leipzig, 1920), 94–95.

8. Ibid., 26.

9. *Arcona,* the ninth Gazelle-class cruiser, was launched in 1903 and was in and out of active fleet service until 1942, when it was moored as a floating antiaircraft battery and radar station. The ship survived both wars and was broken up for scrap in 1946.

10. *Amazone* was originally launched on 6 October 1900, and was refitted and modernized between 1921 and 1923. The ship served in the Reichsmarine fleet until it was stricken the last day of March 1931. *Amazone*'s floating hulk sat in Kiel as a barracks and auxiliary floating platform. At the end of World War II, the rusted hulk was used to house homeless veterans. The hulk was broken up in Hamburg in 1954.

11. The battleship served as a ship of the line for the Reichsmarine and as a training ship for the Kriegsmarine. It was sunk by British aircraft in Gotenhafen seven days before Christmas in 1944. The ship was broken up in 1947, but its bell is on display in the Dresden Army Museum.

12. *Niobe* capsized and sank in a storm on 26 July 1932. Of those aboard, the captain and fifty men were saved; sixty-nine others (thirty-three crewmen and thirty-six cadets) drowned. For a time *Niobe* was commanded by Count von Luckner of World War I fame.

13. *Emden,* launched in 1925, was named after the famous raider ship lost in World War I; it bore a large Iron Cross on the bow in honor of its namesake. *Emden* saw frontline combat service during World War II and was finally scuttled on 3 May 1945, in Heikendorfer Bay.

14. The Königsberg-class cruiser *Karlsruhe* became a Kriegsmarine frontline ship after the training cruise of 1936. A torpedo fired from the British submarine HMS *Truant* on 9 April 1940, caused extensive damage to the ship and killed eleven crewmen. *Karlsruhe*'s captain ordered the ship's destruction three hours later. It was sunk by torpedoes fired from the German boat *Jaguar* and sank in position 58 degrees, 4 minutes north latitude and 8 degrees, 4 minutes east longitude, off Kristiansand, Norway.

15. *Gorch Fock* was sunk in the closing months of World War II off Stralsund. It was salvaged by the Russians in 1948, renamed *Tovarisch,* and given to the Cherson Merchant Marine School in the Ukraine. The ship, homeported in Odessa, now sails with 180 cadets and sixty-six officers and crew.

16. *Albert Leo Schlageter* displaced 1,784 tons, carried 19,132 square feet of sail, and had a mainmast that rose 146 feet above the waterline. The ship survived the war and ultimately ended up in the Portuguese navy as the training ship *Sagres II*. Currently, *Sagres II* leaves its home port of Alfeite twice a year to take its twenty-nine officers, 131 crewmen, and nine cadets on training cruises.

17. Wolfgang Frank and Bernhard Rogge, *The German Raider* Atlantis (New York: Ballantine Books, 1956), 1.

18. "Ever since the founding of the Company it has been Hansa's policy—and their pride—to fit their vessels with the latest equipment and to use the most up-to-date shipbuilding techniques, so as to own absolutely first-class ships" (Leonard Gray, *85 Years of Shipping under the Maltese Cross, Deutsche Dampfschiffahrts-Gesellschaft Hansa*

1881–1966: Portrait of a Major German Shipping Company [Kendal, U.K.: World Ship Society, 1967], 3).

19. Arthur V. Sellwood, *Dynamite for Hire* (London: T. Werner Laurie, 1956), 98.

Chapter 2. A Sheep Becomes a Wolf

1. Bernhard Rogge, "Leadership on Board the Raider *Atlantis*," U.S. Naval Institute Proceedings 80 (February 1963): 43.

2. Rogge held to the German navy's tradition of "unpolitical soldiership" while selecting his crew; enthusiastic adherents to the ideals of the Nazi party were turned away. In *The German Navy in the Nazi Era* (Annapolis: Naval Institute Press, 1990), Charles S. Thomas cites Rogge's unconvincing support for National Socialism by quoting from Rogge's address "Voraussetzungen für den Offiersberuf. Ausarbeitung für die Inspecktion des Bildungswesens der Marine, 1942," wherein he defined the party as "common good before individual good" and "all for one and one for all." Thomas continues: "In the same address, Rogge appears to have stated that the older National Socialists were in part 'crass egotists' and 'pompous asses' and complained about the 'HJ [Hitler Youth] sickness' evident among younger Germans" (209).

3. Letter from Johann Meyer, Bad Segeberg, to author, 16 August 1996.

4. An examination of the attention to detail Rogge gave to just this one item on the list indicates how thoroughly he analyzed and scrutinized everything that would affect the crew once the ship was at sea. The men selected and approved each title to ensure that the library covered as wide a range of interests as possible. The book selections included nonfiction fields ranging from history, nature, and culture, to educational programs and technical courses, to fiction novels, humor, and contemporary and classical literature. Later, as ships were captured, foreign-language titles were added for the benefit of the prisoners.

5. Rogge, "Leadership," 42.

6. Sellwood, *Dynamite for Hire*, 103.

7. The 14,800-ton battleship *Schlesien* was launched on 28 May 1905, and fought with distinction at the Battle of Jutland during World War I. From 1918 to 1940 the ship was used for training and coastal defense. In July 1940 *Schlesien* was withdrawn from service and used as a dormitory ship in Gotenhafen. The ship was put back into service with a reduced crew in early 1941 and used as an icebreaker. Rearmed with smaller guns, *Schlesien* supported minesweeping and other defensive actions until April 1945. *Schlesien* fought at the battle for Gotenhafen in April 1945, then was withdrawn to Swinemünde with more than one thousand wounded men. On 3 May 1945, *Schlesien* hit a mine at Zinnowitz, near Swinemünde, and was beached the next day. Between 1949 and 1956 the remains were blown up and removed for scrap.

8. Rogge, "Leadership," 42–43, 47.

9. See Georg Schwarzenberger, *A Manual of International Law*, 5th ed., 1967, 208: "A clear rule has grown up in accordance with which the use of false flags for the purpose of deceiving the enemy is a permissible war ruse. A man-of-war must, however, hoist her own colours before opening fire." Burdick H. Brittin and Liselotte B. Watson

concur in *International Law for Seagoing Officers*, 1972, 223: "It is not illegal for a naval commander to use such ruses as false colors or disguises of outward appearance to entice an enemy warship or aircraft into action. Before going into action, however, he must always show the warship's true colors."

10. *Hessen* was a 13,208-ton Braunschweig-class battleship built in the Germania yards in Kiel and launched on 18 September 1903. It was the only one of the four Braunschweig-class ships not taken out of the fleet in 1916 and broken up. *Hessen* was finally stricken on 31 March 1935, only to be recommissioned as a target ship on 1 April 1937. *Hessen* survived the war and was surrendered to the Soviet Union in 1946. The Soviet navy renamed the ship *Tsel* and put it into active Soviet service.

11. *U-37* was a small 1,408-ton, type IXA boat commanded by Werner Hartmann, who went on to sink twenty-four ships for a total of 115,616 tons. He was awarded the Knight's Cross on 9 May 1940, and Oak Leaves to go with it on 5 November 1944. Both *U-37* and Hartmann survived the war. The submarine, under the command of Kapitänleutnant Eberhard von Wenden, was scuttled on 8 May 1945, in Sonderburg Bay at latitude 54 degrees, 55 minutes north and longitude 9 degrees, 47 minutes east. Hartmann died on 26 April 1963.

12. Frank and Rogge, *German Raider*, 12.

Chapter 3. *Atlantis* Goes into Action

1. On 14 September 1914, the requisitioned armed merchant cruiser RMS *Carmania*, disguised as the Hamburg Sud Amerika line's *Cap Trafalgar*, met the actual German ship *Cap Trafalgar*, also a requisitioned armed merchant cruiser, disguised as *Carmania*, off Trinidad. During the ensuing battle, *Carmania* sank *Cap Trafalgar*.

2. August Karl Muggenthaler, *German Raiders of World War II* (London: Robert Hale, 1977), 21.

3. The standard radio signals for that time included QQQ, to represent an approaching vessel of suspicious origin; RRR, to signify an enemy surface warship or a known auxiliary cruiser; and SSS, for an approaching submarine.

4. The officer of the watch noted *Scientist*'s final position as 20 degrees, 50 minutes south latitude and 4 degrees, 30 minutes east longitude.

5. The British East India Company first employed Asian seamen in the seventeenth century. Although they came from many different countries, it was the custom at that time to refer to all dark-skinned Asians as "lascars." It is believed that the term derives from the Persian word *lashkar*, which refers to a band of army camp followers.

6. Roy Alexander, *Sea Prison and Shore Hell* (Sydney: Angus and Robertson, 1942), 98–99.

Chapter 4. The Secret Gets Out

1. Gordon Gumming, "The Agulhas Minefield—Its Discovery and Claerance" [*sic*].
2. Frank and Rogge, *German Raider*, 27.

3. *Africana* was a ten-year-old, 308-ton former fishing research vessel pressed into wartime service as HMSAS *Africana*, minesweeper T 01; it was scrapped in 1964. *Natalia* was originally launched in 1925 as a whale catcher. In 1939 the 238-ton ship became HMSAS *Natalia*, minesweeper T 03. The 261-ton steam trawler *Aristea* was launched in 1935 and pressed into World War II service as the minesweeper HMSAS *Aristea* (T 18). *Crassula* was a 261-ton trawler launched in 1935 and scrapped in 1968.

4. Gumming, "Minefield."

5. At the time of the initial message the British Operational Intelligence Center (OIC) had determined that at least one merchant raider was operating in the southern seas. Several months later, near the end of July, the OIC determined that more than one raider was at sea. The British Admiralty then created a new intelligence subsection specifically devoted to gathering information on the raiders. The subsection built a reasonably accurate picture of the raiders' descriptions, locations, and numbers through interviews with survivors and analyses of attack frequency, times, and locations. This information was continually updated and relayed to Allied war and merchant ships.

6. I was unable to determine if the erroneous report was an intentional ploy for intelligence-counterintelligence purposes or simply a mistake caused by wartime confusion. *Abbekerk* was actually sunk at latitude 50 degrees, 5 minutes north and longitude 30 degrees, fifty minutes west on 24 August 1942, by torpedoes fired from *U-604*.

7. Wolfgang Frank and Bernhard Rogge, *Under Ten Flags* (London: Weidenfeld and Nicolson, 1955), 40. *Tiranna* broadcast its position as 18 degrees, 50 minutes south latitude and 67 degrees, 50 minutes east longitude.

8. The references vary in the casualty count of the attack. Some say five were killed; others say six.

9. Frank and Rogge, *German Raider*, 40.

10. Kurt Weyher and Hans Jürgen Ehrlich, *The Black Raider* (London: Elek Books, 1955), 75.

11. The wireless transmissions from the target ship, *Atlantis*, *Eastern Guide*, and the British shore station are outlined in Edwin P. Hoyt's *Raider 16* (New York: World, 1970), 60.

12. A rating on the bridge of *Atlantis* recorded the enemy ship's final position, halfway between Ceylon and Sumatra, as 0 degrees, 16 minutes south latitude and 86 degrees east longitude.

Chapter 5. Captured Sisters

1. *Atlantis*'s fifth victim disappeared from view at 5:53 P.M. on 2 August 1940, at latitude 30 degrees, 30 minutes south and longitude 67 degrees east.

2. *King City* went down at latitude 17 degrees, 35 minutes south and longitude 65 degrees, 28 minutes east.

3. Message transmission texts are quoted from Frank and Rogge, *German Raider*, 62–63.

4. Quotation from Alexander, *Sea Prison*, 81. *Athelking* sank at position 22 degrees south latitude and 67 degrees, 30 minutes east longitude.

5. Although Captain Rogge did not know it, *Benarty*'s radio transmission did reach some British stations. The raider *Pinguin* (*Ship-33*) was outside *Atlantis*'s and *Benarty*'s radio range, but *Pinguin*'s log for 10 September reflects the interception of transmissions calling *Benarty* and others relaying the raider warning.

6. Mohr recorded the position of the sinking as 18 degrees, 40 seconds south latitude and 70 degrees, 54 minutes east longitude.

7. The basic text of the exchange between the two ships is taken from Frank and Rogge, *German Raider*, 71.

8. *Commissaire Ramel* sank at latitude 28 degrees, 25 minutes south and longitude 74 degrees, 23 minutes east.

9. *Tirranna* turned down on its port side, capsized, and sank at latitude 45 degrees, 19 minutes north and longitude 1 degree, 20 minutes west. *Tuna* was a 1,325-ton general service patrol–class British submarine commissioned into the Royal Navy on 1 August 1940. At the time of the sinking it was under the command of Lt. Cdr. M. K. Cavanagh-Mainwairing. The submarine served throughout the war, including landing commandos in canoes at Bordeaux in December 1942 and torpedoing and sinking *U-644* with all hands on 7 April 1944, just northwest of Narvik, Norway, in the North Sea. The submarine was stricken and scrapped in 1946.

10. A memento of *Tirranna* survives today. An Australian seaman picked up one of *Tirranna*'s empty mailbags from *Atlantis*'s deck as he was being transferred to *Durmitor*, intending to use the bag as bedding. The man kept the forgotten bag in his kit and finally returned to Australia with it in his possession. The mailbag is now on display at the General Post Office Museum in Sydney.

Chapter 6. Hell Ship *Durmitor*

1. Frank and Rogge, *Under Ten Flags*, 84. An officer on *Atlantis*'s bridge recorded the location of the capture as 8 degrees, 30 minutes south latitude and 101 degrees, 30 minutes east longitude.

2. Many published accounts of the leave-on-board program say that the crewmen enjoying this leave were not required to wear their uniforms and were excused from saluting. *Atlantis* crewman Johann Meyer recalls: "We had to wear our uniforms and salute, we were still soldiers, just on vacation and we didn't have any civilian clothes to wear" (letter to author, 19 December 1999).

3. *Durmitor* sailed from position 12 degrees, 75 minutes south latitude and 102 degrees east longitude.

4. The Italians eventually sailed *Durmitor* back to Mogadishu. It sat idle there until February 1941, when it was captured by HMS *Shropshire*. The steamer was renamed *Radwinter* and pressed into British merchant service. In 1946 Britain returned the ship to Yugoslavia. Yugoslavia restored the name *Durmitor* and used the ship in active merchant service until 1963, when it was broken up at Split.

5. Leutnant Emil Dehnel exhibited exceptional seamanship in bringing *Durmitor* to a friendly port under the most adverse conditions without loss of life or any bloodshed.

6. Ulrich Mohr and A. V. Sellwood, *Ship 16* (New York: John Day, 1956), 144. *Atlantis* captured the tanker at latitude 5 degrees, 35 minutes north and longitude 88 degrees, 22 minutes east.

7. *Automedon*'s final position was marked in the log as 4 degrees, 18 minutes north latitude and 89 degrees, 20 minutes east longitude.

8. *Atlantis*'s log recorded *Teddy*'s final position as 5 degrees, 35 minutes north latitude and 88 degrees, 22 minutes east longitude.

9. Frank and Rogge, *German Raider*, 81.

10. Timothy J. Runyan and Jan M. Copes note that "the capture yielded important courier posts, including new code tables for the Eastern Fleet and other operational materials of great use to the Japanese" (Runyan and Copes, eds., *To Die Gallantly: The Battle of the Atlantic* [Boulder: Westview Press, 1994], 51).

11. The defense plans for Singapore were among many *Automedon* items provided to the Japanese government. The information proved so valuable that on 27 April 1942, the Japanese government presented Rogge with an elaborate samurai sword in appreciation. Japan presented only three such swords: one to Rogge, one to Reichsmarshall Hermann Göring, and one to Field Marshall Erwin Rommel.

12. *Ole Jacob* was put into German service as the supply ship *Benno*. *Benno* was sunk with bombs and torpedoes from British aircraft on Christmas Eve 1941 off the northwest coast of Spain. Benno is a German nickname meaning "Little Bernhard." The ship was named for Rogge.

13. *Atlantis* could receive and decode Hydra ciphers; however, the merchant raiders, their supply ships, and the blockade-runners normally used Special Cipher 100 (the Kriegsmarine coded it "Triton"; the British called it "Pine"). Special Cipher 100 remained secure throughout the war—it was never broken.

14. John R. Angolia, *On the Field of Honor*, vol. 2 (San Jose: Roger James Bender, 1980), 56.

15. Conditions aboard *Storstadt* were more austere than those on *Atlantis*—so much so, in fact, that an *Automedon* crewman died from pneumonia during the journey to port. *Storstadt* docked safely at Bordeaux on 5 February 1941, and the surviving prisoners were transferred to Front Stalag 221.

Chapter 7. A Nearly Fatal Landfall

1. Oliver E. Allen, *Pacific Navigators*, Seafarers Series (Alexandria, Va.: Time-Life Books, 1980), 96.

2. Most period books, including Mohr's Atlantis: *Kaperfahrt unter 10 Flaggen*, incorrectly state the date of Herrmann's death as 23 or 24 December.

3. Matrosen-Gefreiter Bernhard Herrmann was born just twenty-one years earlier in Schnellewalde Kreis Nuestadt/Oberschlesien. The Volksbund Deutsche Kriegsgräberfürsorge (German War Graves Commission) confirmed that Seaman Herrmann's grave at Port-Couvreux on Gazelle Bay is the southernmost site of interment recorded for any German soldier or sailor during the entire Second World War. When *Atlantis* left the islands in January 1941, the crew removed the grave marker and disguised the

grave to match the surrounding landscape in order to maintain operational security for their mission. Herrmann's grave was relocated in May 1965 with the help of the French government.

4. Frank and Rogge, *German Raider*, 102.

5. Sellwood, *Dynamite for Hire*, 108.

6. An English crewman recorded *Mandasor*'s final position as latitude 4 degrees, 18 minutes south and longitude 61 degrees, 36 minutes east.

7. The ship *Atlantis* sighted was not the *Queen Mary* but the 22,281-ton *Strathaind* from the P&O line. *Strathaind* was indeed escorted by cruisers while performing duty as a troop transport ship.

8. Charles Gibson, *The Ship with Five Names* (London: Abeland-Schuman, 1965), 28.

9. Muggenthaler, *German Raiders*, 97.

10. The location of the capture was noted in *Atlantis*'s war log as 4 degrees, 30 minutes south latitude and 50 degrees, 50 minutes east longitude.

11. Sellwood, *Dynamite for Hire*, 109–110.

12. *Tannenfels* was the sister ship of *Goldenfels*, the merchant ship converted into the raider *Atlantis*.

13. *Tannenfels* was sailing from India to Hamburg in August 1939 when its master, Captain Steuer, received an order from the German Admiralty to proceed to the nearest neutral port because of the threat of war. Steuer shaped course for Italian Somaliland and was detained there by Italian authorities even after Italy joined the war on Germany's side. *Durmitor* arrived on 23 November and was likewise detained. In the confusion of the British army's ground offensive against Somaliland *Tannenfels* was able to take on the German prize crew of *Durmitor* and slip out of the harbor on 31 January 1941.

Chapter 8. A German Battleship and an International Incident

1. At the time of the meeting *Admiral Scheer* was classified as a Panzerschiffe (i.e., an armored ship). *Scheer* and its two sisters, *Admiral Graf Spee* and *Lützow*, were similarly denominated with Germany's other large ships of the line and called pocket battleships. In 1940 the High Command reclassified the two remaining ships (*Scheer* and *Lützow*) as heavy cruisers.

2. *Tannenfels* reached the safety of a full escort at the mouth of the Gironde estuary on 19 April 1941.

3. Kapitän-zur-See Theodor Kranke survived the war. *Admiral Scheer* met its end on 9 April 1945, at 11:35 P.M. in Kiel. While entering the harbor inlet of the Deutsche Werke dockyard, *Scheer* was struck by five bombs dropped by attacking British aircraft; it sank at latitude 54 degrees, 20 minutes north, longitude 10 degrees, 8 minutes east.

4. *British Advocate* was renamed *Nordstern* and pressed into German service. During Allied air attacks on 23 and 24 July 1944, *Nordstern* was bombed and sunk at the Donges pier. The ship was raised on 17 August 1947, and broken up for scrap.

5. *Doggerbank* under Leutnant Paul Schneidewind completed several successful sorties. The ship sowed minefields around Cape Agulhas and was credited with the loss of five Allied ships. As it made its way home to Germany on 3 March 1943, *Doggerbank* was sighted by *U-43* under command of Kapitänleutnant Hans-Joachim Schwantke, who, believing *Doggerbank* was an unescorted British merchant ship, fired three torpedoes that struck amidships. *Doggerbank* exploded and quickly sank in the Atlantic Ocean just west of the Canary Islands (latitude 10 degrees, 34 minutes north, longitude 10 degrees west). Only one man, Matrose Fritz Kuert, survived. Kuert was found by the Spanish tanker *Campoamor* twenty-six days later in a boat, alone and unconscious, at position 15 degrees, 31 minutes north, 51 degrees, 25 minutes west—a full sixteen hundred miles from the site of the sinking. The SKL exonerated Schwantke of error in the sinking and struck the entire incident from the submarine's war log. The blame was placed squarely on Schneidewind, who shot himself while drifting hopelessly in a lifeboat.

6. *Ketty Brøvig* went down at latitude 4 degrees, 50 minutes south and longitude 56 degrees east.

7. *Perla* went back to sea and was operating near Beirut on 9 July 1942, when it was surprised by a British warship. The crew was unable to scuttle the ship in time and *Perla* was captured.

8. The medal is roughly equivalent to the British Distinguished Service Cross or the U.S. Silver Star.

9. Frank and Rogge, *Under Ten Flags*, 133.

10. Charles J. V. Murphy, "The German Raider Caught in the Act of Sinking *Zamzam*," *Life*, 23 June 1941, 26.

11. *Lusitania* was sunk on 7 May 1915, by *U-20* under the command of Leutnant Walter Schwieger. Of the 1,959 passengers, 1,195 lost their lives, including 123 Americans.

12. Murphy, "Raider Caught Sinking *Zamzam*," 71.

13. Ibid., 72.

14. Ibid., 74.

15. Olga Guttormson, *Ships Will Sail Again* (Minneapolis: Augsburg, 1942), 19. The following week Laughinghouse succumbed to his wounds while still aboard *Atlantis*.

16. The arrival of *Dresden* and *Speybank* was reported to Hitler, as shown in the transcript of "Conference of the C.-in-C., Navy with the Führer at the Berghof on 22 May 1941":

> 1. Situation ... (b) Cruiser Warfare in Foreign Waters.—The prize *Speybank* put into Bordeaux on May 11th with a very valuable cargo of 1,500 tons of manganese, 300 tons of rubber, jute, and tea. The supply ship *Dresden* put into a harbour in Southern France with 140 Americans, some of them women and children, who were taken aboard auxiliary cruisers during the capture of an Egyptian steamer. It is inexcusable of the U.S. Government to allow American citizens, including women and children, to travel on ships belonging to belligerents. The captain of *Dresden* treated the American passengers with great consideration so that no protests are likely. (Signed) Raeder

Fuehrer Conferences on Naval Affairs 1939–1945 (Annapolis: Naval Institute Press, 1990), 196–200.

Chapter 9. The Noose Tightens

1. *Nordmark* remained near this location for nearly six months and is credited with replenishing no fewer than forty-five German ships.
2. "I got a convoy off Freetown (Africa) SL-68 and attacked that convoy for about a week along with *U-105*. During this time Kamenz conducted excellent navigation duties working along with my navigational Chief Petty Officer" (Jürgen Oesten, Hamburg, letter to author, 29 November 2001).
3. Kapitänleutnant Kamenz left a present on board *Nordmark* for Kapitänleutnant Oesten that was delivered when *Nordmark* met *U-106* some three weeks later. It was a compass and mounting binnacle from one of *Ole Jacob*'s lifeboats with a brass plate reading: "Die überwasserpiraten den Unterwasserpiraten" (The surface pirates to the underwater pirates) (Oesten, letter to author, 29 November 2001).
4. The British intelligence network was extremely careful to keep the capture of *U-110* a highly guarded secret. Not even the U-boat crew was aware that their ship's code material had been captured. *U-110* sank while under tow, but by that time the British had secured a complete and fully functional Enigma machine with codebooks. The seizure remained a highly guarded British secret until 1958.
5. Despite many instances indicating that the British could read the Kriegsmarine's secret messages, Dönitz and most of the German general staff remained stoutly convinced that the German codes were unbreakable.
6. *Rabaul* ended its twenty-five years of service at position 19 degrees, 30 minutes south latitude and 4 degrees, 30 minutes east longitude.
7. Extracted *Kriegstagebuch* of *Atlantis*, microfilm, National Archives Records Administration, T-1022/3126.
8. The ship sank at latitude 25 degrees south and longitude 14 degrees east.
9. The 42,210-ton battle cruiser *Hood* was sunk on 24 May 1941. The three survivors were Midn. W. J. Dundas, Ordinary Signaller A. E. P. Briggs, and Ordinary Seaman R. E. Tilburn.
10. *Bismarck* was lost on 27 May. Only 103 men from the crew of more than 2,200 survived.
11. One of the ships sunk was *Atlantis*'s support ship *Babitonga*, which was lost on 21 June 1941. *Babitonga* was intercepted by the 13,220-ton heavy cruiser HMS *London* just north of the equator off the West African coast, at latitude 2 degrees, 5 minutes north and longitude 27 degrees, 42 minutes west. When approached by the British cruiser, *Babitonga*'s captain scuttled his ship.
12. *Tottenham* reported its position as 7 degrees, 39 minutes south latitude and 19 degrees, 12 minutes west longitude.
13. Muggenthaler, *German Raiders*, 107.
14. Frank and Rogge, *German Raider*, 128.

15. *Balzac* went down near latitude 12 degrees south and longitude 29 degrees west.
16. Mohr and Sellwood, *Ship 16*, 212.

Chapter 10. Pacific Waters

1. Rogge, "Leadership," 50–51.
2. *Silvaplana* was captured at latitude 26 degrees, 16 minutes south and longitude 164 degrees, 25 minutes west.
3. *Komet* pulled into the port of Cherbourg on 26 November 1941, completing a cruise of 512 days. Admiral Eyssen was reassigned to shore duties at Luftflotte IV and later in the Navy Logistics Office in Oslo. He survived the war and retired. *Komet*, outfitted with new guns and radar, put to sea again under Kapitän-zur-See Ulrich Brocksien on 7 October 1942. The raider was quickly trapped and attacked by five Hunt-class destroyers and eight British motor torpedo boats; either the British shell fire or a torpedo hit *Komet*'s aviation fuel stores, causing the ship to explode and instantly disintegrate without a trace at 2:15 A.M. on 14 October; all hands were lost.
4. The prize crew comprised twenty-six Norwegians, four Swedes, one Dane, and one Pole. The ship was quickly reconfigured, renamed *Irene*, and used as a Kriegsmarine blockade-runner. On 4 October 1943, it was intercepted by the Royal Navy minelayer HMS *Adventure*. The Kriegsmarine crew scuttled *Irene* at latitude 43 degrees, 18 minutes north and longitude 14 degrees, 26 minutes west to prevent the ship from reverting back to Allied control.
5. Frank and Rogge, *Under Ten Flags*, 156–157.
6. Bernhard Rogge, "The End of the *Atlantis*," *Kommando* 6, no. 4 (1955): 8–11.
7. Ulrich Mohr and Arthur V. Sellwood, *Sea Raider* Atlantis (New York: Pinnacle Books, 1975), 236.
8. Mohr, Atlantis, 236.

Chapter 11. *Atlantis* Is Lost

1. Patrick Beesly, *Very Special Intelligence* (London: Hamish Hamilton, 1975), 88.
2. A. W. S. Agar, Epilogue to Mohr and Sellwood, *Sea Raider*, 277.
3. Mohr and Sellwood, *Sea Raider*, 241.
4. Funkgefreiter Johann Meyer, letter to author, 30 May 1996.
5. "Bernhard Rogge: Der Kaperkapitän vom Hilfskreuzer 'Atlantis,'" *Der Landser-Großband* 844, no. 2 (1993): 41.
6. Bernhard Rogge and Wolfgang Frank, *Schiff 16* (Hamburg: Gerhard Stalling, 1957), 316–317.
7. *Atlantis* sank at latitude 4 degrees, 20 minutes south and longitude 18 degrees, 35 minutes west.
8. HMS *Devonshire* survived the war and was used as an English training ship from 1947 to 1953. The ship was finally broken up by Cashmore, Newport in 1954.

Chapter 12. Sunk and Rescued—Twice

1. See the 29 July 1944 issue of *Collier's* magazine.
2. Krooß was killed by a shell burst on a companionway leading to the boat deck when he stood aside to allow an officer to pass by. The pause placed him directly in the path of an incoming explosive round.
3. Karl Dönitz, *Memoirs: Ten Years and Twenty Days,* trans. R. H. Stevens (New York: World, 1959), 179.
4. Johann Meyer, letter to author, 10 March 1996.
5. Mohr and Sellwood, *Sea Raider,* 255.
6. Frank and Rogge, *German Raider,* 142.
7. Kapitänleutnant Ernst Bauer completed five patrols as the commander of *U-126* before moving to shore duty in 1943. He was awarded the Knight's Cross on 16 March 1942, and ended his hunting with twenty-four ships and 108,513 tons of lost British shipping to his credit. He survived the war and retired from the German Bundesmarine in 1972 as a Kapitän-zur-See. *U-126* was lost with all hands on 3 July 1943, at latitude 46 degrees, 2 minutes north and longitude 11 degrees, 23 minutes west as a result of British aircraft attacks.
8. The ship was the 4,850-ton HMS *Dunedin,* a World War I–era cruiser. At a range of more than three miles, *U-124* fired three torpedoes toward *Dunedin* as the cruiser steamed at seventeen knots. Stuart Gill writes in *The War Record of HMS* Dunedin (online at http://www.world-war.co.uk/index.htm [20 August 2000]):

> Two torpedoes hit within seconds of each other, at around 1326 GMT, the first striking amidships, wrecking the main wireless office, the second further aft, probably near the officers quarters. The first hit sent the ship lurching to starboard, the second caused even greater damage dismounting the after 6in gun, and blowing off the starboard screw. . . . *Dunedin* turned on her beam ends and sank in about seventeen minutes.

About 150 men of the ship's complement of 400 survived the sinking, floating on seven Carley floats and pieces of debris. In the afternoon of 27 November, the U.S. merchant ship *Nishmaha* rescued the seventy-two survivors. When *Nishmaha* reached Trinidad, only four officers and sixty-three ratings were still alive.

9. Frank and Rogge, *German Raider,* 142–143.
10. Ibid., 143.
11. Wolfgang Frank, *The Sea Wolves: The Story of German U-boats at War,* trans. R. O. B. Long (New York: Rinehart, 1955), 138.
12. Some period reports relate that Eckermann fired three torpedoes in a single attack; however, most postwar references agree that he launched five torpedoes in two separate spreads.
13. HMS *Dorsetshire* was sunk with HMS *Cornwall* west of Ceylon on 5 April 1942, by bombs from a Japanese carrier aircraft. *Dorsetshire* lost 227 crewman in the sinking.
14. The established course was 330 degrees.
15. The Africa wavelength was the frequency specified for all U-boats operating in the South Atlantic.

16. E. B. Gasaway, *Grey Wolf, Grey Sea* (New York: Ballantine Books, 1970), 177.
17. Mohr, *Atlantis*, 267.
18. Earlier Rogge and the U-boat commanders had intercepted *U-124*'s battle report to the BdU with details of the attack, including the grid coordinates, the date, and the fact that *U-124* had used only three torpedoes. *Dunedin*, like *Dorsetshire* and *Devonshire*, had been hunting for U-boat supply vessels.
19. In fact, Mohr sailed *U-124* off course because he encountered and stopped an American freighter, the twenty-three-year-old *Sagadahoc*, which he sank after determining that it carried contraband. See Clay Blair, *Hitler's U-boat War: The Hunters, 1939–1942*, vol. 1 (New York: Random House, 1996), 407, for more information on the sinking and its aftermath.
20. Frank and Rogge, *German Raider*, 148.

Chapter 13. Back to Germany

1. Mohr and Sellwood, *Sea Raider*, 268.
2. Frank and Rogge, *German Raider*, 149.
3. Because *UA* was a larger, export-type boat, it transferred only fifty survivors while the other boats each off-loaded seventy men.
4. *U-123*, under the command of Kapitänleutnant Reinhard Hardegen, was embarking on the first of two highly successful combat patrols under Operation Paukenschlag (Drumbeat), which targeted the very vulnerable shipping lanes along the U.S. eastern seaboard.
5. The text of the signals between the two U-boats is noted in the ship's official war log, the Kriegstagbuch, *KTB-123*, 23 December, 1941, and cited in Michael Gannon's *Operation Drumbeat* (New York: Harper and Row, 1990), 124.
6. This was the same location where the prize ship *Tirranna* was sunk months earlier.
7. Johann Meyer, letter to author, 10 March 1996.
8. Capitano di Corvetta Antonio De Giacomo was wounded on 16 March 1943, when *Torelli* was surprised on the surface by U.S. Navy Helldiver aircraft off the coast of Brazil. Two of the exposed crewmen were killed and the rest of the bridge watch, including the commanding officer, were wounded. The submarine suffered heavy damage that forced it to make a hasty return to base under the command of the executive officer. Giacomo recovered from his wounds and survived the war. He completed five operational war patrols and sank three Allied merchant ships totaling 25,382 tons. At the war's end he was the sixth most successful Italian submarine commander. *Luigi Torelli* had a very interesting career. The Italian navy homeported the sub with the Betasom flotilla in Bordeaux, France, on 5 October 1940. The boat patrolled from there until it was taken over by the German Kriegsmarine and commissioned as *UIT-25* on 10 September 1943. *UIT-25* was taken over by the Imperial Japanese Navy on 10 May 1945, and commissioned as *I-504*. After the Japanese surrender, the U.S. Navy took possession of the boat and scuttled it.
9. Korvettenkapitän Karl-Friedrich Merten went on receive the Knight's Cross on

13 June 1942, and shortly thereafter became the 147th recipient and only the twentieth naval officer to receive the Oak Leaves on 16 November 1942. Merten survived the war with twenty-nine ships and 186,064 tons to his credit. He died on 2 May 1993. *U-68* was sunk with fifty-six casualties at latitude 33 degrees, 24 minutes north, longitude 18 degrees, 59 minutes west on 10 April 1944, by aircraft from USS *Guadalcanal*.

Hans Eckermann left *UA* on 14 February 1942, to take over as chief of the 8th U-boat Flotilla. He later worked as a staff officer for U-boat Command Norway, then for the U-boat Acceptance Command, and finally as a staff officer at the German High Command Headquarters, Marine Defense Division. In May 1945, then Fregattenkapitän Eckermann entered Allied confinement first as a prisoner of war and later as a "surrendered person"; he was released on 20 July 1947.

UA, originally built for the Turkish navy and commissioned *Batiray*, was the most successful U-boat of nonstandard, foreign design in German service—responsible for the loss of seven ships totaling 40,706 tons. *UA* was taken out of service in May 1944 at Neustadt in Holstein and was scuttled on 3 May 1945, at the Kiel Arsenal and later broken up.

10. Capitano di Corvetta Fecia di Cossato became an extremely successful submarine commander, sinking eighteen merchant ships totaling 86,438 tons. *Enrico Tazzoli* was lost with all hands sometime between 18 and 24 May 1943, while sailing from France to the Indian Ocean. Fecia di Cossato was not assigned to the ship at the time. On 27 August 1944, *Tazzoli*'s former commander shot himself, leaving behind a letter to his mother explaining that his place was with his sailors who rested beneath the ocean. A modern Italian submarine is named *Fecia di Cossato* in his honor.

11. Kapitänleutnant Nico Clausen sank twenty-four ships totaling 74,807 tons. He was awarded the Knight's Cross on 13 March 1942, for sinking seven ships (25,613 tons) during his fourth patrol with *U-129*. Clausen was lost along with all hands (sixty-one men) aboard *U-182* on 16 May 1943, when it was depth-charged in the South Atlantic Ocean by the American destroyers USS *Mackenzie* and USS *Lamb*.

The BdU removed *U-129* from war service at Lorient on 4 July 1944. *U-129* was scuttled in Lorient by sailors just over a month later on August 18, 1944. The ship was raised in 1946, stricken, and broken up.

Capitano di Corvetta Emilio Olivieri commanded *Pietro Calvi* during two operational missions, sinking five Allied ships totaling 29,031 tons in the process. He survived the war as Italy's fifth most successful commander. *Pietro Calvi* was discovered by Allied escorts on the evening of 15 July 1942, as it maneuvered to close on a convoy sailing just south of the Azores. Depth-charged and severely damaged, *Calvi* was forced to surface into a hail of machine-gun and cannon fire. With many of his crew dead and the English coming aboard his submarine, *Calvi*'s commander, Capitano di Fregata Primo Longobardo, ordered the boat scuttled at 2:20 A.M. on 16 July. The submarine took Captain Longobardo and a Royal Navy boarding officer down with it.

12. Capitano di Corvetta Ugo Giudice completed three war missions aboard *Finzi*, sinking three ships totaling 21,496 tons. Giudice returned to Italy on 18 August 1942, to take command of the training sail ship *Palinuro*. He survived the war. *Guiseppi Finzi* successfully completed ten missions, sinking four Allied merchants totaling 26,222

tons. Most older references state that the boat fought a fierce sea battle with British escorts on 20 August 1944. These records relate that the fight ended when *Finzi* was severely damaged and its crew scuttled the boat to avoid its capture. Current sources indicate that *Finzi* in fact came under Kriegsmarine control on 9 September 1943, when the Italians signed the armistice. The ship continued to fly the Italian flag until 14 October, when Italy declared war on Germany. The Kriegsmarine seized the boat and commissioned it as *UIT-21*. The Germans later deemed *UIT-21* unsuitable for operations and placed it in a U-boat pen for repair and overhaul. The boat was scuttled in place on 25 August 1944, to prevent its capture by the advancing Allied army.

Korvettenkapitän Johann "Jochen" Mohr sank twenty-seven ships for a total of 132,731 tons. He was awarded the Knight's Cross on 27 March 1942, and went on to become the 177th recipient of the Oak Leaves on 13 January 1943. Mohr was lost when *U-124* sank with all hands on 2 April 1943, west of Oporto, Portugal, at latitude 41 degrees, 2 minutes north and longitude 15 degrees, 39 minutes west when his ship was depth-charged by the British sloop HMS *Black Swan* and the corvette HMS *Stonecrop*.

13. Frank and Rogge, *German Raider*, 150.

14. There is only one confirmed award of this badge—the one presented to Rogge. A second badge was probably marked for presentation to Kapitän-zur-See Ernst Felix Krüder to coincide with Krüder's posthumous award of the Oak Leaves after he was lost with the raider *Pinguin*, but there is no record of the award being formally entered into the German military record system. A third officer was also qualified for the badge, and there is some evidence that he was being considered. Kapitän-zur-See Hellmuth von Ruckeschell may have received the badge, but on paper only. Rogge must thus be counted as the sole known recipient of the badge.

Chapter 14. After *Atlantis*

1. Charles W. Koburger, *Steel Ships, Iron Crosses, and Refugees: The German Navy in the Baltic, 1939–1945* (New York: Praeger, 1989), 98.

2. In a final irony for Rogge, *Devonshire* was the same ship that had destroyed *Atlantis* three and a half years earlier.

3. Helmut Raumann, "Memories of USS *Prinz Eugen* (IX-300): Life as 'Employed Enemy Personnel,'" in *The "Prinz Eugen" Project*, on line at <http://www.brandes.de/pg/book/Prinze.htm> (20 November 2000).

4. The German surrender marked the end of the epic career of *Prinz Eugen*. The heavy cruiser, which had once sailed with *Bismarck*, was one of only two German capital ships afloat at the time of the surrender. *Prinz Eugen* was taken over by the United States on 14 December 1945, and commissioned USS *IX 300 Prinz Eugen*. The new American warship sailed to Boston with a combined Kriegsmarine and U.S. Navy crew (574 Kriegsmarine sailors and officers with eight U.S. Navy officers and eighty-five enlisted men) on 13 January 1946, arriving on the twenty-sixth. En route, the ship suffered a complete machinery breakdown and came under tow from an escort vessel. The United States later sailed the heavy cruiser to Bikini Atoll to join a research flotilla

made up of seventy-one other ships, including USS *Nevada,* USS *Arkansas,* USS *Pennsylvania,* the infamous Imperial Japanese Navy flagship *Nagato,* and the legendary aircraft carrier USS *Saratoga.* The United States assembled the ships at Bikini as research targets for the Mk3A, Model 1561 Fission Bomb explosions under Operation Crossroads. *Prinz Eugen* survived two detonations of bombs almost identical to the one dropped over Nagasaki without significant damage. The first, Able, was an airburst detonated on 1 July 1946; the second, Baker, was an underwater detonation on 25 July 1946. After the blasts, the U.S. Navy towed the ship to Kwajalein Atoll and decommissioned it. On 21 December *Prinz Eugen* took on a 35-degree list; at 12:43 P.M. on 22 December 1946, the great ship capsized and sank in Kwajalein Lagoon on Enubuj Reef, coming to rest at 9 degrees, 22 minutes north latitude and 167 degrees, 9 minutes east longitude. In August 1979, one of the screws was removed and placed in the German Naval Memorial in Laboe, Germany.

BIBLIOGRAPHY

Correspondents and Interviewees

Allison, Craig, England
Angolia, Lt. Col. (Ret.) John R., USA
Bartholomay, Hans (*Atlantis* crewman), Canada
Birtwhistle, Keith, England
Bredow, Hans, Germany
Burg, Bryan H., Esq., USA
Cappello-Mambelli, Claudio, Italy
Cooper, Harry, USA
de Graaf, Rudolf (*Atlantis* crewman), Germany
Frailey, Don, USA
Helgason, Gudmundur, Iceland
Huber, William, USA
Keller, Heinrich (*Atlantis* crewman), Germany
Kühl, Gerhard (*Atlantis* crewman), Germany
McBride, Graham, Canada
Meyer, Johann (*Atlantis* crewman), Germany
Müller, Wilhelm (*Atlantis* crewman), Australia
Oesten, Jürgen (commanding officer, *U-106*), Germany
Ranieri, Adm. (Ret.) Attilio Duilio, Italy
Ranieri, Lt. Giampiero, Italy
Reiners, Eberhard (*Atlantis* crewman), Germany
Rieper, Helmuth (*Atlantis* crewman), Germany
Rieper, Volker, Germany
Siemers, Heinrich Jr., Germany
Stephen, Michael, Germany
Waßmann, Jürgen, Germany
Waßmann, Willi (*Atlantis* crewman), Germany
Weber, Emil (*Atlantis* crewman), Germany
Williamson, Gordon, England

Wunder, Ludwig (*Atlantis* crewman), Germany
Zscheile, Martin (*Atlantis* crewman), Germany

Electronic Sources

The Avalon Project at the Yale Law School. *Nuremberg Trial Proceedings.* Vol. 13. <http://www.yale.edu/lawweb/avalon/imt/proc/05-13-46.htm> (8 March 2000).

Gill, Stuart. "The War Record of HMS *Dunedin.*" <http://www.world-war.co.uk/index.htm> (22 August 2000).

Grummelharrys Marineseite. "Vizeadmiral Bernhard Rogge." <http://home.t-online.de/home/053032622-0001/rogge.htm> (23 March 2001).

Raumann, Helmut. "Memories of USS *Prinz Eugen* (IX-300): Life as 'Employed Enemy Personnel.'" *The Prinz Eugen Project.* <http://www.brandes.de/pg/book/Prinze.htm> (2 June 2000).

Rusbridger, James. "Ultra and the Sinking of the *Automedon.*" <http://www.john/weedon.btinternet.co.uk/nesa-ultra.htm> (1 May 2001).

"S.S. *Automedon:* The Ship That Doomed a Colony." <http://www.forcez-survivors.org.uk/automedon.htm> (19 March 2001).

Steinberg, Glenn A. "German Admirals and Generals, 13 March 1943." <http://gsteinbe.intrasun.tcnj.edu/ww2/officercorps/Navy/rear-admiral.htm> (23 March 2001).

Wittenberg, Edward. "The Pirate Ships: German Commerce Raiders, 1939–1942." <http://www.kriegsmarine.net/raiders.htm> (1 May 2001).

National Records

National Archives of Australia, Melbourne

Item 4/341: "Bogus Raider Messages."

MP15871/1, Item 153: Alfred Holt and Company, Blue Funnel Line correspondence regarding the loss of the steamship *Automedon.* 4 November 1947.

MP15871/1, Item 153S: "Sinking of *Commissaire Ramel.*" Commonwealth of Australia, Director of Naval Intelligence Reports. 26 May 1941 and 14 August 1941.

MP15871/1, Item 164: "Indian Ocean Raider." Commonwealth of Australia, Director of Naval Intelligence Report. 14 March 1941.

MP 1787/1, Item 164H: "Indian Ocean Raider." Commonwealth of Australia, Director of Naval Intelligence Report. 14 March 1941.

MP 1787/1, "Raider Descriptions." New Zealand Naval Intelligence. 7 February 1941.

MP 1787/1, Report of the Destruction of Enemy Raider No. 16. 9 July 1948.

MP 1787/1, Descriptions of Indian Ocean raiders' tactics obtained from merchant seamen rescued at Merka. undated.

MP 1787/1, "German Raider *Tamesis.*" Royal Australian Naval Intelligence. 10 November 1941.
Weekly Intelligence Report: Raider Supplement. Supplement to WIR 64. 30 May 1941.
Weekly Intelligence Report: Raider Supplement 2. Supplement to WIR 138. 30 October 1942.
Weekly Intelligence Report: Raider Supplement 3. Supplement to WIR 181. 27 August 1943.

Public Record Office, London, England

ADM 234/324: *Battle Summary No. 13: Actions with Enemy Disguised Raiders 1940–1941.* 1942.
ADM 1/9977: *Raiders: Lessons from the Last War.* 28 November 1939.
ADM 1/10294: *Operation of Surface Raiders in the Far East; Japanese Co-operation in German Raider Operations, 1940–1941.*
ADM 1/20004: Publication, as a dispatch, of the report on the destruction of a German raider by the *Devonshire.* 22 November 1941.

United States National Archives and Records Administration, Washington, D.C.

T1022, rolls 2,945 and 3,162: war log of *Atlantis.*
T1022, rolls 3130–3131: war log of *Atlantis,* including operational orders and action reports.
RG 165-390/35/9/7, box 456: Interrogation report of Richard Bulla.
RG 165-390/35/10/1, box 466: Interrogation report of Johann Heinrich Fehler.

Official Publications, Histories, Diaries, Conventions, and Wartime Dispatches

Churchill, Winston. Dispatch 2065, annexes A and B. Declassified message from Prime Minister Churchill to President Roosevelt regarding protection of merchant shipping. 23 May 1941.
Fortnightly Summary of Current National Situations (declassified). U.S. Navy, Office of Chief of Naval Operations, Office of Naval Intelligence, Washington, D.C. 1 December 1941.
"German Raider Tactics." Extract from Chief of Naval Operations Bulletin No. 8 (declassified). U.S. Navy, Office of Chief of Naval Operations, Division of Fleet Training, Washington, D.C. 2 January 1942.
Gumming, Gordon. "The Agulhas Minefield—Its Discovery and Claerance [*sic*]." Undated manuscript. Copy in the author's possession.
Hague VII, Articles 1–12. *Convention Relating to the Conversion of Merchant Ships into War-Ships.* 18 October 1907.

United States War Department. *Recognition Pictorial Manual of Naval Vessels, FM 30-50.* Washington, D.C.: Bureau of Aeronautics, Navy Department, 1943.

Waters, Sidney D. *New Zealand in the Second World War: German Raiders in the Pacific.* Wellington, New Zealand: War History Branch, Department of Internal Affairs, 1949.

Video

Die Piraten de Diktators: Die erfolgreiche Kaperfahrt des Geisterschiffes Atlantis. Hamburg: WDR Studio, 1999.

Books and Periodicals

Alexander, Roy. *Sea Prison and Shore Hell: The Cruise of the Raider* Atlantis, *from the Diary of John Creagh.* Sydney: Angus and Robertson, 1942.

Allen, Oliver E. *Pacific Navigators.* Seafarers Series. Alexandria, Va.: Time-Life Books, 1980.

Anderson, Eleanor. *Miracle at Sea: The Sinking of the* Zamzam *and Our Family's Rescue.* Bolivar, Mo.: Quiet Waters Publications, 2001.

Angolia, John R. *On the Field of Honor.* Vol. 2. San Jose, Calif.: Roger James Bender Press, 1980.

Angolia, John R., and Adolf Schlicht. *Die Kriegsmarine Uniforms and Traditions.* Vols. 1, 2, and 3. San Jose, Calif.: Roger James Bender Press, 1991, 1991, 1993.

Ballard, Robert D. *Exploring the* Lusitania. Toronto: Warner/Madison Press, 1995.

Barnett, Correlli. *Engage the Enemy More Closely: The Royal Navy in World War Two.* New York: W. W. Norton, 1991.

Becker, Rolf O. *Fallen Tarnung!—Feuer frei! Kampf und ende von Schiff 16, dem Hilfskeuzer* Atlantis. SOS Sonderband 19. Munich: Moewig Verlag, 1959.

Beesly, Patrick. *Very Special Intelligence.* Garden City, N.Y.: Doubleday, 1978.

Bekker, Cajus. *The German Navy 1939–1945.* New York: Dial Press, 1974.

Bennett, Geoffrey. *Naval Battles of the First World War.* New York: Scribner's, 1968.

"Bernhard Rogge." *Der Landser-Großband* 844, no. 2 (1993): 3–56.

Blair, Clay. *Hitler's U-boat War: The Hunters, 1939–1942.* Vol. 1. New York: Random House, 1996.

Borkin, Joseph, and Charles A. Welsh. *Germany's Master Plan.* New York: Duell, Sloan and Pearce, 1943.

Bragadin, Marc Antonio. *The Italian Navy in World War II.* Annapolis: Naval Institute Press, 1957.

Braynard, Frank O. *The Tall Ships of Today in Photographs.* New York: Dover, 1993.

Brennecke, H. J. *Cruise of the Raider HK-33*. New York: Thomas Y. Crowell, 1954.

———. *Gespensterkreuzer HK 33 Hilfskreuzer* Pinguin *auf Kaperfahrt*. Hamm: Koehlers, 1953.

Brice, Martin. *Axis Blockade Runners of World War II*. Annapolis: Naval Institute Press, 1981.

Brittin, Burdick H., and Liselotte B. Watson. *International Law for Seagoing Officers*. 3d ed. Annapolis: Naval Institute Press, 1972.

Chantrain, J. P., R. Pied, and R. Smeets. *The German Sailor in World War Two*. London: Arms and Armour Press, 1990.

Chatterton, E. Keble. *Britain at War: The Royal Navy from January 1941 to March 1942*. London: Hutchinson, n.d.

Chesneau, Roger, et al., eds. *Conway's All the World's Fighting Ships 1922–1946*. London: Conway Maritime Press, 1980.

Church, Jim. "The Sunken Fleet of Bikini Atoll." *Skin Diver* 47 (December 1998): 60–67.

Churchill, Winston S. *The Grand Alliance*. Boston: Houghton Mifflin, 1951.

Dickey, George L. Jr. "The End of the *Prinz*." U.S. Naval Institute *Proceedings* 87 (August 1969): 148–151.

Dönitz, Karl. *Memoirs: Ten Years and Twenty Days*. Trans. from the German by R. H. Stevens. New York: World Publishing Company, 1959.

Eyssen, Robert. *HKS Komet: Kaperfahrt auf allen Meeren*. Jugenheim: Koehlers Verlagsgesellschaft, 1960.

Flamigni, Antonio, Alessandro Turrini, and Tullio Marcon. *Sommergibili Italiani: Cento Anni di Vita tra Storie e Leggenda*. Rome: Rivista Marittima, 1990.

Fraccaroli, Aldo. Letter to the Editor. *U.S. Naval Institute Proceedings* 76 (December 1950): 1375.

Frank, Wolfgang. *The Sea Wolves: The Story of German U-boats at War*. Trans. from the German by R. O. B. Long. New York: Rinehart, 1955.

Frank, Wolfgang, and Bernhard Rogge. *The German Raider* Atlantis. New York: Ballantine Books, 1956.

———. *Schiff 16: Die Kaperfahrten das schweren Hilfskreuzers* Atlantis *auf den Sieben Weltmeeren*. Munich: Wilhelm Heyne Verlag, 1968.

———. *Under Ten Flags*. London: Weidenfeld and Nicolson, 1955.

Fuehrer Conferences on Naval Affairs, 1939–1945. Annapolis: Naval Institute Press, 1990.

Gannon, Michael. *Operation Drumbeat*. New York: Harper and Row, 1990.

Gasaway, E. Blanchard. *Grey Wolf, Grey Sea*. New York: Ballantine Books, 1970.

Gibson, Charles. *The Ship with Five Names*. London: Abelard-Schuman, 1965.

Giorgerini, Giorgio. *Almanacco Storico delle Navi Militari Italiane: la Marina e le Sue dal 1861 al 1975*. Rome: Marina Militare, 1978.

Gray, Leonard. *85 Years of Shipping under the Maltese Cross, Deutsche Dampfschiffahrts-Gesellschaft Hansa 1881–1966: Portrait of a Major German Shipping Company.* Kendal, U.K.: World Ship Society, 1967.

Gröner, Erich. *German Warships 1815–1945.* Vol. 1: *Major Surface Vessels.* Annapolis: Naval Institute Press, 1990.

Guernsey, Isabel Russell. *Free Trip to Berlin.* Toronto: Macmillan, 1943.

Guttormson, Olga, and Jane Nelson. *Ships Will Sail Again.* Minneapolis: Augsburg Publishing House, 1942.

Handbuch für den Verkehr mit den ausländischen Marinen. Berlin: E. S. Mittler und Sohn Verlag, 1932.

Hansen, Hans Jürgen. *The Ships of the German Fleets 1848–1945.* New York: Arco, 1975.

Herlin, Hans. *The Survivor: The True Story of the Sinking of the Doggerbank.* Trans. from the German by John Brownjohn. London: Leo Cooper, 1994.

Herwig, Holger H. *The German Naval Officer Corps: A Social and Political History 1890–1918.* Oxford: Oxford University Press, 1973.

Hickam, Homer H. Jr. *Torpedo Junction.* New York: Random House, 1991.

Hillgruber, Andreas. *Germany and the Two World Wars.* Trans. from the German by William C. Kirby. Cambridge: Harvard University Press, 1981.

Hinsley, F. H., E. E. Thomas, C. F. G. Ransom, and R. C. Knight. *British Intelligence in the Second World War.* Vol. 2. New York: Cambridge University Press, 1981.

Hoehling, A. A. *The Great War at Sea: A History of Naval Action 1914–18.* New York: Thomas Y. Crowell, 1965.

Howard, Michael. *British Intelligence in the Second World War.* Vol. 5. New York: Cambridge University Press, 1990.

Hoyt, Edwin P. *Count von Luckner: Knight of the Sea.* New York: David McKay, 1969.

———. *Kreuzerkrieg.* New York: World Publishing Company, 1968.

———. *Raider 16.* New York: World Publishing Company, 1970.

Hughes, Terry, and John Costello. *The Battle of the Atlantic.* New York: Dial Press, 1977.

Jane's Fighting Ships of World War II. New York: Crescent Books, 1995.

Janssen, Jens. *Schicksale Deutscher Schiffe Nr. 196. Schiff 16 = Hilfskreuzer Atlantis: 622 Tage ohne Werft und ohne Hafen.* Munich: Arthur Moewig Verlag, 1960.

Jordan, Roger W. *The World's Merchant Fleets 1939.* Annapolis: Naval Institute Press, 1999.

Koburger, Charles W. *Steel Ships, Iron Crosses, and Refugees: The German Navy in the Baltic, 1939–1945.* New York: Praeger, 1989.

Koop, Gerhard. *Emden Ein Name—fünf Schiffe.* Munich: Bernard and Graefe Verlag, 1983.

Kranke, Theodor. *Pocket Battleship: The Story of the Admiral Scheer.* New York: W. W. Norton, 1958.

Lewin, Ronald. *Ultra Goes to War.* New York: McGraw-Hill, 1978.

"*Life* and *Fortune* Men among Passengers Rescued as Germans Sink *Zamzam*." *Life* 10, no. 22 (2 June 1941): 34.

Littell, Robert. "The Cruise of the Raider *Atlantis*." In *Secrets and Stories of the War*, 1:58–64. London: Reader's Digest Association, 1963.

McLachlan, Donald. *Room 39: A Study in Naval Intelligence*. New York: Atheneum, 1968.

Mielke, Otto. *Hilfskreuzer Orion Rund um den Erdball*. SOS Sonderband 39. Munich: Moewig Verlag, 1954.

Miller, Nathan. *War at Sea: A Naval History of World War II*. New York: Scribner's, 1995.

Mohr, Ulrich. *Die Kriegsfahrt Des Hilfskreuzers Atlantis: Bilddokumente Einer Kreuzerfahrt in Vier Ozeanen*. Berlin-Schöneberg: Riffarth, 1944.

Mohr, Ulrich, and Arthur V. Sellwood. *Sea Raider Atlantis*. New York: Pinnacle, 1975.

———. *Ship 16*. New York: John Day, 1956.

Muggenthaler, August Karl. *German Raiders of World War II*. Englewood Cliffs, N.J.: Prentice-Hall, 1977.

Murphy, Charles J. V. "The German Raider Caught in the Act of Sinking *ZamZam*." *Life* 10, no. 25 (23 June 1941): 21–27, 70–79.

Oiness, Sylvia M. *Strange Fate of the Zamzam: The Miracle Ship*. Minneapolis: Osterhaus, 1942.

Pattee, Richard S. "The Cruise of the German Raider *Atlantis*." *U.S. Naval Institute Proceedings* 75 (December 1949): 1322–1333.

Piekalkiewicz, Janusz. *Sea War 1939–1945*. Dorset, U.K.: Blandford Press, 1987.

"Prison Ship: Nazi Censor Releases *Life*'s Zamzam Pictures." *Life* 11, no. 24 (15 December 1941): 110–117.

Reit, Seymour. *Masquerade: The Amazing Camouflage Deceptions of World War II*. New York: Hawthorn Books, 1978.

Rogge, Bernhard. "The End of the *Atlantis*." *Die Suid-Afrikaanse Kryghistoriese Vereniging Kommando* 6, no. 4 (1955): 8–9.

———. "Leadership on Board the Raider *Atlantis*." *U.S. Naval Institute Proceedings* 80 (February 1963): 40–51.

Roskill, S. W. *A Merchant Fleet in War: Alfred Holt and Company, 1939–1945*. London: Collins Press, 1962.

———. *White Ensign: The British Navy at War 1939–1945*. Annapolis: Naval Institute Press, 1960.

Ruge, Friedrich. *Der Seekrieg: The German Navy's Story 1939–1945*. Trans. from the German by M. G. Saunders. Annapolis: Naval Institute Press, 1957.

Runyan, Timothy J., and Jan M. Copes, eds. *To Die Gallantly: The Battle of the Atlantic*. Boulder: Westview Press, 1994.

Schmalenbach, Paul. *German Raiders: A History of Auxiliary Cruisers of the German Navy 1895–1945*. Trans. from the German by Keith Lewis. Annapolis: Naval Institute Press, 1979.

Schmalenbach, Paul S., and James E. Wise Jr. "*Prinz Eugen* Album." *U.S. Naval Institute Proceedings* 87 (August 1969): 87–102.

Schwarzenberger, Georg. *A Manual of International Law*. 5th ed. New York: Praeger, 1967.

Sellwood, Arthur V. *Dynamite for Hire: The Story of Hein Fehler*. London: T. Werner Laurie, 1956.

Showell, Jak P. Mallmann. *The German Navy in World War Two*. Annapolis: Naval Institute Press, 1979.

———. *U-boat Command and the Battle of the Atlantic*. St. Catharines, Ontario, and Lewistown, N.Y.: Vanwell, 1989.

Swanson, S. Hjalamar, ed. ZamZam: *The Story of a Strange Missionary Odyssey*. Minneapolis: Board of Foreign Missions of the Augustana Synod, 1941.

Thomas, Charles S. *The German Navy in the Nazi Era*. Annapolis: Naval Institute Press, 1990.

Van Der Vat, Dan. *The Atlantic Campaign*. New York: Harper and Row, 1988.

Vicovari, Frank, and Lucian Cary. "I Rode a German Raider." In *One Hundred Best True Stories of World War II*, 793–811. New York: William H. Wise, 1945.

Von der Porten, Edward P. *The German Navy in World War II*. New York: Thomas Y. Crowell, 1969.

Weyher, Kurt, and Hans Jürgen Ehrlich. *The Black Raider*. Trans. from the German by Paul Dinnage. London: Elek Books, 1955.

Woodward, David. *The Secret Raiders*. New York: W. W. Norton, 1955.

INDEX

Abbekerk, 56–57, 58, 61, 235n. 6
Aboukir, HMS, 199
Admiral Scheer, 139–40, 142–44, 146, 226, 238n. 1
Adventure, HMS, 241n. 4
Africa Maru, SS, 145
Africana, HMSAS, 55, 235n. 3
Agar, Augustus W. S., 190–91, 209, 211
Agulhas, Cape: mining of, 51–52; sweeping of, 54–55, 117
Albert Leo Schlageter, 9–11, 232n. 16
Alexander, Roy, 49
Alsterufer, 150, 155–57, 159–60
Amazone, SMS, 7, 232n. 10
Antenor, HMS, 105, 107
Arcona, SMS, 7, 232n. 9
Aristea, HMSAS, 55, 235n. 3
Asta, SMS, 7
Aster, HMS, 203
Athelking, 87–88, 92, 235n. 4
Atlantis: abandon ship ordered, 196–97; aground on granite spike, 120–21; aground in Weser River, 21–22; armaments, 20; and breakout, 28–35; Cape Agulhas, mining of, 51–52; code ciphers, 237; commissioned as a warship, 19, daily routine, 64; departing Kerguelen Islands, 127; through Drake Passage, 185–86; equator-crossing ceremony, 39–40; fatal accident, 125–26; first crew casualty, 97; five hundredth day at sea, 176; at Foundry Branch, 19; fresh water transfer, 123–24; at Gazelle Bay, 122; German propaganda, effect on operations of, 56; Henderson Island inspected by, 185; Kerguelen Islands sighted by, 117; minefield, Allied actions against, 54–55; mission, 24; named by Rogge, 19; need for fresh water, 114; operational areas overlapping with Pinguin, 89; in Pacific Ocean, 174–75; prisoner deception, 52–53; rescued by Python, 205–8; safe return of crew, 223; sailing from port, 24–25; Sci-entist, intelligence gathered from, 50–51; scuttled, 197; sea blockade defenses, 26–27; six hundredth day at sea, 186; Speybank patrolling with, 144–46; status report to SKL, 139; sunk, 198; survivors sail for France, 217; testing hull repairs, 127; under attack, 195–96; Vana Vana rest stop, 182–84; war log, 221; Zamzam prisoner transfer, 155–57. See also Goldenfels; Rogge, Bernhard; Ship-16

Atlantis battles: versus Athelking, 86–88; versus Automedon, 109–11; versus Balzac, 171–72; versus Benarty, 89–92; versus City of Bagdad, 65–68; versus Commissaire Ramel, 93–95; versus Devonshire, 192–94; versus Durmitor, 99–100; versus Kemmendine, 70–72; versus Ketty Brøvig, 136–38; versus King City, 82–85; versus Lieutenant de la Tour, 161; versus Mandasor, 128–29, 130–32; versus Ole Jacob, 106–8, 113; versus Rabaul, 162–63; versus Scientist, 45–48, 50–51; versus Silvaplana, 177–78; versus Speybank, 133–35; versus Talleyrand, 77–80; versus Teddy, 105–6, 112; versus Tirranna, 59–60, 97; versus Tottenham, 170–71; versus Trafalgar, 166–67; versus Zamzam, 151–57. See also Atlantis disguises; Atlantis operational encounters

Atlantis disguises: capabilities, 23; as Abbekerk, 56–57; as Brastagi, 160; as Kasii Maru, 41–42; as Kim, 28; as Knute Nelson, 27; as Polyphemus, 187–88; prisoner deception, 52–53; as Tarifa, 63

Atlantis operational encounters: with Admiral Scheer, 142–44; with Alsterufer, 155–57; with Babitonga, 168; with British Advocate, 146; with Chenonceaux, 149; with City of Exeter, 43–44; with Devonshire, 192–94; with Dresden, 150–51; with Durmitor, 101; with HMS Eagle and HMS Nelson, 163–65; with Ketty Brøvig and Tannenfels, 140–41; with Komet, 179–81;

Atlantis operational encounters *(continued)*: with *Lieutenant de la Tour,* 161; with *Münsterland,* 179–81; with HMS *Nelson* and HMS *Eagle,* 163–65; with *Orion,* 172–73; with *Perla,* 147–48; with *Pinguin,* 115–16; with *Python,* 205–8; with *Storstadt,* 115–16; with *Tannenfels* and *Ketty Brøvig,* 140–41; with *Tirranna,* 75–76, 80–81; with *Troilus,* 135–36; with troopship, 133; with *U-68,* 187; with *U-126,* 191–92
Aubretia, HMS, 161
Automedon, 128, 131, 135, 237n. 7; capture and sinking of, 109–11; intelligence from, 113

Babitonga, 150–51, 240n. 11; *Atlantis* resupply from, 160–61; prisoner transfer, 168
Balme, David, 161
Balzac, 172, 241n. 15
Bari, 231n. 15
Bauer, Ernst, 192, 200–201, 202, 205, 242n. 7
Beesly, Patrick, 190
Benarty, 91–92
Benno, 237n. 12. See also *Ole Jacob*
Bismarck, 167, 168–69, 240n. 10
Bjørney, Finn, 78
Bjørney, Svenn, 78
Black Swan, HMS, 245n. 12
Blackstone, Sir William, 1
Bletchley Park, 161, 190
Borchert, Georg, 79; and air patrols from Vana Vana, 183–84, 188; and attack on *Benarty,* 90–92; and new aircraft assembly, 159–60
Bounty, HMS, 184
Brandon, R. S., 135
Brastagi, 160
Breuers, (*Teddy* prize officer), 106, 135; radio direction-finding, 144–45, 146, 168
British Advocate, 146, 238n. 4
Broadway, HMS, 161
Broder-Peters, S., 29
Brown, William, 94
Bührle, Emil, 205
Bulla, Richard, 28, 42, 57, 76; and air patrols from Vana Vana, 182–84, 188–89; and attack on *Benarty,* 89–92; and attack on *Mandasor,* 128–30; and attack on *Tallyrand,* 79–80, 99, 106, 126, 132; and new aircraft assembly, 159–60
Bulldog, HMS, 161
Burns (*Zamzam* chief engineer), 153
Burns, Cyril, 47

Cameron, D. V., 170–71
Canberra, HMAS, 147
Cap Trafalgar, 234
Carls, Rolf, 6
Carmania, RMS, 234
Chapman, Dick, 94
Charles H. Cramp, 166
Chenonceaux, 149
Christian, Fletcher, 184
Ciliax, Otto, 6
City of Bagdad, 67–69
City of Exeter, 44, 56, 69
Clausen, Nicolai, 208, 215, 244
Coburg, 147
Collmann, Wolfgang, 14
Commissaire Ramel, 94–95, 236n. 8
Conrad, Joseph, 201
Cook, James, 117–18
Cornwall, HMS, 167, 242n. 13
Crassula, HMSAS, 55, 235n. 3
Creagh, John, 49, 88

Dean, F. J., 55
De Giacomo, Antonio, 220, 243n. 8
de Graff, Rudolf, 163
de Kerguélen-Trémarec, Yves, 117
Dehnel, Emil: *Atlantis,* returns to, 140–41; *Durmitor,* prize officer of, 100; sailing to Italian-held port, 101–5, 236n. 5
Dettenhofer, Anton, 202
Devonshire, HMS, 193–99, 227–28, 241n. 8, 245n. 2
di Cossato, Fecia, 220, 222, 244n. 10
Dido, HMS, 227–28
Dittman (Leutnant zur See), 157, 182
Doggerbank, 147, 239n. 5. See also *Speybank*
Dönitz, Karl, 6; *Atlantis* survivors, rescue of, 202–3; eastern front, evacuation of, 226–27; *Python* survivors, rescue of, 213–14
Dorsetshire, HMS, 190, 193; sinks *Python,* 209–11, 242n. 13
Dresden, 150–51, 187, 200, 202, 239n. 16; *Zamzam* prisoners, transfer of, 155–57
Dunedin, HMS, 216, 242n. 8
Duquesa, 144
Durmitor, SS, capture of, 100–105, 109, 114, 140, 238n. 13

Eaddy, C. R., 135
Eagle, HMS, 164
Eastern Guide, 66–67
Eckermann, Hans: *Python,* meeting with, in

UA, 208–9; rescue of *Python* survivors, 212–13, 214–15; sailing on his own accord, 216–17, 244n. 9
Emden, SMS, 7–8, 66, 232n. 13
Engelhardt, Konrad, 226
Enrico Tazzoli, 220–21, 222, 244n. 10
Esso Hamburg, 168
Ewan, W. B., 109
Eyssen, Robert, 179–81, 241n. 3

Fehler, Johann Heinrich, 18, 111, 121, 131–32, 141, 146, 153, 213, 215; as *Atlantis* crewman, 14; and *Atlantis* scuttling, 197; and *Automedon* scuttling, 111; and *Benarty* scuttling, 92; and *City of Bagdad* scuttling, 68; *Scientist*, failed scuttling of, 47–48; mining operation, 51–52; as prize officer of *Ketty Brøvig*, 138–39; and *Mandasor* scuttling, 131–32; and *Python* scuttling, 211; Rogge, first impression of, 12; and *Talleyrand* scuttling, 80; water collection system, 122–24; and Vana Vana landing party, 183; and *Zamzam* survivors
Felchner, Ernst, 205
Ferry (Rogge's dog), 74, 126
Formidable, HMS, 136
Foyn, Mathias, 78
Frank, Wolfgang, 209, 219
Freienfels, 69
Freiwald, Willi, 133
Freya, SMS, 3, 231n. 2
Fröhlich, Herbert, 157
Front Stalag 221, 237

Gazelle (German survey ship), 114
Geierfels, 67
Gerstenhauer, Horst, 202
Giudice, Ugo, 221, 244n. 12
Giuseppe Finzi, 221–22, 244n. 12
Goldenfels, 17, 61, 66, 80; commissioned as warship, 19; conversion, 10–11. See also *Atlantis*; *Ship-16*
Gorch Fock, 8–9, 16, 232n. 15
Göring, Hermann, 237n. 11
Gout, Hugo, 46
Graf Spee, 157, 202, 238n. 1
Grau, Peter, 159
Guadalcanal, USS, 244n. 9
Gundersen, Edvard Hauff, 60–61
Guttormson, Olga, 157

Hansa, 10, 16, 19, 69, 232n. 18
Hardegen, Reinhard, 221, 243n. 4

Hartmann, Werner, 30, 34–35, 234
Hawkins, HMS, 136
Helenus, 111–12
Herrmann, Bernhard, 125–26, 237n. 3
Hessen, 24–25, 234n. 10
Hill, A., 130–31
Hood, HMS, 167, 240n. 9
Hydra cipher, 115, 161, 169, 237n. 13

I-504. See *Luigi Torelli*
Irene, 241n. 4

Jäger, Walter, 150–51, 155–57
Jaguar, 232n. 14

Kamenz, Paul, 15, 33, 35, 71–72, 98 43, 186–87; *Atlantis*, final position of, 189; *Atlantis*, returns to, 159; *Ole Jacob* boarding, 107–8; prize officer of *Ole Jacob*, 113–14; rationing plan, 64
Karlsruhe, 8, 16, 193, 232
Kasch, Lorenz: artillery drills, 25; defensive indirect fire planning, 122, 69; jammed guns, 171; *Kemmendine*, 71–73, 93; *King City* versus, 83–84; and *Rabaul* sinking, 162; *Scientist* versus, 48; *Speybank*, versus, 133–34; *Tiranna* versus, 59–60; torpedo attack on, 70–71
Kasii Maru, 41, 57
Ketty Brøvig: attack on, 137–41; scuttled, 147; used as oiler, 143–44, 148, 239n. 6
Kielhorn, Wilhelm, 31, 64; *Atlantis* flees with one engine, 192, *Atlantis*'s engines refurbished, 81, 95, 122, 188; fire from *Atlantis*'s smokestack, 165; and *Tiranna* repair, 75
Kim, 28, 41
King City, 84–85, 235n. 2
Knute Nelson, 27–28
Koberger, Charles W., 227
Komet (*Ship-45*), 169, 179–81, 241n. 3
Kormoran (*Ship-41*), 139–40, 150–51, 169
Kota Nopan, 179, 181
Kranke, Theodor, 143–44, 146, 238n. 3
Krogh, Lief Christian, 108
Krooß, Willi, 202, 242n. 2
Krüder, Ernst Felix, 115–16, 167, 245n. 14
Kuert, Fritz, 239n. 5
Kühn, Erich: as *Atlantis* crewman, 14; formal inspection, 176, "leave on board" policy, 101, muster of crew, 85, nicknamed "Captain Bligh," 75; preparing to sail, 24–25; problem painting waterline, 41–43; procuring provisions, 19;

Kühn, Erich *(continued):*
shifting ballast aft, 120–21; and *Tirranna* boarding, 60; wounded, 202

Lamb, USS, 244n. 11
Laughinghouse, Ned, 153, 239n. 15
Leander, HMAS, 147
Leicestershire, 153
Lemp, Julius, 161
Lender, Willi, 16, 134
Leopard (E-boat), 29
Lieutenant de la Tour, 161
LIFE Magazine, 154, 156, 195
London, HMS, 240n. 9
Longobardo, Primo, 244n. 11
Lorenzen, Fritz, 14, 42, 64
Lot (French tanker), 145, 168
Lueders, (captain of *Python*) 209–11, 215
Luigi Torelli, 220, 221–22, 243n. 8
Lusitania, RMS, 154, 239n. 11
Lütjens, Günther, 6
Lütken, Thor, 106
Lützow, 180, 226, 238n. 1

Mackenzie, USS, 244n. 11
Mackenzie (master of *Commissaire Ramel*), 95
Mahronda, 171
Mandasor, 130–33, 238n. 6
Marguerite, HMS, 203
Marineschule Mürwik, 3, 4, 6
Marshall, H. W., 84
Master Elias Kulukundis, 165
Merten, Karl-Friedrich, 214, 217, 219, 243n. 9; *Atlantis* meeting with, 186–87; *Python* meeting with, 208–9; rescue and tow of survivors, 212–13
Meyer, Johann, 15, 204–5, 222, 236n. 2
Miller (master of *Rabaul*), 162
Mohr, Johann, 208, 214, 215, 216, 243n. 19, 245n. 12
Mohr, Ulrich: and *Abbekerk* disguise, 56; aboard *Admiral Scheer*, 143; aboard *Tazzoli*, 222; abandoning *Atlantis*, 197–98; *Atlantis*, requisitioned as an officer for, 14–15; *Atlantis* war log carried by, 221; *Benarty*, searching mail of, 92; and *City of Bagdad*, capture of, 67–68; formal inspection of ship, 176; Henderson Island, inspection of, 185, intelligence-gathering from BBC and American news broadcasts, 54, 58, 95–96, 167–68; interviews British prisoners about *Atlantis* mining operation, 53; interview with Captain Gundersen of *Tirranna*, 60–61; and *Kasii Maru* disguise, 40–43; and *Ketty Brøvig* boarding, 137; Kerguelen Islands landing party and, 118–19, *Ole Jacob*, capture of, 107–8; prize crew misconduct, 75–76; provisioning requirements plan of, 18–19; saves *Mandasor* survivors from sharks, 131; and *Scientist* boarding, 47–50; Singapore, defense plans of, 110, *Speybank*, boarding of 134; submarines, on embarking aboard, 218–19; *Teddy*, capture of, 106; *Vana Vana*, sailing for, 181–83; and *Zamzam* boarding, 153–54
Møller, Erling, 137
Moltke, SMS, 3–4, 231n. 3
Monge, 145
Morrow, Andrew, 134–35
Muggenthaler, August Karl, 44, 171
Müller, Heinz, 198, 202
Mund, Louis, 66, 75, 80, 96
Murawjw Amurski. See *Pillau*
Murphy, Charles J. V., 152, 156
Müsterland, 179–81

Napp, Bruno, 147
Natalia, HMSAS, 55, 235n. 3
Nelson, HMS, 164
Nerger, Karl August, 16, 21, 101
Neubert, Kurt, 192, 201
Newell, Cyril, 111
Niagara, 64
Nielson, Niels Stange, 178
Niobe, SMS, 7, 232n. 12
Nishmaha, 242n. 7
Nolan, Edward, 170
Nordmark, 150, 159–60, 187, 240n. 1
Nordstern. See *British Advocate*

Oberkommando der Kriegsmarine (OKM), 2
Oceania, 37
Oesten, Jürgen, 159, 240nn. 2–3
Ole Jacob: captured, 107–9, 237n. 12; meeting with, 111–13, 114
Oliver, R. D., 194–96, 198–99
Olivieri, Emilio, 221, 244n. 11
Operational Intelligence Center, 190, 235n. 5
Orion (*Ship-36*), 25, 38, 168–69, 174, 177; *Atlantis* meeting with, 172–73; North Atlantic action orders, 64
Ott, Franz, 29

Palinuro, 244
Pégase, 145
Perla, 140, 147–48, 239n. 7
Pietro Calvi, 221–22, 244n. 11
Pigors, Wilhelm, 197–98
Pillau, SMS, 4, 5, 231n. 5
Pinguin (Ship-33), 236n. 5, 245n. 14; *Atlantis* meeting with, 115; forwarding message, 81, 89, 95, 128; sunk, 167
Polyphemus, 188, 194–95
Popham, Brooke, 111
Prinz Eugen, 226, 227–28, 245nn. 3–4
Python, 213, 214, 215, 217; *Atlantis* crew, rescue of, 205–7; 187; crews taken aboard subs, 218–19; sinking of, 208–12

Q-Ship, 83–84
Queen Mary, RMS, 133, 238n. 7

Rabaul, 163, 240n. 6
Raeder, Erich, 6; grants Rogge operational leeway, 38, 207, 224, 239n. 16; inspection by, 23
Raumann, Helmut, 227
Reid, E. B., 72–73
Reil, Georg, 15, 49, 58, 72, 201
Reinicke, Hans-Jürgen, 226, 227–28
Resolution, HMS, 117
Reuter, Ludwig von, 5
Rodig, Johannes, 156
Rogge, Bernhard: ammunition and mines, loading of, 23–24; assessing hull damage, 120; assignments, 6–9; *Atlantis* scuttling, 196–98; awarded Knight's Cross, 115–16; awarded Oakleaves, 224; Baltic, actions in, 226; and Bernhard Herrmann, death of, 125–26; book release, 229; Bundesmarine service, 229; Cape Agulhas, mining of, 51–52; changing tide of war, 169; and close call with English warships, 163–65; commissioning warship, 19–20; crew additions approved by, 156–57; crew arrives in France, 223; crew debriefing, 62–63; crew rescue tow plan, 202–5, 212–17; crew selected by, 15–16; decision to leave ship, 197–98; decision to return to Germany, 185; decision to stop at Vana Vana, 182; departing Kerguelen Islands, 127–28; departing shipyard, 24; equator-crossing ceremony, 39–40; evacuation of Eastern areas, 226–27; Eyssen, meeting with, 179–81; and *Goldenfels* conversion, 16–19; and gunnery exercises, 25–26; Iron Crosses, awarding of, 73, 85, 116, 149; "leave on board" policy of, 101; movie release, 229; mustering survivors, 201, 212; North Atlantic area, ordered to, 168; officer training, 3–5; officers selected by, 13–15; ordered to refuel U-boats, 186–87, 191–92; oversees hull repair, 124–25; and prize crew misconduct, 75–76; rationing plan of, 64; sailing against blockade, 26–36; samurai sword, award of, 245; on SKL, 97; on strict inspection regime, 176; submarines, Italian, 220–21; surrender and aftermath, 227–28; technology's effect on operations, 150; Vana Vana rest stop, 182–84; Weyher, discussions with, 173; writing raider action report, 225. See also *Atlantis*; *Atlantis* battles; *Atlantis* disguises; *Atlantis* operational encounters
Rogge, Elsbeth, 229
Rommel, Erwin, 237n. 11

Sagadhoc, 243n. 19
Sagres II. See *Albert Leo Schlageter*
Savery, P. W., 111
Scapa Flow, 5, 6
Schäfer, Johann, 202
Scherman, David E., 154–55, 158, 195
Schlesien, 19, 233n. 7
Schleswig-Holstein, 7
Schneidewind, Paul, 146–47, 239n. 5
Schwantke, Hans-Joachim, 239n. 5
Schwieger, Walter, 239n. 11
Scientist, 47–50, 52–53, 162, 234n. 4
Seeger, Karl, 97
Ship-16, 10, 12, 14, 16, 17–18, 19; mail collection, 25; receives ammunition and mines, 23, 114, 192. See also *Atlantis*
Shropshire, HMS, 236n. 4
Silvaplana, 177–79, 181–82, 241n. 2
Smith, William Grey, 153
Special Cipher 100, 175, 237n. 13
Speybank, 139–40, 168, 239n. 16; *Atlantis*, sailing with, 144; capture of, 134; France, arrival in, 147; radio direction-finding, 145–46
Sprung, Hans-Bernhard, 15, 49
Starling, Robert, 153
Steuer (master of *Tannenfels*), 238n. 13
Stewart, D., 109
Stonecrop, HMS, 245n. 12
Storstadt, 115–16, 237n. 15
Stralsund, SMS, 4, 231n. 4

Strathaird, HMTS, 238n. 7
Strauberger, Georg, 133

T-153 (torpedo boat), 6
Talleyrand, 78–80, 89, 97
Tamesis, 127, 158, 160, 195
Tannenfels, 139–41, 143–44, 146–47, 238n. 2
Tantalus, 133
Tarifa, 63
Taronga, 32
Task Force Rogge, 226
Teddy, 108, 113, 114; *Atlantis* meeting with, 111; capture of, 105–6; sinking of, 112
Thomas, Charles S., 6
Thysville, 43
Tirranna: capture of, 60–63, 65; departure of, 80; discipline problems on, 75–76; sinking of, 96–97, 74; with sister ship, 78–79, 82, 85–86, 98, 124, 235n. 7, 236nn. 9–10, 243n. 6
Tomkins, A. E., 87–88
Tottenham, 170–71, 189
Tovarisch. See *Gorch Fock*
Trafalgar, SS, 167
Triton cipher, 237n. 13
Troilus, 135–36
Truant, HMS, 232n. 14
Trummer, Hans, 29
Tsel, 234n. 10. See also *Hessen*
Tuna HMS, 96, 236n. 9

U-20, 239n. 11
U-37, 29–30, 33–35, 53, 234n. 11
U-43, 239n. 5
U-68, 209, 214, 216, 219, 222; *Atlantis* meeting with, 186–87; France, arrival in, 222; fueling *U-126*, 217; *Python* meeting with, 208; survivors, rescue of, 212–13; survivors, transfer to *Tazzoli*, 220–21
U-106, 159, 240n. 3
U-110, 161, 240n. 4
U-123, 221, 243n. 4
U-124, 203, 221, 222, 243n. 18, 245n. 12; *Dunedin*, sinking of, 207; France, arrival in, 222; *Python* meeting with, 208; survivors, rescue of, 213–17
U-126, 186, 194, 213, 242n. 7; *Atlantis* meeting with, 191–92, survivors, rescue of, 200–201; survivors, towing of, 203–6
U-129, 203, 208, 217, 221, 244n. 11; France, arrival in, 222; survivors, rescue of, 213–15
U-182, 244n. 11
U-644, 236n. 9
UA: forwarding wireless messages, 81; *Python* meeting with, 208; survivors, rescue of, 212; survivors, towing of, 214–17, 209, 220, 221, 222, 243n. 3, 244n. 9
Uebel (master of *Müsterland*), 179
UIT-21, 245n. 12. See also *Giuseppe Finzi*
UIT-25, 243n. 8. See also *Luigi Torelli*

Vana Vana, 182, 184
Versailles, Treaty of, 5, 67
Vicovari, Frank, 153, 200–201, 219–20
von Luckner, Felix Graf, 232n. 12
von Ruckeschell, Hellmuth, 245n. 14
von Wenden, Eberhard, 234n. 11
Wachtfels, 16
Waldmann, (Leutnant zur See), 61–62, 80, 85, 96
Watson (first officer of *Scientist*), 47
Watt (master of *Benarty*), 92–93
Wenneker, Paul, 180
Wenzel, Adolf, 14, 68, 73, 81, 88, 90
Wesemann, Heinrich, 26, 73, 143
Weyher, Kurt, 64, 172–73
White, Armstrong, 67, 69, 72, 75–76
Widder (*Ship-21*), 25
Wilhelm II, Kaiser, 2, 3, 5, 231n. 6
Willis, Algernon, 190
Windsor (master of *Scientist*), 47, 50, 53
Witthoeft-Emden, Robert, 7
Wolf, SMS (auxiliary cruiser), 16, 21, 84, 169
Wolf (E-boat), 29
Woodcock, Albert E., 170
Wooge (Leutnant zur See), 156
Zamzam, 153–56, 158, 160, 174, 200, 219–20

ABOUT THE AUTHOR

A native of Pittsburgh, Pennsylvania, Capt. Joseph P. Slavick has served in the United States Air Force for more than twenty years. He began as a security policeman in 1982, and ten years later he was commissioned a personnel officer. As a security policeman he served in Egypt, the Netherlands, Crete, and Greece. As an officer he has held posts at Andersen Air Force Base in Guam and the Presidio of Monterey in California. Captain Slavick also holds a bachelor's of science degree in management from the University of Maryland. He is currently stationed at Eglin Air Force Base near Fort Walton Beach, Florida, where he lives with his wife and three children. This is his first book.

The Naval Institute Press is the book-publishing arm of the U.S. Naval Institute, a private, nonprofit, membership society for sea service professionals and others who share an interest in naval and maritime affairs. Established in 1873 at the U.S. Naval Academy in Annapolis, Maryland, where its offices remain today, the Naval Institute has members worldwide.

Members of the Naval Institute support the education programs of the society and receive the influential monthly magazine *Proceedings* and discounts on fine nautical prints and on ship and aircraft photos. They also have access to the transcripts of the Institute's Oral History Program and get discounted admission to any of the Institute-sponsored seminars offered around the country.

The Naval Institute also publishes *Naval History* magazine. This colorful bimonthly is filled with entertaining and thought-provoking articles, first-person reminiscences, and dramatic art and photography. Members receive a discount on *Naval History* subscriptions.

The Naval Institute's book-publishing program, begun in 1898 with basic guides to naval practices, has broadened its scope to include books of more general interest. Now the Naval Institute Press publishes about one hundred titles each year, ranging from how-to books on boating and navigation to battle histories, biographies, ship and aircraft guides, and novels. Institute members receive significant discounts on the Press's more than eight hundred books in print.

Full-time students are eligible for special half-price membership rates. Life memberships are also available.

For a free catalog describing Naval Institute Press books currently available, and for further information about subscribing to *Naval History* magazine or about joining the U.S. Naval Institute, please write to:

Membership Department
U.S. Naval Institute
291 Wood Road
Annapolis, MD 21402-5034
Telephone: (800) 233-8764
Fax: (410) 269-7940
Web address: www.navalinstitute.org